*Nira Yuval-Davis, Professor, Director of the Research Centre*
on Migration, Refugees and Belonging (CMRB),
University of East London, UK

'Meticulously documenting state crime, harm and violence targeted against women seeking asylum, Canning skilfully deploys her academic-activist feminist standpoint to explode the myth of the refugee 'crisis'. At the same time, she insists that the silence which is integral to state power can be and is being challenged through collective social action: *Gendered Harm and Structural Violence in the British Asylum System* is part of that resistance movement.'
Steve Tombs, Professor, Head of Social Policy & Criminology at the
Open University and Co-Director of the International Centre for
Comparative Criminological Research, UK

'In this book, Canning provides a thoughtful, contextually grounded and meticulous critique of the British asylum system that is searing in its potency. Canning reminds us that Britain's asylum systems and structures compound trauma, produce harm and perpetrate violence on those who arrive seeking humanitarian protection. A decade of research and advocacy has contributed to this book and the considered analysis offers immense value to researchers, advocates and practitioners.'
Alison Gerard, Associate Professor in Law and Director of the Centre
for Law and Justice, Charles Sturt University, Australia

'This is a must read for anyone who wants to gain understanding of the structural harms and violence inflicted on people seeking asylum by the British state and its corporate allies. In this book, Canning has conducted an excellent feminist analysis of torture and harm, and given voice to the voiceless, drawing narratives of survival and resistance. This is a necessary and much needed contribution to critical criminology and feminism.'
Dr Monish Bhatia, Lecturer in Criminology,
Abertay University, UK

'In this beautifully written yet powerful and moving account of women's experiences as they seek protection from persecution, violence and human rights abuse, Victoria Canning paints a complex picture that challenges the assumption that conditions for those seeking asylum in the UK are better than in other countries of Europe. In weaving the accounts of women through the book, she illustrates the structural gender violence that permeates the system but also stories of survival and resistance that challenge the representation of women asylum seekers as vulnerable and dependent. A must read!'

Heaven Crawley, Professor, Centre for Trust, Peace and
Social Relations, Coventry University, UK and author
of Refugees and Gender: Law and Process

Gendered Harm and Structural Violence in the British Asylum System

Britain is often heralded as a country in which the rights and welfare of survivors of conflict and persecution are well embedded, and where the standard of living conditions for those seeking asylum is relatively high. Drawing on a decade of activism and research in the North West of England, this book contends that, on the contrary, conditions are often structurally violent. For survivors of gendered violence, harm inflicted throughout the process of seeking asylum can be intersectional and compound the impacts of previous experiences of violent continuums. The everyday threat of detention and deportation; poor housing and inadequate welfare access; and systemic cuts to domestic and sexual violence support all contribute to a temporal limbo which limits women's personal autonomy and access to basic human rights.

By reflecting on evidence from interviews, focus groups, activist participation and oral history, *Gendered Harm and Structural Violence* provides a unique insight into the everyday impacts of policy and practice that arguably result in the infliction of further gendered harms on survivors of violence and persecution.

Of interest to students and scholars of criminology, zemiology, sociology, human rights, migration policy, state violence and gender, this book develops on and adds to the expanding literatures around immigration, crimmigration and asylum.

Victoria Canning is a Lecturer in Criminology at The Open University, UK. For the past decade she has been involved in feminist and asylum rights campaigns in the North West of England. She is co-ordinator of the Prisons, Punishment and Detention Working Group with the European Group for the Study of Deviance and Social Control and, among other affiliations, is an activist with Merseyside Women's Movement.

Routledge Studies in Criminal Justice, Borders and Citizenship

Edited by Mary Bosworth, Katja Franko and Sharon Pickering
University of Oxford, University of Oslo and Monash University

Globalising forces have had a profound impact on the nature of contemporary criminal justice and law more generally. This is evident in the increasing salience of borders and mobility in the production of illegality and social exclusion. *Routledge Studies in Criminal Justice, Borders and Citizenship* showcases contemporary studies that connect criminological scholarship to migration studies and explore the intellectual resonances between the two. It provides an opportunity to reflect on the theoretical and methodological challenges posed by mass mobility and its control. By doing that, it charts an intellectual space and establishes a theoretical tradition within criminology to house scholars of immigration control, race and citizenship including those who traditionally publish *either* in general criminological *or* in anthropological, sociological, refugee studies, human rights and other publications.

Gendered Harm and Structural Violence in the British Asylum System

Victoria Canning

Routledge
Taylor & Francis Group

LONDON AND NEW YORK

First published 2017
by Routledge

2 Park Square, Milton Park, Abingdon, Oxfordshire OX14 4RN
52 Vanderbilt Avenue, New York, NY 10017

Routledge is an imprint of the Taylor & Francis Group, an informa business

First issued in paperback 2019

British Library Cataloguing-in-Publication Data
A catalogue record for this book is available from the British Library

Library of Congress Cataloging-in-Publication Data
Names: Canning, Victoria, 1984– author.
Title: Gendered harm and structural violence in the British asylum
system / Victoria Canning.
Description: 1 Edition. | New York: Routledge, 2017. |
Series: Routledge studies in criminal justice, borders and citizenship; 9 |
Includes bibliographical references and index.
Identifiers: LCCN 2016044965 | ISBN 9781138854659 (hardback) |
ISBN 9781315720975 (ebook)
Subjects: LCSH: Women—Violence against—Great Britain. |
Political refugees—Great Britain. | Power (Social sciences)—Great Britain.
Classification: LCC HV6250.4.W65 C355 2017 | DDC 362.88082/0941—dc23
LC record available at https://lccn.loc.gov/2016044965

ISBN: 978-1-138-85465-9 (hbk)
ISBN: 978-0-367-19905-0 (pbk)

Typeset in Times New Roman
by codeMantra

This book is dedicated to the many women who have survived situations beyond adversary, only to be faced with more in sanctuary.

Contents

Figures

Tables

Series editor introduction

Mary Bosworth

In this important new book, Victoria Canning adds vital new evidence to the debate over asylum policies in Britain. Drawing on many years of research and activism, she maps out how the British asylum process is structurally violent, re-victimising those who seek sanctuary, even while proclaiming a commitment to safeguarding them. Whereas much of the critical literature on migration control focuses on the work of non-state actors, usually in the private sector, who do so much of border control, Canning trains her attention on the state itself, examining the logic, practice and impact of asylum policy.

The book draws on interviews with service providers as well as people seeking asylum. Such testimonies flesh out aspects of the everyday nature of the asylum system and ground the conceptual analysis and literature. Wary of appropriating people's stories, Canning opted to work closely with one woman in particular, who is referred to in the text as Hawwi.

Hawwi's story lies at the heart of the project Canning has set herself: to depict the human impact of this complicated and unfamiliar legal system, without losing track of the wider structural factors. By concentrating on one life history, supplemented by interviews with practitioners, Canning is able to document and critique the forms of structural violence in play. Hawwi's experiences, in other words, although her own, come to stand in for others. In so doing, they illuminate how broad structural matters like race, gender and class, as well as state policies shape people's experiences and justify the system. These matters constrict people's options and shape their treatment, but are not uniform nor entirely fixed.

As British politicians and public figures, like their contemporaries elsewhere, adopt an increasingly hostile rhetoric and policy approach to asylum and migration, this book urges us to act. The public has a role to play, as Canning makes clear, in speaking out about the treatment of others and the logic behind border control.

While this book is sobering, it is not a litany of woes. Canning's own biography as well as the ideas she sets out within this account offer an inspiring and thoughtful blueprint for critical engagement. Hawwi's story makes it quite clear that we must act. Current policies are not inevitable, she points out, nor are they just. They are instead political choices that could be made otherwise.

Acknowledgements

This book encompasses years of research and activism, thus it has had input, support and dedication from many people – activists, practitioners, academics, support staff and friends who have contributed in uncountable ways. Most important is the input from women awaiting refugee status who have shared stories, opinions, jokes, songs, coffee and insight to life seeking asylum in Britain. I am most thankful.

Particular thanks to the following people and groups (in alphabetical order):

Monish Bhatia, Andrea Beckmann, Jon Burnett, Bree Carlton, Helen Churchill, Vickie Cooper, the Danish Institute Against Torture (DIGNITY), Deborah Drake, the European Group for the Study of Deviance and Social Control, Jacqui Gabb, Steve Garner, Mimoza Gashi, Paddy Hillyard, Janet Jamison, Andrew Jefferson, Rhianne Jones, Martin Joorman, Evgenia Iliadou, Liz Kelly, Liverpool John Moores University's Criminology and Sociology Departments, Migrant Artist's Mutual Aid, Dan McCulloch, Helen Monk, TsiTsi Munodawafa, the women of Merseyside Rape and Sexual Abuse Centre, Merseyside Refugee & Asylum Seekers Pre & Post Natal Support Group, News from Nowhere, Operation Bobbi Bear, Sara Parker, Jackie Patiniotis, Simon Pemberton, Amina Rafique, Hannah Ryan, colleagues and friends at Sahir House, David Scott, Joe Sim, Ann Singleton, Kay Standing, The Open University's Social Policy and Criminology Department, Steve Tombs, Frances Webber, David Whyte, Jennifer Verson.

Thanks to my family, especially Mum, Dad, Steven and Ryan, Mags and Den, Cara, Violet and in particular to my sister Samantha who has always read and commented on my work (however tedious that task may have been). Thanks also to the Douglas lot for their continual support, my nieces and nephews for uplifting distractions and to Sarah Currie and Paula Moore for their decades of friendship.

Special thanks to Samantha Fletcher, a woman whom I am lucky to call a colleague, critical thinker, fellow *Shah's* enthusiast and close friend.

As always, Andrew Douglas has supported this work from the very beginning. Everything from reading draft articles to emergency dog walking has been covered by Drew (not to mention enduring spontaneous absences and some unconventional hours of working!). I am forever grateful.

Introduction

Introducing *Gendered Harm and Structural Violence*

Shortly after giving a conference presentation in 2011 regarding the state of asylum in Britain, a colleague undertaking similar research began her own presentation with an indirect challenge, stating, 'if you think England is bad, you should see asylum in Greece'. It was an interesting and provocative start. Greece is situated close to contemporary conflict zones. Like many other Eastern and Southern European countries, its borders have been geographically instrumental in responding to those fleeing conflict, not only those *leaving* Middle Eastern regions but also historically sitting as a gateway to Middle Eastern refugee camps for some fleeing Nazi persecution.

Greece has long sat at the spatial coalface of conflict and political turmoil, perhaps now more than ever. As we enter 2017 and with no foreseeable end to the so-called refugee crisis,[1] the spatial significance of Greece, Turkey and Italy is ever more present as more people arrive at Europe's borders, and more people die trying to cross them (IOM, 2016). Britain on the other hand sits comfortably away from the areas of first response, instead surrounded by sea and ocean and with 3740 miles of landmass between the nearest point in the Middle East and its own soil, and around 2500 miles to even the most Northern point of Africa. The increasingly militant policing of borders around Calais and the ports of Northern France continue to stem immigrants' moving through the last leg of a long journey to Britain, instead restricted by law (through carrier sanctions and visa controls), increased border and riot policing, and a 16 foot razor wire fence. In short, Britain is well guarded. The relatively few who make it to Britain to claim sanctuary usually do so by plane, or long and arduous overland journeys. As such, and reflecting on my Greek colleague's earlier contention, it may be fair to say that the landscape of asylum in Britain does not necessarily seem remarkable. Her point, to me, is incontestable – problems in Britain's asylum system are not unique and when looked at from the surface, conditions do not even seem all that poor.

Britain does not hold a particularly high place in global asylum application rankings in relation to its Western European neighbours. To give an example, in 2015 there were 38,878 applications for asylum in the whole of the United Kingdom out of over 1.1 million refugees entering Europe at the same time (Red

Cross, 2016). Where countries such as Greece and Italy are often the first port of call by sea or land for refugees and economic migrants fleeing persecution and poverty in North and Sub-Saharan Africa or the Middle East, the British Isles are not. Its privileged geographic position means that no crowded boats wash up at its shores, and British beaches remain untouched by the lifeless bodies of refugees. Coastal towns are not scrambling to provide makeshift homes in United Nations High Commissioner for Refugees (UNHCR) tents to house those fleeing persecution, poverty or conflict. Indeed, conditions are often categorically worse in 'Other' European areas, where influxes of people seeking sanctuary are not (or for economic reasons cannot be) met with adequate infrastructure, housing, schooling, healthcare or nutrition.

Yet, when we speak of survivors of conflict or persecution who arrive in Britain, the trajectory of their journey is often overlooked. An Iranian woman may face daily struggles in a border camp in Greece that her counterpart living in England does not, but what is to say that the woman in England did not first live for some years in Greece? While Britain may not be comparatively dreadful in terms of over-crowded conditions for refugee groups, its responses to those seeking sanctuary are uniquely problematic, for it is not only Britain's geographic placing that evades it from immediate responsibility, but its neo-colonial legislative and securitised land-scape which – as many border researchers have documented – spread well beyond the English Channel (Carr, 2012; Webber, 2012; Weber and Pickering, 2011). Britain is cushioned from the aftermath of conflict-related migration with laws and conventions that effectively offshore and outsource responsibility to other – predominantly economically poorer – Middle Eastern, North African and Southern European regions and countries. And yet Britain is simultaneously more affluent than most European states, ranking at number five of the Gross Domestic Product (GDP) indices (in comparison, Turkey is at number 18 and Greece at number 45, World Bank, 2014) and stands directly or indirectly accountable for inducing or maintaining conditions of conflict or instability that affect regions where some of the highest rates of asylum seekers come from including Iraq, Afghanistan and Syria.

This book thus aims to contest the assumption that those seeking asylum in Britain face few challenges. Whilst I am willing to accept that physical conditions are poorer, in some regions dire, in comparison, *Gendered Harm and Structural Violence* argues that policy, legislation and an increasingly anti-immigration ideological turn makes life in Britain's asylum system extremely difficult for many of the people that pass through it. I will also argue that rather than mitigating harm or alleviating the impacts of previous harms, such as physical or sexual violence, domestic abuse or torture, the complexities of the asylum process and the time that is spent in it can actually exacerbate physical and mental health problems. As the following chapters address, practices such as dispersal, detention, deportation or the threat of deportation, and the high levels of poverty, destitution and exclusion that people seeking asylum are met with, have the capacity to induce significant social and emotional harms. Since many of these harms are avoidable, and the outcomes of them are often easily anticipated, I will argue that the decisions taken to inflict these equate to structural violence on the part of the British state. These harms, as I will also demonstrate, have gendered consequences and are experienced differentially across intersectional groups in society.

Researching gendered harm and structural violence

The issues and points raised throughout stem from a decade of undertaking interviews, focus groups, oral history and activist participation, mostly in the North West of England. Britain consists of three nations: England, Scotland and Wales but is often conflated with the United Kingdom, which encompasses these nations and in addition Northern Ireland. This book focuses specifically on Britain rather than the United Kingdom for two reasons: first, because this research has been based primarily in England and although there are regional policy differences between England, Wales and Scotland (even regions *within* England), the legal landscape is predominantly centralised to Westminster. Thus the socio-political conditions under which people seeking asylum live are broadly similar although, as the following chapter will highlight, refugee policy and practice can differ (particularly in Scotland, which has worked to separate itself from some punitive political decisions regarding immigration). I have not included Northern Ireland, and thus the UK, primarily because it has a rather different landscape, both in terms of political power holding and in relation to its experience of immigration, which is more strongly influenced by European migration than by asylum (the latter of which sat at a 'record number' of less than 500 applications in 2015, see McCulloch, 2015). As someone from Northern Ireland, I acknowledge the limitations of placing minimal focus on a region that is often obscured from research on Britain, but would argue instead that further case study analysis would be more beneficial than placing it as an add-on without sustained investigation. Unless directly specified as the UK within a given context, the main focus of this book is Britain.

Second, and more broadly, Britain is used as a case study for exploring the impacts of border controls, denial of autonomy, and lack of support services for people seeking asylum precisely because the extent of harms in British asylum are seldom acknowledged beyond those experiencing them or those who work within the parameters of asylum and immigration support. Some aspects of its immigration controls are seen as positive in other areas which mirror its sovereign attitude to restrictive borders for asylum seekers, including Nordic countries such as Denmark and Norway, but also Australia, New Zealand and North America. As I have found over the years, Britain arguably gains the privilege of having an illusion of choice and freedom in a country often represented as a global beacon of human rights. The reality that meets most people seeking asylum is rather different: one of temporal suspension, legal restrictions and an increasingly xenophobic climate. These are difficult to define because they are *invisible*: knowable only to those who become caught in the complex web of the British asylum system, and who experience the limbo that it can induce. This book therefore documents the everyday harms of the British asylum system, focussing on the lives of women awaiting asylum.

The primary case study region has been Merseyside, a county of around 1.38 million people, a key area for asylum dispersal[2] and which until 2009 had held one of two asylum processing offices before it was centralised to London. It has a small but increasing asylum population, is one of five initial accommodation sites, and assesses anywhere between 1400–3000 people seeking asylum in Initial Accommodation Centres at any given time (BBC, 2015a; MacPherson, 2014). As of 2015, the Local Authority registered fourth highest in proportion of their neighbourhoods being in the most deprived nationally on the English Index of Multiple Deprivation (Department for Communities and Local Government, 2015). In the same year, UK Visas and Immigration announced that the Complex Casework Directorate in Liverpool city centre would now take on further submissions for post-appeal rights. Basically, those whose asylum claims had been exhausted, and who would be submitting further evidence for their claim, would have to do so in person in Liverpool.

The findings from numerous projects included in this book began with the undertaking of a PhD in 2008 which focussed on the impacts of conflict-related sexual violence on women seeking asylum, and the forms of support available (or not available) to survivors. This subsequently developed into a project[3] with Dr Helen Churchill, also based in Merseyside, with which we investigated women's experience of perinatal care. Other projects have included localised exhibitions (such as 'Women Seeking Sanctuary', 2012), a post-doctoral investigation of support for survivors of sexual torture in Denmark (see Canning, 2016a), activist participation in community-based arts groups and photography projects, and practitioner-led projects focussing on support for survivors of violence or torture. In all, the findings for this book draw on thousands of hours of activist participation with organisations and people seeking asylum, around 70 interviews with practitioners, psychologists, rape support counsellors; and around 10 focus groups with women – some receiving perinatal care, and some awaiting asylum appeal outcomes. While many of the findings and concerns raised from the original research will form the base of later arguments, the process itself has perhaps formed the more radical and critical points to be made. Time spent with women seeking asylum shifted focus from the past, to the problems of the present and in particular how these problems are compounded by the states actions, or indeed inactions, to respond to the lives of women in any way other than neoliberal forms of social control. As research unfolded, I quickly realised that my own interest in the histories of women needed significant bridging to recognise the interests and priorities of women themselves – to gain enough funds to survive, tackle poor housing conditions, avoid losing their home (or in most cases for single women, a small room in shared accommodation).

As we will see, policies and legislation developed to ensure that 'genuine' asylum seekers gain access to liveable conditions have in fact impinged on the majority of those who are legally limited by outsourced visa controls and restrictions, dispersal orders, inadequate welfare and limited access to healthcare. For many women, dispersal orders – introduced by the Labour government in 1999 – meant that choosing the house or indeed the city they lived in were out of their hands. Welfare allowances, which in 2015 amounted to £5.36 per day, were managed and stretched in any way that could avoid destitution or going hungry. Women walk for miles to meet in social groups to discuss strategies for survival and resistance, to shop in the designated places forced on them by restrictions laid out by pre-paid supermarket, or Azure, cards. This is not due to the lack of transport available through Merseyside's over 200 bus routes, but because a day travel pass was, at the time of writing, £3.80 – almost 75 per cent of a single person's daily expenditure. In short, the objectives of each of the projects undertaken became stretched and obscured by the many other problems faced by women seeking asylum which transpired as the projects, and my activist involvement with multiple groups[4], evolved.

Some of what is included stems from witnessing the long-term impacts of everyday harms. On completing PhD research in 2011, I chose not to publish the original thesis in full precisely because I could not quite identify exactly what I was seeing in the wider political context of immigration and asylum. The insidiousness of harms and structural violence make recognising them almost impossible in such a short space of time. Hopefully the arguments throughout will do justice to the points women have raised over the years in challenging the problems that the process of seeking asylum can cause.

The politics of voice

The portrayal of lives and experiences are, rightly, contentious ventures in the social sciences. The precarious histories of 'research from below' in critical criminology (Becker, 1967; Gouldner, 1968) and women's voices within feminist research and activism (Kelly *et al.*, 1994; Maynard and Purvis, 2004; Stanley and Wise, 1993) have long grappled with the concept of power inherent to academic research. As Kelly and Radford pointed out 30 years ago, 'All feminist work on sexual violence, from working in refuges and Rape Crisis centres, to organising demonstrations and campaigns, to designing research methodology, to theorising, has roots in experience' (1987: 238). This is true and intentions are often well meant, but as the crisis at Europe's borders continues, so does the proliferation of research into the lives of women migrants, some of which might arguably open the door to voyeuristic and semi-exploitative conditions for the value of social acknowledgement. Representations of bare life (Agamben, 1998) have superseded those of survival and resistance, and individualistic tales of oppression are relied upon to draw public sympathy and support. In an era of conflation between immigrant and criminal, one of sympathy fatigue for the oppressed, this is perhaps understandable, but the position of the researched (or the Whiteness of the researcher) is not always fully considered.

Therefore at the very heart of this book is the question of voice – who has the right to be heard when it comes to the rights and lives of women seeking asylum? As Black, Asian and Indigenous feminists have long pointed out, much of what is discussed about the lives of Black, Minority Ethnic and refugee women is portrayed through the knowledge of White bystanders (Amos and Parmar, 1984;

Crenshaw, 1991; hooks, 1981, 1984, 1990). What can ensue is a voyeuristic gaze to the seemingly less powerful in society, something which inadvertently has the capacity to objectify rather than empower. As a White Northern Irish woman, this is a risk inherent to the process, but as the scope for detention or deportation of people seeking asylum is increased, and considering the ever more restrictive measures placed against resistance and protest in Britain (see Gilmore, 2010; 2012), critical friends are perhaps more necessary than ever. As the conclusion will highlight, there are many examples of resistance from autonomous refugee groups across the UK and indeed the world and it is worth borrowing a phrase from RISE (Refugees, Survivors and Ex-Detainees, based in Melbourne) who advocate 'nothing about us without us' (see Rise, N.D.). From a feminist and critical criminological perspective, the agenda of those made most powerless should be central and the academic or activist: a supportive conduit for challenging social injustice.

This book does not aim to lay findings out as a springboard for voyeuristic sympathy, or to further the impression of women seeking asylum as vulnerable and dependent. This is a danger I implicitly aim to avoid. As such a fine balance between participants' voices and academic interpretation has been drawn when undertaking research with women, and the objective throughout has been to balance how women see violence, support or life in asylum, and how I have interpreted these experiences. A number of strategies have been employed to do this. The most obvious has been the amount of time spent with women and support organisations to gain as full an insight as is possible, but others have included joint interpretation (such as in undertaking an oral history with Hawwi, more information on which is included in Chapter 5), in developing joint presentations at activist and academic conferences, and in facilitating access to my written work for women who have been involved in the research process and who have subsequently fed back on any issues for clarification. What I hope to do is weave the voices of women and the concerns of practitioners into a critical analysis of the state and the state's responses to survivors of persecution, torture and abuse. Thus rather than accepting dominant discourses of vulnerability, this book will tell two stories: one of women's experiences of survival, migration and lives in asylum, and one of structural violence, harm and ultimately state power.

This is therefore a story of the state – specifically the British state – and its role in perpetuating oppression and structural violence. From time spent with women seeking asylum, I am increasingly aware of the sprawling controls of the state, including in detaining and deporting women whose claims for refugee status have been refused, and that this has facilitated a form of social silencing that leaves women vulnerable, particularly those who speak out. Unlike citizens or other British-born activists, asylum activists face the threat of forced return to their country of origin, despite the historic promise of non-refoulement (see Kelly, 2012). So ultimately, while this book hopes to avoid speaking on behalf of women seeking asylum as a collective, it does aim to be a vehicle for voices that have been structurally silenced by a state intent on dissolving dissent, critique and the demand for rights that many of the women involved in weaving this narrative have stood for.

The contours and boundaries of Gendered Harm and Structural Violence

Just as the title suggests, this book addresses violence, power and harm in Britain's asylum system. Needless to say, these are complex concepts. Gender and state power each have their own histories of academic discussion and contestation. This book does not aim to reiterate long-running epistemological debates about concepts, but instead focusses on the implications that identities and individuals involved in the research process experience based on the multiple realities of harms which are disproportionate in prevalence among certain social groups, and which have unequal gendered consequences.

There are most definitely limits to what has been included. It does not fully consider the lives of children seeking asylum, a complex area of concern that requires its own thorough analysis (see Allnock *et al.*, 2015; Hynes, 2010, 2015). Perhaps the other most obvious limitations relate to the lack of representation given to those in governmental organisations, and the inability for this book to encompass all the ongoing changes and challenges the United Kingdom faces in the aftermath of the EU Referendum of June 2016, which saw a 51.9 per cent majority of voters out of a 72.2 per cent turnout opt to leave the European Union. To the first point, arguments made throughout do not mean to detract from the complexities of handling or working with asylum processes, nor do they aim to silence the state. I have on many occasions attempted to engage caseworkers (at the time, United Kingdom Border Agency staff) and was denied access. I only gained one interview with one regional director who subsequently limited what I could publish through a clause. This book unapologetically adopts an approach that facilitates the voicing of people who have fewer opportunities to be heard, and whose everyday experiences of harm are invisible to most. However, although the voice of the state is heard through media and political discourse on a daily basis, there is arguably a gap in knowledge regarding the experiences of those working directly with asylum cases, and who are required to implement policy in often strenuous circumstances (see Weber, 2005).

To the second point, as anyone who was present in the run up to the EU Referendum can attest to, much of the debate surrounding 'Brexit'[5] was premised on immigration and border control. As this book was coming to completion, so too was a long-running debate on the sovereignty of border controls in Britain. Media and public opinion in the final three months at least were particularly vitriolic against immigration, from the EU as well as the impending 'threat' of the refugee crisis and the impacts that this might have on future increases in immigration. In the final weeks of writing, the whole political landscape of the United Kingdom changed completely: former Prime Minister David Cameron resigned, Home Secretary Theresa May took up his role, and the whole Conservative Cabinet underwent a reshuffle. As much of this book has been edited to keep pace as is possible, but as with all issues of a contemporary nature, it is likely that more changes will come. While there is little scope for addressing the issue of the referendum itself, it is fair to say that coming changes will no doubt impact further on the rights and experiences of immigrants in Britain, refugees and asylum seekers included.

Therefore to begin with, the first chapter will lay the foundations of the process of seeking asylum in Britain, from applying for asylum or leave to remain, to asylum refusals and appeals. Although this may seem straightforward, Chapter 1 highlights the social and legal obstacles that people face on claiming asylum, and is concerned with the increased illegalisation of asylum and the impacts that punitive policies can have on immigrant groups. The second chapter opens up the broader trajectories of violence in the lives of refugees, specifically considering gendered violences against women as a continuum. By documenting research findings and arguments made within border studies, Chapter 2 establishes an intersectional continuum of violence across different identities, times and spaces.

Chapter 3 steers us towards identifying structural violence in the British asylum system. Utilising the work of Johann Galtung (1969) in reflection of practitioner arguments and women's experiences, and considering policy and practice within the asylum process, this chapter sets the structural context of those that follow. Chapter 4 then picks up on the micro-level implications of structurally violent decisions and practices by addressing the concerns raised by women in focus groups, interviews and activist circles. Ultimately, this chapter documents the harms that women face in everyday capacities, focussing specifically on social harm, emotional harm, physical harm, autonomy harm and relational harm.

As we move to Chapter 5, the micro-level impacts of trajectories of violence and their combination with the process of seeking asylum are voiced through the experiences of a woman named Hawwi. Having gotten in contact with me in 2011 through a refugee support organisation, Hawwi asked to participate in the research I was undertaking at the time and did so through oral history. The objective of this chapter is to highlight the lived experience of gendered violence, and address the value and limitations of seeking asylum, and support for survivors of sexualised violence. From this we move to Chapter 6, which encompasses the points raised so far in considering ways in which harms are alleviated, mitigated, or exacerbated when women seek asylum in Britain. This chapter places particular focus on ways in which survivors of violence – primarily women survivors of sexual violence or torture – are responded to by practitioners, non-governmental organisations and the British state.

The complex issues raised up until Chapter 6 do little to grapple with *how* power works to instil the harms highlighted in the overall research. Chapter 7 adopts two key critical concepts, silence (Mathiesen, 2004) and denial (Cohen, 2001), to deconstruct the ways in which harms can be knowingly inflicted but social silenced, ignored or denied. This penultimate chapter challenges the way in which short-term solutions are embedded in structural and organisational responses to the harms and violences of the British asylum system, and critically considers the role of corporations in doing this. The final chapter then moves to recognise the ways in which women seeking asylum organise to support themselves and each other, and to campaign against the problematic actions of state and state/corporate relations that silence them. Resistance has been integral to refugee and asylum activist groups who fight hard for the rights of individuals and families escaping persecution. Some groups are autonomous and self-organising, others are part of unions and women's rights groups. In any case, as I will argue, while campaigning might range from protest to practitioner-based interventions, it is perhaps through survival itself that resistance is most deeply embedded.

Notes

1 I say 'so-called refugee crisis' here because I contest the use of the term 'crisis' in this context. A crisis is unforeseeable or unpredictable. The events unfolding at Europe's borders have been wholly predictable: conflict, country occupation and economic dismantlement of any given region creates influxes in migration, and Greece and Turkey had already been experiencing significant increases in refugee populations since the 1990s. We also know that when legal routes are closed, refugees will find more danger routes through which to move, leading to increased deaths at borders (Weber and Pickering, 2011). As such, the Refugee Crisis is arguably more aligned to militarised neoliberal border mismanagement than an unforeseeable crisis (See Canning, 2018).

2 The Immigration and Asylum Act 1999 removed the option for people seeking asylum to choose where they would live while their claim was under review. This introduced dispersal, which effectively moves people away from London, often to poorer Northern, Welsh or Scottish cities such as Liverpool, Sheffield, Leeds, Cardiff and Glasgow.

3 Funded by the British Academy and entitled: Migrancy and Maternity: Experiences of Maternity Care Amongst Women Seeking Asylum in Merseyside.

4 For reasons of anonymity I won't name the groups I have been involved with. Broadly, however, these include three refugee women's groups, one Darfuri community group, a Rape Crisis centre, a women's rights group, an LGBTI asylum support group, an HIV support organisation, and a number of social justice collectives.

5 The term given to Britain's exit from the European Union – a term which clearly excludes Northern Ireland even though it actually refers to the whole of the United Kingdom leaving the Union.

1   Asylum in Britain (an illusion of sanctuary?)

The aim is to create here in Britain a really hostile environment for illegal migration.

Prime Minister Theresa May, then Home
Secretary (2012, quoted in Kirkup and Winnett, 2012)

Introduction

Hostility towards illegal immigration is nothing new in Britain's political land-scape. The gradual increase in immigration to Britain – in net migration, asylum applications in the 1990s, and immigration from the EU – has firmly placed the 'immigration debate' centre stage in public consciousness. As we will see, these have most recently manifested in debates around the control of 'our borders' where the EU is concerned. However, illegal immigration seems akin to a hei-nous crime in contemporary Britain, with employers colluding with the Home Office to catch out 'illegals',[1] a constant barrage of stories on illegal migration in daily news, and increasingly punitive sanctions for those who enter Britain 'illegally'. However, as this chapter shows, and as Stumpf (2006) and Weber and Pickering (2011) have argued, migration is not inherently illegal. Instead aspects of mobility have been *illegalised*, bound within civil and criminal law and in-creasingly restrictive social policy. Importantly (for this book at least) the same agendas which illegalise migration have not only illegalised the movement of people fleeing poverty and destitution, but also for refugees and those seeking asylum (see Canning, 2016b).

As has been indicated, this book will begin by outlining the political and so-cial context of seeking asylum in Britain. As a first step, this chapter will give an overview of the process of seeking asylum, simultaneously considering the flecks of problems that each step to gaining refugee status carries for those applying. To do this, it will contextualise the current challenges facing 'Fortress Europe' and outline Britain's increasingly punitive approach to border controls. In all it aims to highlight some of the key legislations which have facilitated the limitation of access to the asylum system itself over a period of time.

In doing so, I am acutely aware that readers of this book will come from a spec-trum of knowledge bases. Some will know the British asylum system inside-out, some will be vaguely familiar. As such, this chapter offers a broad overview of the asylum system, processes of illegalisation, relevant legislation and welfare considerations. Towards the end, it will set out key developments in responding to women seeking asylum, within both the British context and the wider European narrative. However, it also aims to avoid replicating the many intricate analyses of the social and legal contexts of seeking asylum which are well documented elsewhere and some of which form the basis of this chapter.[2] What follows is an overview, before moving to the more empirical aspects of this book in the remaining chapters.

Setting the scene

The legislative regulation of immigration to and from the UK was arguably first established in the Aliens Act of 1905, which embedded border control powers into the Home Office and facilitated the detaining and deportation of immigrants who were not 'self-sufficient'. Perhaps the first step in deterring poorer migrants and refugees from Britain, this aimed primarily at reducing the intake of poor Jews evading Russian pogroms from the late 1800s. This agenda continued, particularly in the lead up to the Second World War when further restrictions were placed on primary immigration and cases examined individually rather than by persecuted group (see Canning, 2016b).

It was (at least in part) the collective guilt of leading powers across international nations, which had inadequately intervened or appropriately responded to the massacre of Jewish and Roma people, people with disabilities, and Prisoners of War under Nazi occupation, that instigated the development of the International Declaration of Human Rights (1958) and the 1951 United Nations Convention Relating to the Status of Refugees. The latter of these, termed the Refugee Convention, declared that:

> As a result of events occurring before 1 January 1951 and owing to well-founded fear of being persecuted for reasons of race, religion, nationality, membership of a particular social group or political opinion, is outside the country of his nationality and is unable or, owing to such fear, is unwilling to avail himself of the protection of that country; or who, not having a nationality and being outside the country of his former habitual residence as a result of such events, is unable or, owing to such fear, is unwilling to return to it.
>
> (United Nations, 1951, Article 1, Part 2,
> subsequent Protocols in 1967)

It is unlikely that this convention will be new to the reader, nor will the agenda of its implementation. The millions of lives lost in the years leading up to and including the Holocaust were hard felt by an international community that had arguably turned a blind eye to impending atrocities. Prevention through sanctuary would become paramount in future times of crisis. Despite this remorse, this would not be the last time that the inactions of many of the same countries – Britain included – would result in the same kinds of gaps of consciousness. If we step four decades forward, the consequences of non-intervention during the Bosnian War (1992–1995) and the Rwandan Genocide of 1994 led to further collective guilt and promises of change. In the aftermath of a war leaving over 20,000 dead on Europe's doorstep, and a genocide resulting in the deaths of around 800,000 Tutsis and moderate Hutus, a plethora of United Nation Security Resolutions ensued. While there is no scope to delve into the politics of intervention here (so heavily discussed has it been in international politics) it is fair to say that inaction induced further political regret.

However, intervention in conflict, genocide and war is very different to actively, and legally, deterring the survivors of it. In considering the movement of refugees to safety, the significance of immigration law and border practices become more central to discussing the role of international actors in responding to women, men and children who are persecuted in conflict or under torturous regimes; to Lesbian, Gay, Bisexual, Transgender and Queer people who are persecuted and face abuse or murder under oppressive governments; and to religious or political opponents who are actively targeted in regions across the world. As political events in the 1980s and 1990s unfolded in Rwanda, Romania, the Former Yugoslavia, Kosovo, and Iraq – to name just a few – so too did the British governments' objectives to reduce access to sanctuary in the UK by outsourcing visa checks, establishing carrier sanctions and introducing restrictions for non-European immigrants (Webber, 2012). By the mid-1990s, a climate of unity across Europe was being established through the introduction of a new and fresh European Union (in 1993), while freer movement for European citizens was being instigated in Luxembourg by the Schengen Agreement,[3] through 28 countries. The United Kingdom and Ireland opted to stay out of the Schengen Agreement, instead choosing to regulate their own borders: perhaps a political omen of things to come, for this would not be the last political opt-out by the UK in the name of immigration.

The challenge to fortress Europe

If we step forward again, this time by over two decades to 2017, the shift from positivity and unity to fear and control in Europe has been quite astounding. The death of 2977 civilians in four attacks across the United States on 11 September 2001 gained unprecedented international condemnation and military response. Only now, over 15 years later, are the impacts of 9/11 and the subsequent occupation of Iraq (2003–2011) and the War in Afghanistan (2011–2014) truly visible. Economic destabilisation in parts of the Middle East, infrastructural destruction and political radicalisation are a few of the outcomes of conflict within the countries themselves. Like countries which neighboured Rwanda, the regional implications of conflict have been devastating and include increased unrest, the development of an international Islamic State terror network, and further justifications for countries in the West to inflict airstrikes, drone surveillance and the militarisation of countries in the region. Perhaps most notably, these countries include Syria, a country that has now been in armed conflict since 2011 and holds a death toll of around 250,000, and where almost five million people have been forced to flee.[4]

Unlike Iraq or Afghanistan, Syria's conflict stems heavily from autonomous resistance and revolution from within: generations of people who came together to challenge a repressive political system under President Bashar Hafez al-Assad's dictatorship, in what contributed to the Arab Spring of 2011. However, alongside airstrikes from Assad's military, the USA, Russia, the UK and France, has been the growth of Islamic State (IS, ISIS, or Da'esh). As this continues to ensue, questions are increasingly raised about the role of Western superpowers in its development, and the role they take to ensure the safety of refugees who flee violence from the region. Consider, for example, that former Prime Minister Tony Blair recently admitted that the occupation of Iraq contributed to the formation of IS. When asked if the Iraq War was 'the principal cause' of the rise of Islamic State, he replied that 'I think there are elements of truth in that' (in Osley, 2015). Britain – manipulated by Blair's alliance with George Bush and the Bush administration (see The Iraq Inquiry, 2016) – has arguably played its role in perpetrating violences that have facilitated further violence in regions from which hundreds of thousands of people have now fled.

Drawing this back to Europe, and to echo the sentiments of Michalowski:

> National leaders in these countries [in US, European Union and Australia] condemn genocide and war crimes in poor nations while simultaneously deploying strategies of border militarization and internal immigration enforcement that results in deaths, injuries, and dehumanisation for millions of immigrants seeking to escape the 'severe breakdowns of economic, political and social structures' resulting from the neoliberal global economic policies of the very nations to which displaced people are now fleeing.
>
> (Michalowski, 2013: 218)

The past five years have seen a movement of people that is akin to numbers mobilising up to and throughout the Second World War. At the time of writing, the surge of refugee numbers into Europe had peaked at around 1,000,573 in 2015 (UNHCR, 2015) and sea arrivals sat at over 204,000 for the first six months of 2016 (IOM, 2016). It has perhaps only been since 2015 that the term 'refugee crisis' has been common in public discourse and yet, as border research undertaken by Ruben Andersson (2014), Matthew Carr (2012) and Leanne Weber and Sharon Pickering (2011) all show, the militarisation of 'Fortress Europe'[5] has long been in train. The hopes of fluid borders set out in 1993 have been gradually eroded by increased (and increasingly militant) borders guards, displacement camps, detention centres and wire fencing. Importantly, this was not only started in the aftermath of refugee movements from Syria, as contemporary media commonly suggests.

It is true that there has been significant intensifications of control as numbers increase, and that these are regularly more akin to violence than protection, but the legal narratives and modes to control non-European Union (predominantly non-White) citizens are much more engrained. These have included internal controls to act as deterrents to would-be asylum applicants across Europe. As Weber and Pickering argued before the term 'refugee crisis' even took hold:

> Across the Global North, governments are increasingly engaged in efforts to reduce the access of illegalized migrants to public services and regulated labour markets. In Europe, Australia and North America, eligibility restrictions on the provision of essential housing, health and education services, and legal sanctions on employers who hire undocumented workers, are being systematically introduced.
>
> (Weber and Pickering, 2011: 112)

Corroborating this from a criminalisation agenda, Dauvergne also points out:

> Criminalisation of asylum seeking has been in train since the 1990s and is apparent in provisions such as safe third country agreements, carrier sanctions, visa requirements, safe country of origin requirements, restricted access to welfare benefits, and the imposition of 'eligibility' provisions as a precondition of access to domestic asylum systems.
>
> (2013: 76)

At a time when mobility has been made easier than ever for people from rich Northern nations, for poorer demographics, particularly people from the Global South, migration has become increasingly restrictive and significantly more dangerous. Due in part to inequalities in the global distribution of wealth, fewer people are able to travel for leisure, and substantial working restrictions are in place in countries such as the UK, US and Australia. For people from Africa, Asia, the Middle East and South America, travel is further restricted by visa stipulations. Henley and Partners – the self-defined global leaders in residence and citizenship planning – have developed a 'Visa Restriction Index' which indicates how many countries citizens can visit without a visa. They found that those from Germany, Finland, Sweden, the USA and the UK are able to travel freely to 174 countries without needing to obtain a visa before entry, whereby citizens from Afghanistan, for example, can only travel to 28 countries visa-free (Pemberton, 2015).

The invisible border

As we will see, controls through legislation and social policy have been more insidious and less visible than the physical barriers set against those fleeing persecution, conflict and poverty. These have included the Dublin, Dublin II and Dublin III Regulations,[6] which requires the first country that a person arrives in to take responsibility for their claim for refugee status, meaning they should not attempt to claim in a second country and may be returned to the first

European country they arrived in if they do so. Since many people move overland from Middle Eastern or North African regions, this can mean that countries such as Italy and Greece are held responsible for a high number of applicants. Many Northern states have therefore increased restrictions on obtaining a visa, including requiring travellers or migrants to have visas processed *prior* to entering the country.

This is inevitably very difficult for migrants such as asylum seekers, who may not be able to apply in advance due to circumstances relating to state persecution or conflict. The alternative to legal travel becomes illegalised migration, and the increased criminalisation of immigrants in criminal justice systems. According to Aas and Bosworth (2013: vii), in Europe alone:

> rapidly growing foreign populations represent on average 20 per cent of prison inmates, reaching extraordinary highs in countries such as Switzerland (71.4 per cent), Luxembourg (68.8 per cent), Cyprus (58.9 per cent), Greece (57.1 per cent) and Belgium (44.2 per cent).

Importantly, many of those are imprisoned based on immigration policy or legislation violations rather than for violent crimes or other offences.

The reader might well question how effective militarisation or criminalisation actually is as a deterrent, since the numbers of people entering Europe have not declined and more recently have instead increased. The answer to this is simple: border controls cannot prevent the efforts of people mobilising whose alternative is poverty, conflict and persecution. What the militarisation of borders does instead is shift forms of mobility into clandestine migration (Andersson, 2014) where more people die taking unsafe routes of travel, or where borders entrap people into a kind of 'stuckness' (Turner, 2010) by preventing onward (and sometimes even backward) travel. As Weber and Pickering have detailed in depth, this facilitates high numbers of border-related deaths including by drowning, starvation, sunstroke and suicide (2011). They are clear to point out that these deaths are not unavoidable, but are the direct or indirect product of punitive border controls that aim to keep out unwanted, or undeserving, immigrants. As Table 1.1 evidences, rather than being able to travel safely, people are increasingly forced into more dangerous forms of travel, particularly by haulier or sea.

Table 1.1 Border-related deaths, 2014–2016

Region of origin	Total border-related deaths per year in the Mediterranean	Total border-related deaths per year globally
Number of deaths: 2014	3279	5262
Number of deaths: 2015	3673	5604
Number of deaths: by end of November 2016	4699	6198

Bordered Britain's island mentality

This brings me to the crux of this chapter: the role that Britain contemporarily plays in responding to refugees. Applications for asylum in the UK began increasing between the 1970s and 1990s, peaking in 1991 and 1995, with 44,840 and 43,965 applicants respectively (Blinder and McNeil, 2016). This escalated to just over 84,000 applications in 2002, prompting border panic across Britain and encouraging populist calls for further restrictions on asylum. The result would be a gradual decline in applications.

As regional conflicts intensify and more people flee Middle Eastern, African and Asian countries in pursuit of safety, European countries have been forced to reflect upon their status as host states. Countries that border these areas such as Greece, Turkey, Italy and (as people continue journeys on foot or by train) Macedonia, Bulgaria, Hungary and Croatia, are predominantly the first to respond to refugees themselves. However, the opening of this book challenged the assumption that Britain's geographical distance is the primary reason for its relatively low numbers of asylum applications, even as the contemporary crisis has developed. Perhaps the most obvious way to delineate this myth is to compare the number of people offered temporary or permanent status in other European states, none of which border conflict regions in the way that Greece, Turkey or Italy do. Looking at 2015 as an example, Blinder and McNeil demonstrate significant disparities in asylum applications. Germany received 476,510 applications for asylum, Hungary received 177,135, and Sweden received 162,450. By comparison, the UK show a yearly increase of only 20 per cent from 32,344 in 2014 to 38,878 in 2015, even though this year had seen unparalleled migration into Europe since the Second World War (Blinder and McNeil, 2016).

Considering that more people are able to make it to Scandinavian countries than to the UK, the question of accessibility is brought to the fore. Sweden and Germany in particular took 'open door' approaches, at least in the formative stages of the refugee crisis and with particular emphasis placed on sanctuary for those fleeing Syria. The UK offered up 20,000 places in Britain for those in the 'Syrian Vulnerable Persons Resettlement Programme' to be granted between 2014–2020 and simultaneously introduced the increasingly draconian Immigration Act 2016 (see Table 1.2 below). Likewise, the opt-out of the Schengen Agreement outlined earlier was premised on the sovereignty of Britain's right to control its borders, and subsequent treaties and agreements have facilitated the outsourcing of responsibility to countries close to 'problem borders'. The Calais border agreement, or *Le Touquet* Treaty, for example allowed British border guards to undertake passport checks at certain French and Belgian channel borders, effectively stopping 'undesirable' migrants from entering through the physical British border. As Table 1.2 indicates, carrier sanctions have increased and visa requirements tightened, but deterrence strategies within the UK have also reduced migrant rights to seeking asylum as well as access to other aspects of society including work and welfare.

As in many parts of Europe, law and social policy have become increasingly punitive towards immigrants. As Ana Aliverti has shown, while 70 immigration offences were passed in the UK from 1905 to 1996, 84 new immigration

Table 1.2 An outline of Acts relevant to asylum in the UK[7]

Act passed	Outline of objectives and restrictions set
Immigration (Carriers Liability) Act 1987	Carriers, including airlines, became liable to civil penalties if carrying passengers without valid visa into the UK.
Asylum and Immigration Appeals Act 1993	Introduced 'fast-track' procedure and facilitated detention of asylum seekers while claim is under review.
Asylum and Immigration Act 1996	Made employing a person without legal permission to work in the UK a criminal offence.
Immigration and Asylum Act 1999	Created 35 new immigration-related offences. Extended use of civil and criminal sanctions including expanding existing offences of entering country by deception; Increased carrier sanctions (included lorries); Use of force for immigration officers introduced. Also removed choice for accommodation by introducing dispersal orders, swapped cash provision to vouchers, and increased the number of airline liaison officers based abroad to reduce the number of people arriving in UK on forged papers.
Nationality, Immigration and Asylum Act 2002	Offences included assisting unlawful immigration by non-EU citizens and knowingly helping asylum seekers to enter the UK.
Asylum and Immigration Act 2004	Criminalised individuals entering the UK without a valid travel document (or reasonable excuse not to have one); Reduced asylum appeal possibilities and increased potential for removal of support.
Immigration, Asylum and Nationality Act 2006	Introduced civil penalty of £2000 on-the-spot fine to employers of illegal workers; Restricted appeal for those refused entry to the UK for work or study; Allowed the Home Secretary potential to exclude person deemed a terrorist or major criminal from the Refugee Convention and remove citizenship from dual nations if deemed this would be 'conducive to the public good'.
Immigration Act 2014	Reduced possibilities to appeal asylum decisions from 17 to 4; Individuals deemed 'harmful' can be removed before appeal; Introduced provisions requiring landlords to check immigration status of tenant; Introduced NHS surcharges for non-European Economic Area (EEA) migrants; Introduced new powers to revoke citizenship for individuals deemed 'prejudicial' to the UK.
Immigration Act 2016	Employers of illegal immigrants now face criminal sanctions; Introduced 72 hour limit for detaining pregnant women; Introduced five year possible prison term for landlords who rent to an illegal immigrant; 'Deport first, appeal later' introduced the possibility of deporting any immigrant who was awaiting the outcome of an appeal, instead requiring them to appeal from their country of origin.

offences were created from 1997 to 2010 (in Zedner, 2013: 410). Although not all of these relate to asylum, opportunities to enter Britain or indeed the UK have reduced for non-EU citizens. The outcome has met the intention, since applications for asylum have decreased significantly, even as the need for sanctuary relating to the Refugee Convention has increased:

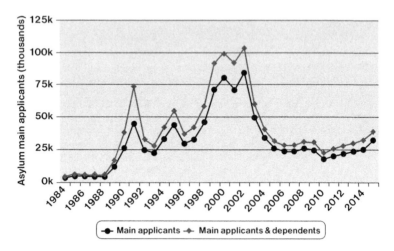

Figure 1.1 Asylum applications and estimated inflows, 1984–2015.[8]

Perhaps the strongest indicator of how immigration, asylum and the 'refugee crisis' has recently been further politicised in the UK was in the run up to the UK's EU Referendum.[9] As anyone living in or visiting the UK in the weeks and months before the vote was carried out can attest, the central premise of leaving the EU would be 'regaining' control of British borders, and challenging the role of the EU in domestic issues relating to immigration or indeed human rights. The image of the then leader of the United Kingdom Independence Party (UKIP), Nigel Farage, standing before a billboard with an image of a queue of non-White migrants and the words 'Breaking Point: the EU has failed us all' gained widespread criticism in Europe. However, it arguably epitomised the climate of xenophobia embedded in the Leave campaign itself, and echoed wider suspicions regarding the intentions of refugees when claiming asylum, exacerbating the perpetual assumption that all migrants are economic migrants.

As Francis Webber argues, however, 'although governments claim that most asylum seekers are disguised economic migrants, the country of origin statistics for those claiming asylum tell a different story, reflecting all the zones of repression and conflict' (2012: 12). Most people seeking asylum in Britain have fled conflict or areas of serious political unrest. We only need look to the highest nationalities seeking asylum in Britain to see that the one commonality among all is that their country of origin is in conflict or unrest. According to the Home Office:

> In the year ending June 2015, the largest number of applications for asylum came from nationals of Eritrea (3,568) followed by Pakistan (2,302) and Syria (2,204). In the same period, the number of asylum applications from Sudanese nationals almost doubled to 1,799, from 938 in the year ending June 2014.
>
> (Home Office, 2015a)

While country profiles can be examined in more depth elsewhere (UNHCR, 2016), it is worth saying that each of these have experienced or are currently experiencing high levels of repression and/or civilian mortality. Regions of Pakistan and Syria are notably facing airstrikes from internal government aggressors, as well as US airstrikes in both countries, and UK, Russian and Turkish airstrikes in Syria. Furthermore, in the case of refugee women, it is notable that thousands of women in the UK asylum system have fled conflict regions where sexual violence is identified as being at epidemic levels, including the Democratic Republic of Congo, Sri Lanka, Somalia and Darfur.[10] In Merseyside, women participants in research and activist groups are most commonly from Pakistan, Bangladesh, Syria, Eritrea, Ethiopia, the Democratic Republic of Congo, India and Nigeria, many of which have experienced conflict or where violence against women is noted as endemic (Bastick *et al.*, 2007).

The process of seeking asylum

The responsibility of 'managing Britain's borders' falls to the Home Office, which develops policy and influences legislation relating to Britain's borders. In practice however, the role of border management is undertaken by a range of agencies and private companies. From 2008–2013, this had been the primary responsibility of the UK Border Agency (UKBA) until their status was removed. Absorbed back into the Home Office, the UKBA was split into UK Visas and Immigration and Immigration Enforcement, and the frontline arm of border policing undertaken by Border Force[11] (since 2012). As well as this, border officers can be employed from the private sector, including G4S, Securitas and Serco – an issue that will be developed later in this book.

Defining the British asylum system can be a complex feat. To make it as clear as possible, the term 'system' in this book relates to all aspects of seeking asylum: relevant laws and immigration or welfare acts; the application process; living in initial accommodation; and practices such dispersal, detention or deportation. This is therefore a system in the broadest sense, something that encompasses the whole process of seeking asylum, and within which people are dependent on an impending decision made by the state. Unlike the overall system, the *process* of seeking asylum *seems* comparatively simple. A person arrives to the UK from another country, applies for asylum or right to remain (generally in relation to the 1951 Refugee Convention and its 1967 Protocols) either at the port of entry or, if they have been in the UK for any length of time, at Lunar House in Croydon. Then they wait the decision outcome, which is ideally to be made within around two to six months.

Linear though it seems, the *system* is so entangled with the *process* that that the practice of seeking asylum becomes more complex. As Figure 1.2 shows, once an application for asylum is lodged, the first interview is undertaken during the 'screening' process, an interview that may include discussing reasons for the application, including forms of persecution. Although the screening process aims to establish the identity and Country of Origin of an applicant, the Home Office point out that 'you will be asked why you want asylum', a difficult question to

Figure 1.2 The process of seeking asylum.

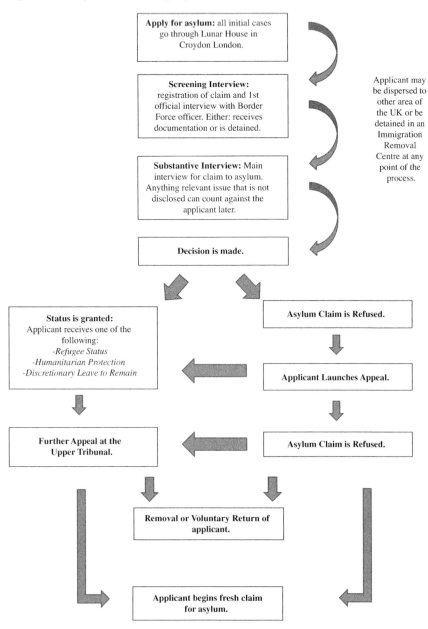

Apply for asylum: all initial cases go through Lunar House in Croydon London.

Screening Interview: registration of claim and 1st official interview with Border Force officer. Either: receives documentation or is detained.

Substantive Interview: Main interview for claim to asylum. Anything relevant issue that is not disclosed can count against the applicant later.

Decision is made.

Applicant may be dispersed to other area of the UK or be detained in an Immigration Removal Centre at any point of the process.

Status is granted: Applicant receives one of the following:
-Refugee Status
-Humanitarian Protection
-Discretionary Leave to Remain

Asylum Claim is Refused.

Applicant Launches Appeal.

Further Appeal at the Upper Tribunal.

Asylum Claim is Refused.

Removal or Voluntary Return of applicant.

Applicant begins fresh claim for asylum.

answer for survivors of violence. During this, fingerprints and photographs are taken and the individual's passport and any documentation will be retained. For those requesting asylum at ports or Lunar House in Croydon, the process can seem more reflective of criminalisation rather than sanctuary. As Imogen Tyler elucidates, seeking asylum in Britain is a complex and adversarial process that increasingly harbours measures to securitise borders, rather than protect persecuted individuals or groups:

> Once an asylum-seeker is identified, they are issued with an asylum seeker's identity card, become subject to detention, dispersal and electronic tagging, barred from access to paid work and have limited (if any) access to education, health care, social housing and income support. For the asylum-seeker, the first and most critical stage moment in this process is being identified as an asylum-seeker.
>
> (Tyler, 2006: 188)

The Home Office request that people bring with them to the screening interview: passports, travel documents, any other documents, police registration certificates (if necessary), medicines, evidence of accommodation and luggage (*up to* a maximum of two pieces of luggage per person – see UK Visas and Immigration, 2014a). In all, this can be difficult since some depend on falsified documentation to enter due to increased Visa restrictions or have had limited access to obtaining official documentation in times of conflict or unrest.[12] For those with adequate documentation, the screening interview asks how and why you have come to the United Kingdom and simultaneously requires you to answer 'questions relating to any criminal offences and national security' (UK Visas and Immigration, 2014b). This mixed 'border security/asylum' discourse is perhaps an odd combination of narratives to begin processing an application requesting sanctuary from persecution.

Under the 2007 New Asylum Model, the applicant should in theory be offered an interviewer of the same sex although the Home Office state that this might not be feasible (Visas and Immigration, 2016). As Asylum Aid (2011) have noted, this means that survivors of sexual violence or sexual torture can be expected to disclose their subjections to abuse to a stranger of the opposite sex. It is also at this point that applicants are given their Application Registration Card (ARC) or standard acknowledgement letter (SAL) for obtaining welfare, and all individuals should be allocated a 'case owner' who is in theory[13] responsible for their application until the final decision. Subsequent meetings should occur in the period leading up to the main interview, the significance of which is highlighted by the Home Office in stating, 'You must tell the caseworker everything you want them to consider or *it can count against you*' (Visas and Immigration, 2015, own emphasis added).

As well as extracting information given by the applicant, a case owner has access to 'Country of Origin Information' (COI, see Home Office, 2010a), which is meant to provide current, reliable and up to date information regarding the country from which the applicant has fled. These should be contemporary and cover a wide range of political issues, including status of women. However, a recent inspection of COI found that documents often did not reflect the whole country situation, some countries had limited or no information and subsequently case owners used inconsistent approaches to fill information gaps. Of 84 refusal letters, 13 per cent included information that was 'at best tangible to the issues relevant to the asylum claim' (Vine, Independent Chief Inspector of the UK Border Agency, 2011: 3). Once the initial statements are taken, the substantive interview is completed soon after (usually within the period of a month). Depending on their age[14] the individual will either be moved to an Immigration Removal Centre while their claim is under review; refused and deported; or dispersed to another area of the UK and assigned initial accommodation. This is usually a shared flat or dormitory which, as addressed in the introduction, are often in some of poorest and most economically deprived parts of the country.

While awaiting an asylum decision, or if the decision taken has been a refusal, asylum seekers are not entitled to work in the UK unless they have been resident or the application has been ongoing for more than one year (UK Visas and Immigration, 2014), despite access to employment being a basic human right (United Nations, Article 23 of the Declaration of Human Rights, 1948). Even then, dependents (most of whom are women and/or children) of the main applicant cannot apply to work. Briscoe and Lavender argue that this further increases social exclusion and ability to integrate (2009) but also ultimately renders individuals state dependent and increases poverty within asylum communities (Burnett and Whyte, 2010). In terms of depriving people seeking asylum the right to work and increasing the likelihood of destitution, the Joint Committee on Human Rights went as far as to say that, 'the government's treatment of asylum seekers breaches the Article 3 ECHR (European Convention on Human Rights) threshold of inhuman and degrading treatment' (2007: 5). In 2015, individual asylum seekers over the age of 18 were eligible to receive £36.62 per week, which amounts to just over £5 per day. This money is to pay for food, clothes, travel and any other expenses. Importantly, it is much less than other benefit recipients. For example, in 2015, people living as British citizens and receiving Jobseeker's Allowance received between £57.35 and £72.40 per week. It is also worth noting that although hearings are held in immigration courts across the whole of the UK, all cases will continue to be processed in London until a point at which a fresh claim is made in Liverpool (when all other options are exhausted). Although seemingly a minor detail, applicants must pay their own travel expenses when attending interviews. Needless to say, paying their way is extremely difficult for people receiving the equivalent of £5.36 per day when train or bus travel prices are at an all-time high.

The accounts given in the screening and substantive interviews become indicators of what the Home Office deem as 'merits' and consistency in the story. If for example a person were to disclose experiences of torture, domestic abuse or sexual violence – all sensitive areas for discussion for survivors – in the second interview but not the first, consistency is questioned and the person's claim can be seemed less credible. Considering that women are disproportionately affected by sexual and domestic violence, this clearly has gendered implications. Following the substantive interview, the Home Office aim to make decisions on each application within six months. As Chapters 3, 4 and 5 attest, this is not always the case.

If an applicant is accepted, they may gain asylum status, which can have limitations (for example, the right to remain for up to five years, after which the case may be reviewed) or their claim may be refused. If the latter they have the chance to appeal the decision, an opportunity that has been significantly reduced by three issues. First, the introduction of 'deport now, appeal later' in 2016 means that the appellant may be removed to their country origin and expected to engage in the legal process from there, whatever state that might be in. Second, access to legal aid has been reduced by financial cuts and legal restrictions introduced in 2016. Third, if the appellant is held in detention, their capacity to engage in the legal process can be spatially and mentally reduced (since those held in detention can experience depletions in support, self-esteem, self-worth, and increased anxiety and mental health problems – see Bosworth, 2014).

All of this takes us only to the point at which an application is decided upon, or another appeal lodged. The process itself continues, sometimes for years, and can incur significant legal and financial challenges. At any time up until deportation or the granting of status, the applicant can be placed into detention in an Immigration Removal Centre (IRC). Only after one year of living in the UK is the applicant eligible to apply for the right to work – which is not always granted – otherwise the person remains welfare dependent and with reduced entitlements to non-emergency healthcare and state or privately run housing (contracted out by the Home Office to corporations such as G4S or Serco).

As we can see then, both the process of applying for asylum and the system within which this sits can be highly complex. The aspects drawn out above in this section will be addressed in much more depth as this book develops but, in the meantime, we will move now to the gendered aspects of seeking asylum in Britain specifically, and the UK more broadly.

Gendered conventions and legislative advancement

The very nature of asylum has changed substantially over the past century, particularly the latter half of the twentieth century in terms of responses from states to post-conflict resolution. The two World Wars exposed voids in international responses to victims and survivors of conflict, making way for policy developments (Canning, 2010; Woodiwiss, 2005). The 1951 Refugee Convention recognises five key reasons for an application for refugee status: race, religion, nationality, membership of a particular social group, or political opinion. As refugee women and feminist advocates have long pointed out (Asylum Aid, 2011; Crawley *et al.*, 2011, Freedom from Torture, 2009, Girma *et al.*, 2014), this is not necessarily reflective of the forms and founded fears of persecution that many women face. The impacts of sexual violence, for example, are significant, variable and encompass social, physical and emotional harms with the potential to span the duration of the survivor's life. Furthermore, the use of public and systematic sexual violence in conflict can instigate further social harms for women, resulting in social ostracism, shame and stigma, shattering communities and potentially forcing migration, therefore increasing the need for asylum (Leatherman, 2011).

In response to this recognition, a number of key Conventions have been developed, many of which stemmed from the Beijing Declaration in 1995 at the Fourth World Conference on Women. Numerous attempts have been made at global levels to address gendered responsiveness to asylum applications, including the potential for women to apply for status under the 'Particular Social Group' (PSG) for gender-related violence claims. Perhaps the most substantive material can be found in The Convention on the Elimination of All Forms of Discrimination Against Women (CEDAW), which was established by the United Nations in 1979. General recommendation No. 32 on the gender-related dimensions of refugee status, asylum, nationality and statelessness of women makes this case:

> Women asylum seekers are entitled to have their rights under the Convention respected; they are entitled to be treated in a non-discriminatory manner and with respect and dignity at all times during the asylum procedure and thereafter, including through the process of finding durable solutions once asylum status has been recognized by the receiving State.'
>
> (CEDAW recommendation no. 32, point 24)

This statement stems from and is set within a much larger narrative that outlines considerations for states responding to refugee women. Across the 63 recommendations made, guidelines cover the treatment of women through from application to refugee status, and relate to asylum interviews, detention, non-refoulement, recognition of gendered violence and access to welfare and support. The United Kingdom has ratified the Convention and as such should work within the limits of its recommendations.

In acknowledgement of women's experiences of persecution as part of a PSG, the UKBA issued the document *Gender Issues in the Asylum Claim* (UKBA, 2010) to introduce a gendered focus when assessing women's claims, particularly in relation to approaching personally and politically silenced issues such as rape, sexual violence and domestic abuse. The document outlined some key points to consider during interviews, such as offering a female interpreter, and highlighted sociocultural norms that may be common in women's countries of origin. While this was a positive development, women continue to be routinely disbelieved, receive little if any support in the aftermath of sexual violence and are still expected to discuss instances of sexual violence in the first interview in an official environment with a stranger (Asylum Aid, 2011; Bögner *et al.*, 2010; Freedom from Torture, 2009). As pointed out earlier, the credibility of the applicant's account is also questioned if sexual violence is not discussed in the interview which in turn reduces the possibility of being granted asylum, and therefore increases the chances of refusal, detention or return. Ultimately, survivors of violence are socially silenced.

As reflected in the dissolution of the UKBA in 2013, research by a number of non-governmental organisations in the UK has consistently demonstrated instances of erroneous decision-making and adversarial rigour which have been more detrimental to the applicant. Smith (2004a) highlighted serious discrepancies in asylum interviewing and reasons for refusal, including overlooking facts about individual cases, unreasonable expectations of knowledge and unfounded assumptions by UKBA staff. More recent reports by Asylum Aid (2011), Rights of Women (2010) and the Refugee Council (2009) confirmed Smith's findings and highlight that the inadequate implementation of gendered review can have serious impacts on women. The lack of a gender sensitive approach can lead to denial of necessary support, create barriers to domestic violence refuges and problematise access to the criminal justice system, if needed. As such, it can result in an unfair review of claims for women applying for asylum in the UK, perpetuating harm against women socially, politically and emotionally through marginalisation and exclusion. The impacts of this, and of the system as a whole, will be unpacked as we move through the rest of this book.

Chapter conclusion

This chapter has outlined the contemporary climate of asylum and immigration in Europe, and the role of Britain in facilitating, exacerbating and responding to this. Having established what the 'asylum system' is, how the process works, and what problems can be created by it, the following chapter progresses into considering the gendered elements of seeking asylum. Importantly, we will move away from considering *process* to discussing gendered *experience*, specifically in relation to violence and harm.

Overall, Chapter 1 has presented the current state of immigration and asylum controls, one which is framed as a contemporary problem within the realms of a 'refugee crisis'. What follows will challenge the idea that a 'crisis' in responding to refugees is new, it is instead a long-running battle for those seeking asylum, with specific consequences for survivors of sexualised and domestic violence: problems which are disproportionately experienced by women.

Notes

1 To give a recent example, in July 2016, Byron Burger, a national restaurant train, recently undertook an exercise whereby targeted individuals without the right to work who were in Byron's employment were told they were being sent to a meeting to discuss the dangers of medium and rare cooking with burgers. On arrival in London, they were met with immigration officers who had already obtained documents from the employer, and who had photographs of the individuals. To date, 35 attendees have been deported (O'Carroll and Jones, 2016). Although supporters of the moves have emphasised that people were working illegally, the example gives a clear indication of how far the control of borders sprawls in contemporary Britain, where Home Office agendas are increasingly entwined with broader aspects of society including low-paid work, even if destitution is the alternative.

2 For in-depth discussion and analysis of many aspects of immigration and asylum in the UK, please see Aas and Bosworth (2013), Aliverti (2012, 2013, 2015), Asylum Aid (2011), Bacon (2005), Bloch and Schuster (2002, 2005a, 2005b), Bosworth (2008,

2014), Freedom from Torture (2009, 2011, 2013), Gibney (2008, 2013), Morris (2010), Pickering (2005), Pickering and Weber (2013), Somerville (2007), Webber (2006, 2012), Weber (2005, 2015), Weber and Pickering (2011).

3 The Agreement was signed in 1985 and took effect in 1995. It currently comprises 26 countries, 22 EU members and four non-EU members.

4 It is difficult to imagine that the implications of ongoing strikes will be any more fruitful than those invested in Iraq or Libya. At the time of writing this chapter (July 2016) reports were released that indicate that a US airstrike in Manbij, Syria, has alleged to have killed 73 civilians (Ackerman, 2016).

5 'Fortress Europe' was historically a military term used during the Second World War, but it is also often used to describe the ways in which European borders are policed to keep migrants out or to criminalise those who do not fit the regulations outlined in the legislations and policies discussed throughout this chapter. For further discussion, see Carr (2012).

6 The Dublin Regulation is an EU law, signed in 1990 and in force from September 1997.

> It establishes the Member State responsible for the examination of the asylum application. The criteria for establishing responsibility run, in hierarchical order, from family considerations, to recent possession of visa or residence permit in a Member State, to whether the applicant has entered EU irregularly, or regularly.
>
> (European Commission, 2016)

Quite basically, Dublin Regulation countries aim to take fingerprints on arrival. If the person subsequently moves across borders, they can be returned to the first European country they arrived in as that country is responsible for their claim under the regulation (since 2008, the Dublin III Regulation).

7 For further details and analysis, see Immigration Act 2016, Canning (2016b), Morris (2010), Somerville (2007), and Webber (2012).

8 Permission to reprint sought from Migration Observatory. Further information available at Blinder and McNeil (2016).

9 In line with a party political promise on re-election of the Conservative Party, former Prime Minister David Cameron called a referendum to decide whether the United Kingdom would remain as part of the European Union. The referendum was held on 23 June 2016. Having backed the 'Remain' campaign, Cameron stepped down as PM when the 'Leave' (or 'Brexit') campaign won, with a 51.9 per cent majority voting to take the UK out of the Union. Former Home Secretary Theresa May took up the role of Prime Minister. May had facilitated around 15,000 changes to legislation affecting immigration during her six years as Home Secretary.

10 In interviews with people working with asylum seekers, countries identified included China, Sri Lanka, Zimbabwe, Cameroon, South Africa, Iraq, Iran, Uganda, the Democratic Republic of Congo, Pakistan, Afghanistan, Malawi, Nigeria, Sudan, Nigeria, Guinea, Ukraine, Georgia, Ivory Coast, Eritrea, Somalia and Ethiopia. A notable correlation is that most of these countries are in states of conflict, post-conflict or civil unrest, with many identified internationally as areas where sexual violence has been employed as a tool of conflict and/or oppression (Bastick *et al.*, 2007).

11 Note the change of tone in the names of relevant agencies, from 'agency' to 'force' and 'enforcement' – a clear reflection of the overall shift in border management agendas.

12 Article 31 of the 1951 Refugee Convention prohibits states from penalising a refugee for illegal entry when the purpose of their entry is to claim asylum.

13 As you will see from Hawwi's experience in Chapter 5 this is not always the case, a problem that can have serious implications for the presentation of the applicants' case.

14 In 2010, the Conservative/Liberal Democrat Coalition announced an end to the detention of children and unaccompanied minors, although 2015 statistics show that over 600 children entered detention between 2010 and 2015 (Owen, 2015). From July 2016 a new dispersal scheme is to be launched to move this group to areas of the UK other than Croydon or Kent.

2 Intersectional continuums of violence

Introduction

Now that the socio-political landscape of asylum in Britain has been set in the context of international responsibilities and obligations, it is important to move to the broader picture of gendered aspects of migration and indeed reasons for migration. This chapter will address the ways in which specific acts of violence impact on women and men differently, and identify ways in which states have come to recognise these shifts, including the development of various Security Resolutions. It bridges the gap between the following chapters that address asylum in Britain and the lived experiences of women. I will thus focus on three points: the trajectories of violence that women seeking asylum can face prior to and during migration; the gendered implications and consequences of such subjections; and the importance of recognising intersectional experiences within these continuums.

The aspects highlighted here aim to represent the broad spectrum of women's lives rather than assign identities as though migrant women are a monolithic group – not all women experience these forms of violence, and not all violence is incorporated here. Furthermore it hopes to avoid confining women's identities to victimhood: the ascription of victim status can undermine the levels of survival and agency that women embody when fleeing violence or living in its aftermath (Jensen and Rønsbo, 2014; Mythen, 2007; Stanley and McCulloch, 2013). This is a complexity that weaves through responses to women – on one hand is the recognition that women as a social group do face disparate levels of violence at the hands of violent men in many, if not most, global regions (Ali *et al.*, 2012; Anthias and Yuval-Davis, 1989; Bastick *et al.*, 2007; Copelon, 2004; UN Women, 2016). On the other hand, this identification has capacity to depoliticise women who might have survived long and arduous journeys both geographically and emotionally. I therefore aim to draw these together, recognising the prevalence of violence against refugee women, but centralising the aspect of survival.

The context of gendered persecution

As is now well established in legal and socio-political literatures, persecution and migration are strongly gendered (Crawley *et al.*, 2011). The lens through which conflict, torture and persecution is viewed has historically been limited to a kind of male-centric gaze, focussed predominantly on the public and political spheres and almost inherently linked to state-level abuses of power and violent infliction (Canning, 2010, 2011a; Mackinnon, 1994, 2006). Indeed, there has been a grow-ing recognition that persecution in relation to the Refugee Convention (1951) is often defined by state violence or political identity, but that the forms of violence to which refugee women can be subjected might stretch across life trajectories, rather than singular experiences (Arcel, 2003; Bastia, 2014).

As such, the landscape in which states, councils and international organisations respond to women who have experienced persecution has changed substantively since the inception of post-World War Two Conventions. As this chapter high-lights, gendered aspects of persecution and conflict-related violence have been increasingly centralised in human rights discourses, particularly since the 1990s (Collier, 2007). European responses to women refugees have consolidated efforts to address state-level recognitions of sexual violence, domestic violence, female genital mutilation and trafficking. While the Refugee Convention (1951) and its Protocols (1967) do not themselves recognise gender as a lone-standing reason for the provision of refugee status, women survivors of gender-related violence may make cases for status under the category of PSG in some circumstances. This does not specify group status but can encompass women fleeing sexual violence, among other social, religious, ethnic and political demographics. This also does not *guarantee* refugee status, and the rates of non-disclosure of sexual violence, particularly in the initial interview, can affect women's likelihood of being believed and thus being granted asylum (Asylum Aid, 2011, see Chapter 6).

Women remain disproportionately affected by sexual and gendered violence prior to conflict, when facing political persecution, during conflict, throughout the migratory process, and when awaiting asylum. In 2008, the then UN Deputy High Commissioner L. Craig Johnstone argued that refugee women are more affected by violence against women than any other women's population in the world due to conflict-related violence and violence during migration (in Refugee Council, 2009, see also Burnett and Peel, 2001). Indeed, there are a number of population groups who may be disproportionately affected by certain forms of sexual violence (such as trafficked women or women with disabilities). This vio-lence is highly sexualised, perpetrated across spectrums of social actors, includ-ing government forces, militia, smugglers, traffickers, allies, friends and partners and husbands (Wood, 2006, 2009). Where sexual violence data exists in relation to women seeking asylum in Europe or Britain, perpetrators are almost always male (Rape Crisis Network Ireland, 2014).

Women and asylum: an intersectional continuum

Although around half of the world's refugee population are women (United Nations, N.D.), the majority of main applicants for asylum in Britain are young adult men. In 2013, just over 72 per cent of applicants were male and just over 27 per cent were female (The Migration Observatory, 2015), while in 2011 around

77 per cent of spouse applications over the age of 18 were women, a fairly consistent figure for this demographic (Refugee Council, 2013). While the gendered population of people seeking asylum in Britain does not reflect the broader global picture of refugees, particularly bordering states of conflict regions, similar demographics can be seen across Europe (Ali *et al.*, 2012).

According to gender disaggregated data, countries with high claims from women also include China (44 per cent), and Nigeria (50 per cent) (Refugee Council, 2013: 10). This perhaps gives us a small insight into the different patterns of women's asylum, as these two countries are noted for comparatively high levels of trafficking in persons, and specifically sexual and domestic exploitation which predominly affect women[1] as we can see in the National Referral Mechanisms' end of year statistics:

Women who apply for asylum in Britain and the UK do so for many reasons: some as active political agents who have been targeted by state or non-state actors, some as part of ethnic or religious minorities, and some as supporters of politically active partners or husbands (Bloch *et al.*, 2000; Freedom from Torture, 2009; Refugee Council, 2009). In areas where homophobic violence is

Table 2.1 National Referral Mechanisms' end of year statistics

Claimed exploitation type	Female	Male	Trans-sexual	Unknown	Total 2015	2014–2015% change
Adult – Domestic Servitude	292	61	0	0	353	50.9%
Adult – Labour Exploitation	161	734	0	0	895	53.3%
Adult – Organ Harvesting	1	1	0	0	2	100.0%
Adult – Sexual Exploitation	813	48	2	0	863	28.2%
Adult – Unknown exploitation	98	73	0	0	171	–3.4%
Minor – Domestic Servitude	44	25	0	0	69	–2.8%
Minor – Labour Exploitation	21	267	0	0	288	39.8%
Minor – Organ Harvesting	0	3	0	0	3	200.0%
Minor – Sexual Exploitation (non-UK national)	89	23	0	0	112	20.4%
Minor – Sexual Exploitation (UK national)	95	10	0	0	105	64.1%
Minor – Unknown exploitation type	130	273	0	2	405	71.6%
Total	1744	1518	2	2	3266	

Source: (National Crime Agency, 2016: 3).[2]

commonplace, gay, lesbian or bisexual people flee abuse, assault and the fear of death. In short, women may apply for asylum for many of the same reasons that men do. However, as Asylum Aid (2011), Canning (2011b, 2013, 2014a), Collier (2007); Crawley *et al.* (2011) and Women for Refugee Women (Dorling *et al.*, 2012; Girma *et al.*, 2014) have intricately noted, the role of non-state perpetrators of violence against women is commonly the central factor in women's need for asylum. Where this is coupled with other reasons for her claim, such violence often becomes secondary to the main categories under the 1951 Refugee Convention.

It is these points which draw us to considering violence in women's lives as part of a social continuum (Kelly, 1988) rather than the often simplistic and unilateral interpretations made by the Home Office (Canning, 2011b, 2013) or indeed other host states across Europe (Ali *et al.*, 2012). The prolific nature of sexual violence in the domestic sphere, in conflict, in refugee and Internally Displaced Persons Camps, in detention, and during genocide are well documented (Amnesty International, 1997; Askin, 1997; Bourke, 2007; Chigwada-Bailey, 2004; Girma *et al.*, 2014; Herman, 1992; Human Rights Watch, 1996, 2004; Kelly, 1988, 1990, 2000; Meintjes *et al.*, 2001; Mookherjee, 2010; Nesabai, 2005; Peel, 2004; Refugee Council, 2009, 2010; SVRI, 2015; Stiglmayer, 1994). However, there remains disparity in what is defined or acknowledged as persecution, leading to gaps in recognition and response to women who have faced or continue to face violence in the domestic sphere. This arguably facilitates a tiering of severity, and where little physical or written evidence can be given with regard to sexual violence or domestic abuse, women's claims may go unfounded against the standard of proof (Asylum Aid, 2011).

Trajectories of violence

Evidence pertaining to women's claims for asylum in Britain commonly indicates that refugee women who experience violence may do across temporal spaces rather than as one-off events (Asylum Aid, 2011; Girma *et al.*, 2015; Refugee Council, 2009). In an activist-based advocacy capacity, my experiences of women's asylum claims are similar, but also suggest that there is a lack of depth provided for detailing women's experiences of violence in asylum claims themselves. There are many possible reasons for this: that women do not wish to detail experiences in any depth; that women choose not to disclose instances of violence to someone they do not know or trust in the way they may choose to with a confidante; that women do not wish to discuss it at all; or that inadequate space is given in the substantive interview and claim to recognise the complexity of multiple violences. Although cases do differ significantly, broadly speaking (and reflecting on the cases I have followed over the years) I would suggest that the broken link lies across all of these points.

Having a role in various activist capacities places me a position of trust where women disclose experiences of violence in general discussions or in relation to their case. As a researcher, a fine line has to be drawn between advocacy and academic knowledge creation, otherwise such insight facilitates exploitation. Similarly, in formal research interviews with women, sexual violence is only discussed on women's terms rather than being instigated: the backbone of this research is the *impacts* of violence and the conditions under which these might be ameliorated in the British asylum system (which more often than not has become a focus on what compounds impacts, as will be discussed in the following chapters). This mitigates exploitation, but also aims to avoid the voyeuristic pressure put on women to disclose interpersonal histories if and when she does not want to.

That said, in my experience many women *do* wish to speak to their histories in their own time and in safe spaces.[3] From those who do wish to speak, it is clearly evident that violence reflects broader pictures of abuse: rape by militia or border guards, sexual trafficking, or as a form of violence in conflict. Other women I have spoken with report experiencing forced participation in pornography, rape by husbands, and rape fleeing conflict. Likewise, in interviews with practitioners such as rape support counsellors or psychologists, I always ask what forms of violence that refugee women they support have been subjected to. Most indicate rape as torture in detention, almost all address sexual violence at the hands of partners, and many support women who have been beaten or whipped before or after rape (including with electric cables), or raped with objects (see Canning, 2014a, 2016a).

As we can see, women hold a globally precarious status in relation to gendered experiences of violence. While any individual may be subjected to violence and abuse at varying times, the key to recognising gendered differences in violent subjections is in the disproportionality of experiences of sexual or sexualised violence within and outside of domestic spheres (CEDAW, 2014). This is not to say that all women experience sexual violence or that no men do, but that forms of persecution more commonly take sexualised characteristics against women; that the predominant perpetrators of such violences are men; and that in the absence of sexual violence there still lies a socio-structural consciousness in that women may be subjected to sexual violence. An important recognition within this is the intersectional nature of trajectories of violence.

Although intersectionality is definable by 'dimensions of difference' (Grzanka, 2014: xvi), in terms of multiple systems of inequality and their relationship with intersections of identity (Anthias and Yuval-Davis, 1983, 1989; Crenshaw, 1989, 1991; Yuval-Davis, 2006b), as will be discussed in more depth later, it also relates to temporal intersections across individual women's lives. Childhood abuse, socio-structural exclusions, female genital mutilation, transactional sex or forced prostitution: all might affect different women at varying points of her life, as might the impacts of such violences. Likewise, women may experience none of these. In short, while there are often correlations in women's accounts, the importance is to recognise that there is no set trajectory and each is different for each woman.

Conflict-related sexual violence

The fairly recent upsurge in documentation of rape in conflict since the Bosnia War (1992–1995) and Rwandan Genocide (1994) has centralised conflict-related sexual violence in global humanitarian agendas. The scale and consequence of sexual violence against women in countries such as the Democratic Republic of Congo, Sierra Leone, Sri Lanka, Uganda and Columbia set the topic of rape in conflict as an integral issue in the international security agenda, facilitating the development of Security Resolutions 1325,[4] 1820[5] and 1960.[6] The historical silencing of rape and sexual violence in war – by states as well as perpetrators – has been intermittently shattered in various regions. For example, the extent of such violence in Bangladesh was addressed through compensation to (some) women, and the public identity of 'war heroines' being ascribed to survivors.[7] Later, the public and systematic nature of sexual violence in Bosnia and Rwanda meant that denial was no longer a possibility in the aftermath of conflict. Later still, endemic rapes against women in the Democratic Republic of Congo drew global attention as a humanitarian problem, a gendered problem, and due to fistula, rape-related births, and HIV transmission, a public health problem (Karumba, 2010).

As such, conflict-related sexual violence is also increasingly recognised as a contributor to women's forced migration (Palmary, 2005, 2007), an issue which is well-documented in asylum and immigration detention literatures (Canning, 2014b; Girma *et al.*, 2014), as well as in torture and psychological support litera-tures (Freedom from Torture, 2009; Patel and Mahtani, 2004; Peel, 2004; Refugee Women's Strategy Group, 2014; Smith, 2004b). However, there arguably remains a disconnect between the speed at which the urgency to impose resolutions on coun-tries in conflict, and the speed at which the countries (specifically Northern na-tions) developing resolutions make ground-level connections between women's or men's experiences of war-related sexual abuse and the reasons for which asylum is sought. Sexual violence is in a way a political anomaly in refugee law: although it might be recognised within the PSG category of the Refugee Convention, it sel-dom guarantees refugee status unless perpetrated alongside other forms of torture (Asylum Aid, 2011; Canning, 2011a; Freedom from Torture, 2009). As will be un-packed more fully in Chapter 6, the standard of proof for claiming on such grounds is high. Along with the stigma and social and self-silencing of sexual violence, and the implications of credibility in the asylum claim, barriers remain between the somewhat popular discourse of rape in conflict as leading politicians see it, and how it is responded to at ground level in the asylum process. Perhaps this was most publicly manifest at the Global Summit to End Sexual Violence in Conflict. Held in London in June 2014 and co-chaired by Angelina Jolie as Special Envoy for the UN High Commissioner for Refugees and William Hague MP as then Foreign Secretary, the Summit 'was the largest gathering ever brought together on the sub-ject, with 1700 delegates and 123 country delegations including 79 Ministers. The Summit agreed practical steps to tackle impunity for the use of rape as a weapon of war, and to begin to change global attitudes to these crimes' (Gov.uk, N.D.).

A positive recognition though this no doubt was, irony was not lost on the fact that the event was co-chaired by a White male Conservative MP who has for a long time advocated increasingly restrictive border controls from precisely the countries most affected, or that the event cost £5.2 million to host (Townsend, 2015a). But perhaps the greatest indicator of the disconnect between Britain's acknowledgement of conflict0related sexual violence and the impacts it has had on many women who have lived through the asylum system was G4S's entry block against protesters advocating an end to immigration detention and deportation. As Women Against Rape put it at the time, 'While the Summit claims to support "courageous survivors", women seeking asylum and protection in the UK are detained, abused including sexually by Serco guards, and deported back to the very war zones where they were attacked' (Women Against Rape, 2014, see also Westmarland, 2014). As we will see later in this chapter, the impacts of such violence can be far reaching; recognition, rather than disconnect, is vital.

Gendering torture

As with conflict-related sexual violence, a number of Conventions are pertinent to discussing torture. The United Nations Convention against Torture or Other Cruel, Inhuman or Degrading Treatment or Punishment (United Nations, 1984) is most commonly recognised as the international backbone to understanding what is meant by the term 'torture'. According to the Convention, torture is:

> any act by which severe pain or suffering, whether physical or mental, is intentionally inflicted on a person for such purposes as obtaining from **him** or a third person information or a confession, punishing **him** for an act **he** or a third person has committed or is suspected of having committed, or intimidating or coercing **him** or a third person, or for any reason based on discrimination of any kind, when such pain or suffering is inflicted by or at the instigation of or with the consent or acquiescence of a public official or other person acting in an official capacity. It does not include pain or suffering arising only from, inherent in or incidental to lawful sanctions.
>
> (United Nations, Article 1, 1984, own emphasis added on gendered terms)

As argued elsewhere (Canning, 2016a), torture is highly gendered, but the recognition of torture is often ambiguous. There is not always agreement on the ground for what constitutes torture, especially in terms of understanding women's experiences of violence and terror outside of state mandates, which definitions of torture – like that above – usually rely upon (Green and Ward, 2004; Kelly, 2012; MacKinnon, 2006; United Nations, 1984). Whether sexual violence should be seen as a form of torture generally in view of its impacts, potential for pain infliction, and inherent capacity to degrade and humiliate tends to be contested. For example, the UN Convention's emphasis on the involvement of a state official is often central to wider definitions as it offers the classification of state crime (Green and Ward, 2004). Where women are sexually abused by state actors, on a state's behalf, or with state complicity or responsibility, torture might be more clearly recognised. In the context of asylum, this is not necessarily an anomaly: as a psychologist who had been supporting survivors of torture for 18 years told me, *'They may have been raped in conflict, raped as a method of torture. Many of the women who visit here have come from rape camps in Central Africa. They've been raped more times than I can even imagine.'*

However, torture, as it stands in the UN Convention, arguably does not adequately recognise or represent women's experiences of sexual violence paramount to torturous violence (Copelon, 2004; MacKinnon, 2006; Smith, 2004a). Although on the surface a definitional issue, research suggests that women's experiences of torturous violence outside of state-sanctioned abuse can be overlooked in asylum claims (Girma *et al.*, 2014; Refugee Women's Strategy Group, 2014). Certainly some women are subjected to torture at the hands of militia, but many women who come through the British asylum system have experienced similar forms of pain infliction over periods of years at the hands of husbands and partners within domestic spheres. In my experience, this is particularly common – either historically and as reason to flee her country of origin, or contemporarily and are either attempting to leave abusive partners or have recently left and so try to make a fresh claim independently, rather than as a spouse. These may not be viewed as 'torture', but the consequences are similar (Herman, 1992).

Although under-researched, sexual torture against men is often exacerbated in prisons, as a way to humiliate, degrade and ultimately silence the men who are abused (Sivakumaran, 2007; Zawati, 2007). This latter objective is particularly the case in repressive regimes and areas where homosexuality is illegalised, thus men who speak out risk criminalisation which can in some regions include the death penalty (Peel *et al.*, 2000; Sivakumaran, 2007). Men who are subjected to sexual violence are most commonly victims of male violence themselves, including during conflict and when tortured in areas of confinement and detention. As the Sexual Violence Research Initiative (2011: 2) highlights, 'In the Democratic Republic of Congo (DRC), according to a study of 998 adults conducted in 2010, 23.6% of the study's 405 men had experienced sexual violence during their lives, 64.5% of whom had experienced it in the context of the country's civil wars. Of these cases, 92.5% of the perpetrators were men, and 11.1% were women, mostly women combatants.'

Men who have been held in state prisons in Iraq and Iran have drawn attention to the use of sexual violence as terror, including in the use of weapons (Allen, 2010). This was similarly noted in Iraq prison camps such as Camp Bucca and Abu Ghraib, where Iraqi detainees were similarly subjected to sexualised degradation at the hands of US soldiers and allegedly with the knowledge of the British Army (Caldwell, 2012; RT, 2014a; Zawati, 2007). As survivors have indicated, the impacts of these abuses are far reaching – shame and stigma, threat of criminalisation. However, it is important to note that – unlike abuse in the domestic sphere – sexual violence at the hands of the state is more recognisable as torture. Since those detained are often incarcerated for political affiliation or religious reasons, and since those who incarcerate are commonly state affiliated, there is clearer cause to recognise fear of persecution on return within the mandate of the 1951 Refugee Convention. That said, as for many women, men survivors of sexual abuse in detention may not disclose such instances of violence to the Home Office or border guards.

Impacts of torturous and sexual violence on refugee women

Thus the forms of violence that people seeking asylum have experienced can include physical abuses, witnessing of violence, sexual violence, torturous violence and, before and during the asylum system, structural violence (which will be unpacked in depth in the following chapter). While some examples have been addressed above, violence itself encompasses a depth of historical debate and research (Arendt, 1969; Bestemann, 2002, Demmers, 2012) as does the psychosocial impacts thereof, so while it is not possible to address all aspects of violence, there is scope to consider the way in which impacts of violence are broadly responded to during the asylum system.

Although there can be similarities across refugee experiences of violence, there is no set experience. Indeed, certain violences may be disproportionately perpetrated against variable social identities, including sexual violence, transphobic abuse or publicly perpetrated torture, but these are neither universal nor unilateral. Similarly, the impacts that violence has on people is not deterministic: people survive in many ways and the social, emotional and physical consequences can effect individuals in very different capacities.

Surviving torture

As international organisations such as the Danish Institute Against Torture, Freedom from Torture, and the International Rehabilitation Council for Torture Victims have documented in depth and over decades, torture has profound and often lifelong impacts on its survivors.[8] In criminological literature, torture has perhaps been overlooked to some degree, although the past decade or so has seen a proliferation of debate (Green and Ward, 2000; Stanley, 2008). Even so, while legislative analyses have increased knowledge and awareness of torture, there is still arguably a disjuncture between torturous practices on the body and the longer-term implications of them. Perhaps this is due to the disparity in disciplines that this relates to, including psychology, psychosocial criminology, international relations, and trauma-related counselling and practice. However, the kinds of violence that can be inflicted through torture should arguably be more central to the concerns of critical social scientists and scholars of border studies in their analysis of the consequences of state crime on torture survivors considering that the bodies that endure it, and the impacts thereof, transcend border, space and time. As Green and Ward point out:

> The extent of port-torture suffering is extensive and involves somatic sequelae (gastrointestinal disorders, rectal lesions and sphincter abnormalities, dermatological disorders, organic brain damage, cardiovascular disorders, difficulties in walking etc.); psychological sequelae (anxiety, depression, psychosis, lethargy, insomnia, nightmares, memory and concentration impairment, hallucinations, sexual problems, alcohol intolerance etc.) and

social consequences of the somatic and psychological sequelae (inability to work, impairment of social personality, negative self-image, inability to relax, inability to relate positively with family members etc.)

(Green and Ward, 2004: 139)

In any case, the provision of support for survivors of torture can be complex: in looking at responses to survivors of conflict-related violence and torture, practitioners and organisations may adopt strategies based on levels of torture-related trauma. In describing her theory of 'complex Post-Traumatic Stress Disorder', Judith Herman highlights that 'prolonged, repeated trauma' (1992: 119) can have multiple impacts that are 'best understood as a spectrum of conditions' (ibid.). Arcel argues that 'war-based trauma is one of the most complex traumas if not *the* most complex because of the many potential traumatising events experienced by the individual before' (2003: 20). Although this will be discussed more critically later on in this book, it is nonetheless clear from research and practitioner-based evidence that torture has capacity for long-term emotional, physical and psychological harm (Baker and Rytter, 2014; International Centre for Health and Human Rights, 2014).

Surviving sexual torture

While defining sexual violence as torture may be important in relation to some asylum claims, it is the impacts of sexual violence which are central to the lives of survivors. As Ussher argues, rape and sexual abuse is 'associated with reporting of psychological distress, that can persist for a number of years following the incident, and will remain long term for approximately 50% of women, even in the presence of counselling or therapy' (Ussher, 2011: 124). Women and men who are subjected to sexual violence in any capacity can be affected in a multitude of ways – again, there is no narrowly prescribed reaction. Some individuals may consider themselves as survivors or victims, and some may feel they can 'cope'[9] while others struggle for long periods of time to recover, if they ever fully do (Herman, 1992). Experiences can negatively affect sleep patterns, concentration, eating habits, social interaction and sexual relations later in life.

To give insight into the consequences of sexual violence on refugee women who survived torture, Freedom From Torture (then the Medical Foundation for the Care of Victims of Torture) analysed the case histories of 100 women survivors from 24 countries seeking asylum in Britain. They found that:

Women in the study exhibited high levels of depression, sleeplessness, nightmares and flashbacks requiring ongoing treatment, counselling and support. Thirty-eight had scars, typically on their faces, breasts and genital areas, Twelve had fistula or other forms of damage to their reproductive organs compatible with having been raped with a sharp instrument, while seven women who had undergone testing had contracted sexually transmitted diseases, including three who were HIV+.

(Freedom from Torture, 2009: 3)

The additional levels of scarring here perhaps indicate the nature of certain forms of sexual violence and torture, specifically the sustained bodily injuries which can accumulate over periods of time, such as when held and abused in detention over weeks, months or years; and the consequences of sexual violence where abuse is sustained, systematic and/or committed by multiple perpetrators which can lead to more physical injury (Ullman, 2007). While these reflect the injuries on some women's bodies, it is not to say that all forms of sexual violence result in them, nor that violence or torture are even necessarily evident on the body. Regarding the impacts of sexual violence, Gregory and Lees pointed:

> typical reactions include helplessness, sleeplessness, flashbacks, nightmares, anger, suicidal feelings, phobic reactions, depression, mood swings, fear of being alone, relationship problems (in particular not enjoying sex), anorexia, loss of concentration and self-esteem and blaming oneself.
>
> (Gregory and Lees, 1999: 136)

Few of these are outwardly visible, and yet there remains an expectation that survivors of sexual violence are able to document abuse as part of their claim. As will be discussed in the following chapters, the social silencing around disclosure creates a significant barrier to this, but so too can the Home Office's standard of proof for evidencing torturous persecution. And yet, as a psychologist managing a torture support organisation informed me:

> *My experience working with survivors is that it leaves people profoundly traumatised, always, and they respond to that in many, many different ways. I don't think I've ever worked with a survivor who hasn't felt high levels of shame, who hasn't struggled to find different ways to block out the emotion and pain that it has caused.*

While women and men may both be subjected to sexual violence, key differences in sexual violence as a means of torture include: a) the broader gendered disproportionality of subjection to sexually torturous abuse that women can experience beyond the remit of the state (for example in domestic relationships, or as part of gendered violence during conflict); b) the gendered physiological impacts of sexual torture, particularly pregnancy and; c) forms of violence during incarceration that are less likely to be seen as politicised or state instigated as imprisonment, such as domestic enslavement or sexualised captivity.

The obvious gendered disparity in outcomes is pregnancy. To quote from an interview with a Danish psychotraumatologist:

> *the difference is often anatomical ... when you rape a man he will not get pregnant. When you rape a woman, she might get pregnant ... The primary psychological bond between a parent and a child is compromised if a woman is forced to give birth to a rape child.*

In any case, survivors of sexual torture can experience deeply entrenched feelings of shame, a social aspect that has obvious potential to hinder disclosure of previous abuses during interviews for asylum. As Zawati argued (2007), this shame can relate to the stigma of engaging in homosexual activity for men from some culturally or religiously restrictive identities, as well as evoking the feeling of emasculation[10] for male survivors of abuse. In interviews with psychologists working in torture rehabilitation in Denmark, participants referred to the loss of bravado or respect for some men, and the social silencing inherent on torture generally and sexual torture explicitly.

Violence in the aftermath of violence

Thus far we have focussed primarily on conflict-related violence, torture and persecution all of which are temporal and commonly occur prior to migration and in one's country of origin or neighbouring region. However, as Meintjes *et al.* argued, 'there is no aftermath for women' where conflict and persecution are concerned (2001: 3–18). In a time of growing research and literature on the aftermath of conflict, when ideas around community transformation and transitional justice were being embedded in international relations and global politics, this was a bold statement to make. Of course, it did not aim to distract from the significance of formal cessations on conflict-related violence, but rather emphasised that whether women leave their communities or stay during times of peacebuilding and reconciliation, forms of violence can simply change rather than truly dissipate.

In many ways, this is also an accurate statement in relation to women seeking sanctuary. As Amnesty International pointed out some time ago:

> Many refugees, especially women, are abused during their flight in search of sanctuary. Smugglers, border guards, pirates, members of armed groups, even other refugees have all been known to abuse refugee women while they are in search of safety. Afghan women trying to reach Pakistan are frequently raped and tortured by members of armed groups and border guards. Vietnamese refugees on boats have been attacked by pirates and robbed, raped or killed. Convoys of refugees fleeing the Russian attack on the Chechen Republic have been deliberately sprayed with bullets and mortar shells.
>
> (1997: 22)

Move forward to contemporary issues in International Relations, and these problems have not gone away. Instead, the non-governmental organisations (NGOs) working on border areas have increasingly made attempts to draw global attention to the violences of migration: abuse and exploitation in Internal Displacement Camps including by United Nations Peacekeepers (Annan, 2005), so-called 'transactional sex' for safe passage during flight, and increasing reports of sexual violence in refugee camps and border camps. On the latter point, Amnesty International have only recently highlighted women's experiences of harassment, exploitation, fear of sexual violence, subjection to police violence, and instances of sexual abuse for women making journeys to Europe though Turkey, Greece, Hungary and Germany, staying at border camps on the way (Amnesty International, 2016a). Abuse and sexual assaults have been reported in German refugee camps, where women-only space is not available and where some women have been prostituted for 10 Euros (Joshi, 2015; Spiegel, 2015). In Athens, men have reportedly engaged in transactional sex for small amounts of money and the use of showers in the absence of hygiene facilities (McVeigh and Smith, 2016). In any case, the combination of destitution, life in limbo and the lack of intervention from European Union leaders arguably exacerbates the potential for sexualised exploitation, and diminishes the likelihood of making money to survive by any other means.

As the following chapter evidences, similar tales of sexualised abuse have become evident in Immigration Removal Centres in Britain, where migrant women have been detained and sexually exploited by private contractor security guards. On the other side of world, reports of sexual abuse against women, men and children as young as six have emerged from Nauru Regional Processing Centre,[11] as have increasing instances of unrest within the centre (The Guardian Australian, 2013). The centre, which detains around 1000 people, (Human Rights Watch, 2015) is largely comprised of migrants fleeing religious and political violence in South East Asia, as well as intense levels of poverty in some regions (ibid., 2015). Reports from a former worker with Save the Children alleged that sexual exploitation was 'common knowledge', and sexual encounters with detainees had been filmed by officers and distributed among staff (Brooks-Pollock, 2015). In my own meetings in Melbourne with lawyers working at Nauru, issues raised included the lack of access to reproductive healthcare, restrictions on abortion, and instances of transactional sex for longer showers and access to cigarettes (field notes, July 2015).

Intersectional identities among refugee women in Britain

As we can see then, inequality and exclusion can be experienced by women in differing ways from men and from each other, and often sit at intersections of inequalities, including race and ethnicity (Crenshaw 1989, 1991; hooks, 1981, 1984; Rice, 1990; Yuval-Davis, 2006a, 2006b). Feminist studies on intersectionality have facilitated the recognition of further points of marginalisation inherent to many women's lives, which can be diverse in relation to wider social characteristics, such as ethnicity, class, religion, ability and sexuality (Sokoloff, 2008; Yuval-Davis, 2006b). Walby *et al.* (2012) provide a useful analysis of the intersections of inequalities at different and fluid points, rather than as stagnant identities. Expanding on this, and while emphasising gendered power relations as a key contributor to sexual violence, it is worth noting that life in asylum sits as another prominently racialised identity that further compound oppression and exclusion for women (Rice, 1990), potentially having serious effects on working through conflict-related trauma. Dispersal, for example, can be precarious for women who have been able to access support for traumatic experiences including sexual violence, as well as informal support networks (Dumper, 2002; Human Rights Watch, 2010).

As CEDAW determined in Recommendation 32, 'gender-related claims for asylum may intersect with other proscribed grounds of discrimination, including age, race, ethnicity/nationality, religion, health, class, caste, being lesbian, bisexual or transgender and other status' (CEDAW, 2014, Point 16). Indeed, this acknowledgement is possibly one of the most fundamental applications of intersectionality (Crenshaw, 1989, 1991) into any Convention relating to refugee status in Europe, moving the concept out of the realms of academic inquiry and more firmly into application and legal practice. This is particularly important in gendered responses to women's asylum applications. Although accused at times as being a concept of identity 'add-ons' whereby oppression becomes an inexhaustible list (see Yuval-Davis, 1994) the complexity of migrant identities can be undermined by broad and sweeping generalisations of experience. Although also criticised for shifting from structural analyses to micro-level accounts through individuals' multiple identities (see Bastia, 2014: 244), I would argue that the opposite is true: by focussing on individual aspects of experience we are able to gain insight into the multiple workings of structural hegemonic power relations which affect or limit the way in which women or indeed men live their lives. This aspect will be drawn upon in more depth in Chapter 5, where the multiple oppressions inflicted through cultural, legal and socio-political inequalities will be deconstructed through oral history analysis. To contextualise the intersectional nature of refugee women's lives, this section will now turn to experiential identities and difference.

Lesbian, gay, bisexual, transgender and queer identities

In February 2014, the *Observer* newspaper received a leaked Home Office document which revealed that a bisexual asylum seeker had been asked questions during his interview which included: 'Did you put your penis into x's backside?' and 'When x was penetrating you, did you have an erection? Did x ejaculate inside you? Why did you use a condom?' (Taylor and Townsend, 2014). This reopened discussion on the way in which the Home Office treat the claims of people seeking asylum. In his subsequent inquiry, John Vine (then Independent Chief Inspector of Borders and Immigration) found that over a tenth of substantive interviews contained questions of an 'unsatisfactory' nature, and that this was twice as common in Detained Fast-Track (DFT) interviews which 'included questions likely to elicit explicit responses or querying the validity of same-sex relationships' (2014: 3). This is an important point – DFT processed claims quickly in cases that were not considered to be complex and were unlikely to be upheld as justifiable cause for seeking asylum, thus the applicant was deemed not to have a 'well-founded fear' of persecution. Legal challenges from pressure and campaigns groups including Detention Action and The Helen Bamber Foundation from 2014 until the time of writing had eventually led to the suspension of DFT, and by 26 June 2015, 323 people were released after the system was declared unlawful. As Detention Action noted, 'The Detained Fast-Track as we knew it – a system which, at its height, was detaining one in four asylum seekers for the duration of their asylum claims and was registering 99% rejection rates in the assessment of these same claims – had been defeated' (Detention Action, N.D.).

While the original case alludes to that of a male applicant, subsequent evidence emerged indicating similar conditions under which women are also expected to disclose their sexuality of claiming fear of persecution during an asylum interview. For example, Nigerian Lesbian, Gay, Bisexual, Trans and Queer (LGBTQ) asylum rights activist Aderonke Apata (whose claim for asylum has been refused by the Home Office) argued that the threshold becomes so high that the only alternative to questioning has been to provide recorded sexual evidence (ibid.). The gendered threat of return to countries where 'corrective rape' has been documented as a means to heterosexualise gay women, such as Uganda or South Africa, is not lost on women fearing forced return or internal relocation.

As with racism and xenophobia, the nature of homophobia is such that the experiences of LGBTQ people seeking asylum is not only affected by those at the border, but also those within it. While this inherently means society more broadly, it also includes some people living in the asylum system. The nature of asylum accommodation, for example, often places with differing identities and interpretations of equality. This is a particularly complex issue: while it is sometimes assumed (perhaps understandably) that people from similar regions or which share languages and cultural beliefs may which to live in networks (Bosworth, 2014), for LGBTQ people who may have fled restrictive or intolerant belief systems, this can be even more problematic (Stonewall, 2010).

In my experience, where fundamentalist religious beliefs hold significant influence over cultural attitudes to sexuality, people identified as LGBTQ can face levels of exclusion that heterosexual people do not. For example, in discussing the impact of HIV transmission through rape with a devout Christian woman, she conveyed her dismay and the impact the diagnosis had on her life by emphasising that she was heterosexual, and as such was undeserving of such a diagnosis. As a researcher, the politics of this are particularly complex: the woman I was speaking to had herself lived through multiple oppressions, and her HIV status had affected her mental health significantly. Her time in the asylum system had been stressful and impacted negatively on her already deteriorating self-esteem, and as such I empathised with her deeply. As an LGBTQ rights activist and volunteer with an HIV support charity, however, this belief at least temporarily affected my responses to her: had any other person made such a comment, I would likely have entered intense debate. Instead we resolved to discuss and unpick the idea that HIV can have deserving and undeserving people live with the virus, but certainly this experience encouraged my recognition that intersectional oppression not only exists for women, but among women.

Living in close quarters with people who see non-heterosexual identities as deviant promotes silencing or, at worst, has the capacity to increase experiences of verbal or physical homophobic abuse. But the much bigger picture is the threat of deportation to the country from which LGBTQ women or men flee. Currently 41 out of 54 Commonwealth Countries have criminalised consensual gay sex, and it remains illegal to be gay in at least 75 countries globally (Carroll and Itaborahy, 2015). Although some of these countries and regions have received significant review and criticism for governmental abuses of LGBTQ people, such as Uganda, Nigeria, Iran and Iraq, people seeking asylum from these countries have been faced with disbelief by Home Office staff in some cases (Stonewall, 2010). According to Richard Bartram, an immigration solicitor, questions related to LGB claims specifically are 'biologically intimate' and commonly investigate what 'turns you on' about other women/men (Channel 4 News, 2014). Thus people with any sexual identity beyond heteronormative identities are faced with multiple barriers to asylum, support, the threat of homophobic abuse or spatial social exclusion, and ultimately the real potential of violence if returned to countries which do not safeguard the rights of LGBTQ groups and individuals (International Commission of Jurists, 2016).

Living with HIV

HIV has long been a topic of debate in the management of borders. Britain, indeed the United Kingdom, has consistently rejected the use of entry restrictions for HIV positive immigrants, even when some countries across the Northern hemisphere advocated restrictions or in the case of some, outright bans. This is perhaps one of the more positive tales to tell from the British immigration estate, particularly since HIV stigmatisation is so deeply entrenched in racist and indeed homophobic ideologies.

However, the exclusionary discourses around immigrants living with HIV pervade, and there is an increasing gap in support for HIV positive people seeking asylum due to so-called austerity measures. The former of these recently reared its head in public debates prior to the UK's general election, when Nigel Farage, former leader of the right-wing UKIP, called for a ban on HIV positive immigrants entering the UK (RT, 2014b). Although clearly an extreme suggestion from a far-right commentator, an amendment to the Immigration Bill (2014) was also proposed by Dr Phillip Lee of the now ruling Conservative Party, and backed by 20 party members (Wright, 2014).

The latter of these directly affects the care of women seeking asylum who are HIV positive, and the care of HIV positive people more generally. Since the economic downturn (or banking crash) of 2008/2009, the British government's introduction of austerity measures has disproportionately affected some of the most intersectionally disadvantaged people in society (Cooper and Whyte, 2017), and this has been the case for HIV positive people. HIV positive people already face significant levels of stigma in contemporary society, and considering the strong connection between sexual violence and HIV transmission (Sexual Violence Research Initiative, 2015) women, particularly those from countries with high HIV prevalence rates, are at risk of non-treatment or indeed self-silencing to avoid sexual violence disclosure or discussion.

(dis)Ability and bordered immobility

As with the above identities, the experiences of people living with disabilities in the British asylum are under-researched and gain little academic attention. This is a significant deficit for a host of reasons: women with disabilities are generally more likely to be subjected to recurring or multiple instances of sexual abuse than women without disabilities (Mays, 2006; Ward *et al.*, 2008) and as such the intersections of race, asylum status and ability, as well as possibly gender or sexual identity, have the potential to impact on support networks to prevent or respond to violence. From a border studies perspective, even the capacity for mobility is reduced for women or men who migrate if they are affected by access to medication or indeed depend on carers or use mobility aids, thus barriers are set before people make it to Europe at all (Mirza, 2011). From a mental health perspective, the disproportionate levels of trauma-related disabilities affecting psychological wellbeing among people seeking asylum also warrants in-depth discussion (see Chapters 4 and 5).

Lifelong disabilities that require sustained medical attention or intense social or personal care can affect women and men's ability to seek asylum. Furthermore, and as outlined earlier, the nature of asylum means that persecutory violence is inherent to some claims. Disabling injuries can be the outcomes of violent acts, as Harris (2003) has previously found. In her study with 38 asylum seekers and refugees, she found incurred disabilities included blindness and mobility impairment due to gunshot wounds, mobility impairment, organ failure or paralysis due to overwork or torture, and deafness due to electric torture (Harris, 2003: 399–401). As I will go on to argue later and as argued elsewhere (Canning, 2015), mental and bodily traumas or disabilities can be compounded by the stresses incurred in the asylum system itself, including the ways in which interviews are undertaken even if and when applicants are acutely unwell.

From what minimal research there is on disability and asylum in Britain, a picture of complexity is painted: barriers to social support due to language problems; a lack of knowledge of rights or entitlement to welfare; and few violence support provisions to respond to the specific needs of women seeking asylum who have disabilities (Roberts and Harris, 2002; Ward *et al.*, 2008). As with non-immigrant women, most abuse that disabled women face is perpetrated by carers or partners. Similar to women living in domestically violent relationships with spouse visas, the complexities of dependency are exacerbated for women with disabilities since the person who undertakes care may also be the person a woman depends on to ensure safety in asylum (Amnesty International and Southall Black Sisters, 2008). Stigmatisation from family members as well as society is additionally harmful (Bywaters *et al.*, 2003), and barriers to social participation are incurred by the gap in knowing women need support, and some women's capacity to know where this might be found (Ward *et al.*, 2008).

Broader aspects of exclusion

The 1951 Refugee Convention specifies that people applying for asylum should hold a well-founded fear of persecution. As the examples above show, and not deflecting from the high levels of sexual violence against women in most societies generally (Bourke, 2007), refugee populations are consistently shown to have experienced higher levels of physical and psychological violence than non-refugees (International Centre for Health and Human Rights, 2014; Wilson and Drozdek, 2004). Considering the country profiles of many people seeking asylum outlined earlier, it is no surprise that women, men or children who access support do so as a means of working through trauma related to violence or abuse.

However, there are other contributory factors that affect the wellbeing of people seeking asylum. An inherent stipulation for refugee status is the movement from ones' country of origin. With this can come significant feelings of loss: loss of networks, social status, job or community roles, possibly the loss of ones' home and belongings. For survivors of conflict, loss can be human and include family, friends or even children. Even migration itself can draw loss: the rigid controls placed across European borders has arguably affected families' abilities to travel as a unit, and as such men are finding increasingly precarious ways to enter before attempting to raise funds to move partners or children across state lines and sea (Crawley and Sigona, 2016).

These issues may seem separate or disjointed from the mandate of the Home Office to provide sanctuary where people are deemed to fear persecution, but in fact they are also intricately connected. While the UK is obliged to legally allow applications for family reunion, so that families that have been separated during conflict or migratory processes might be brought back together. However, various structural obstacles have been placed affecting refugees which means that this is made all but impossible for some. Perhaps the most limiting of these has been the withdrawal of legal aid for family reunion, a decision that was taken by the British government in 2013. This effectively means that the possibility of reunion is near impossible for most – although the Red Cross indicate that they were able to reunite around 250 families in 2014, the changes have hindered this opportunity for most people (British Red Cross, 2015). Considering almost 95 per cent of those waiting to come over were women or children (ibid.) this has a specifically gendered dimension as fewer women are unable to reach asylum in Britain, and those who have can be affected by the distance between themselves and their children. The latter of these points has been clear among the women's groups I have worked with: to date, I have only ever seen one successful reunion among research participants, and many women I have spoken with convey their feelings of loss and anxiety for children that they either cannot reach, or have no capacity to reunite with.

Chapter conclusion

This chapter has conveyed the complexities of gendered violences and their impacts on multiple identities in asylum, establishing an intersectional continuum that women can be faced with prior to, during and after the migration or asylum process. This has scratched the surface of much greater issues that have increasingly been addressed by feminists and social scientists in relation to gendered violence. That said, I do acknowledge that there has been limited scope to focus on other aspects of exploitation, such as sexual trafficking. However, what has been demonstrated throughout is that survivors of violence can be faced with further problems to negotiate when seeking asylum, some which are related to both the personal and the political and many that are reflective of interpersonal and systemic gendered oppressions in women's lives.

It is the political element of this that we will now focus on in the context of structural responses to refugee groups, with particular focus on women seeking asylum. As we have seen, survivors of torture, sexual abuse or persecution have no set monolithic experiences of violence. There are, however, commonalities of experience when seeking asylum in Britain. Destitution, threat of deportation, detention and other aspects of social control can collectively limit individuals' autonomy, and ultimately exacerbate the impacts of previous abuses or experiences. The following chapters will thus unpack policy and practice in the asylum system and argue that deliberate strategies to deter or deport people seeking asylum do, in reality, inflict serious harms. Through the incorporation of women's voices and practitioner concerns, and in structurally analysing the experience of Hawwi who sought asylum in Merseyside, we will move towards addressing and defining structural violence in Britain's asylum system and document the harms that are, I argue, intentionally inflicted on those seeking asylum.

Notes

1 The last point here, however, certainly should not be taken as an indication that men are not exploited. Instead, men are more commonly exploited through public labour in low or no pay environments and with long working hours with poor labour conditions, and face controls through the threat of criminalisation for working illegally (Bhatia, 2014; Burnett and Whyte, 2010).

2 Although now (perhaps problematically) being viewed as a stereotypical identity, I have interviewed or participated in focus groups with a number of Nigerian women who identify as having been trafficked than any other nationality, and according to a UKBA Director: 'the vast majority of sexual exploitation cases are female and the vast majority by nationality are Chinese. I don't think we've had any male sexual exploitation cases in the North West'.

3 By safe spaces, I am referring to rooms or spaces where individuals have the time and trust capacity to discuss instances of violence or other experiences or fears of persecution, torture or abuse. Although understandings of this might vary culturally, I am referring to spaces where individuals feel comfortable enough to discuss whatever they wish to, which for survivors of violence takes time, privacy and confidentiality. Freedom from violence or intimidation is integral, particularly for women survivors of male violence, lesbian, gay or bisexual survivors of violence or homophobia, and

trans survivors of violence or transphobia. Much of this is in short supply, particularly during the initial screening interview. As I will discuss further in Chapter 6, trust and time are also crucial.

4 First to recognise disproportionate effects of some conflict-related violences on women, and advocated women as key to peacebuilding.

5 Identified sexual violence as a war crime and threat to peace and security.

6 Recalled earlier Resolutions, and moved to end rape in war; to end all acts of sexual violence; and to end impunity for perpetrators. See United Nations *Women, Peacekeeping and Security* for full information (UN, N.D.).

7 As Mookherjee argued, however, this indentation in public memory was not as accepting at the local level as more contemporary global lore recalls, and instead localised receptions included sanctions and public scorn (Mookherjee, 2006).

8 Substantial documentation can be accessed at the Danish Institute Against Tortures' library, which is the biggest library of its kind in the world. I spent time researching documents there in 2013, and later in 2014. See World Without Torture (2014).

9 I use the term 'cope' here to suggest survival, but do not include it uncritically or without acknowledgement to resistance and survival more broadly. For further discussion, see Jefferson (2014).

10 I use this in the context of hegemonic and heteronormative assumptions of masculinities (Connell, 1987). I am, however, critical of the inherent assumption of emasculation when men are sexually abused for two reasons: that it is an inadvertent assumption that masculinities are universal; and that it undermines women's experiences of having their sexual autonomy removed when raped, as if this is somehow more acceptable or less harmful for a woman to be raped by a man because her sexuality is not compromised by heterosexual penetration. This is even more complex when considering the sexual violation of LGB and T survivors, some of whom are deliberately targeted to challenge their sexual orientation (such as 'corrective rape' in South Africa).

11 The Nauru Regional Processing Centre is administratively complex. Situated in the South Pacific, it is an offshore processing centre for migrants and asylum seekers otherwise aiming to migrate to Australia or New Zealand, but is run on behalf of the Australian government. Opened in 2012, it has been subject to allegations of violence, abuse and human rights violations almost since its inception.

3 Structural violence in the British asylum system

Almost everything that's done feels under resourced. And you just struggle … Sometimes we have to turn destitute people away because we've got no food, no accommodation, no money, and I cringe when we have to do that.

(Interview with asylum support organisation manager, 2010)

It is the invisibility of human culprits, rather than the presence or absence of intention to cause harm, that best defines structural violence.

(Weber and Pickering, 2011: 94)

Policymakers consistently fail to acknowledge or respond to deepening poverty, while public opinion has become more detached from reality and more hostile to the provision of sanctuary.

(Allsopp et al., 2014: 35)

Introduction

The forms of violence addressed so far are quite specific: all have focussed on violence to the body of some kind, with torture, sexual torture and sexual violence evidencing profound impacts and psychological or emotional harms, often in the longer term. In the domestic sphere, violence is heavily associated with coercive violence and emotional control (Kelly and Westmarland, 2016), yet it is still inflicted at the micro-level, with individual perpetrator(s) albeit systematically and in endemic proportions across societies. But violence more broadly is a notoriously difficult concept to define. Whether violence should be understood as hierarchal in nature, where physical violence is seen as most severe and other lesser bodily harms as less 'violent', has been heavily debated among scholars and practitioners (Green and Ward, 2000, 2004; Kelly, 1988; Tilly, 1985). Likewise, the concept of power is central and yet in criminological terms it is contested: is the infliction of violence evidence of holding power (Weber, 1946, 2002) or evidence of losing power and fighting to regain it (Arendt, 1969)?

While there is no space in this chapter to fully unpack the long-running debates raised in the studies of violence and suffering, it will attempt to map evidence of multilateral forms of violence which cause physical, social or emotional harm, or indeed death, to people seeking asylum. Moving a little away from the arbitrary infliction of pain, physical and sexual violence, it highlights forms of violence in Britain's asylum system that are avoidable but politically implemented as a means not only to control and deter asylum populations (Allsopp *et al.*, 2014; Bloch and Schuster, 2002, 2005a, 2005b; Wilson, 2015), but to cause harm. As such, this chapter encompasses feminist definitions of everyday violence (Bates, 2014; Kelly, 1988; Kelly and Westmarland, 2016; Stanko, 1985, 1990) and Galtung's definition of structural violence (Farmer, 1996; Galtung, 1969). In looking at policy and practice relating to destitution, detention, housing and deportation as case studies, this chapter argues that violence is structural, intentional and deliberate; that the outcomes of certain policies are *foreseeable* and *foreseen*; and that the implications of practices stemming from structural implementations have gender-specific consequences for women seeking asylum.

Addressing structural violence in the British asylum system

In 1969, in an era of emerging academic nuance that reflected the political and social climate of the time, Johan Galtung's seminal essay *Violence, Peace and Peace Research* introduced the concept of structural violence, whereby:

> Violence is here defined as the cause of the difference between the potential and the actual, between what could have been and what is.
>
> (Galtung, 1969: 168)

Across international politics and humanitarian studies, structural violence is commonly associated with states which are defined as 'corrupt', where state officials and greedy politicians in Southern nations use power to their own advantage[1] (see Whyte, 2015), accumulating wealth while poorer populations whither. Scholars of state crime have, on the other hand, historically focussed on violence as the 'infliction of pain, injury or death in contravention of legal or moral norms' (Green and Ward, 2009: 116). The focus of structural violence becomes state's *facilitation of suffering*, and in particular the non-alleviation of avoidable harms as being a form of violence in and of itself; shifting attention from action and intent to inaction, poor decision-making and their subsequent consequences. Where there is capacity for people to live free from suffering, but no political will exists to implement change to alleviate such suffering, structural violence is present.

The first thing to emphasise in relation to structural violence is that it can be unforeseen, in that conditions to alleviate suffering or violence might not have been recognised in advance of them developing even if there may have been capacity to change the outcome (Farmer, 1996). This reflects inaction, and thus remains as violence. However, I argue that this is not the same as the forms of structural violence in the British asylum system. The outcomes of macro-level decisions, legislation and policy implementation and subsequent harmful practices are not accidental or unpredicted, but deliberately decided. As Cooper has pointed out in relation to so-called 'austerity measures' imposed by the Conservative–Liberal Democrat Coalition government between 2010–2015 and the Conservative government then onward, violence and the harms which stem from it are often bureaucratised and logistically imposed (Cooper, 2015). Similarly, the forms of structural violence in asylum relate to very specific political agendas that maintain hegemonic intentions to both reduce asylum applications and intakes, and increase border controls – and thus everyday securitisation – with limited contestation from a majority of the public.

Furthermore, in unpacking forms of structural violence, this chapter documents the failings of the British asylum system from a critical perspective – that the system does not work to protect people who fear persecution, and in fact conditions can exacerbate impacts of previous harms. However, this stance is fairly humanitarian, beguiled on the expectation that the British asylum system is supposedly in place to be 'helping the most vulnerable people in the world's most dangerous places' (Theresa May, in *The Independent*, 2015). If we look at it from a deterrence-based perspective (Bloch and Schuster, 2005a, 2005b; Fekete, 2001; Weber and Pickering, 2011), although the system has long appeared to be in crisis, it is in fact working well for its own intents and purposes. If we take it that the process is in place to deter and restrict refugees, rather than to support them or adhere to the Refugee Convention then the outcomes generally meet the objectives. After all, as we saw in Chapter 1, asylum applications have indeed dropped substantially since the late-1990s even in the face of 'the worst refugee crisis since the Second World War' (Amnesty International, 2015). Meanwhile, the physical and ideological securitisation of the British border has facilitated ever increasing forms of illegalisation of non-European Economic Area (EEA) migration, keeping out the non-White other, and therefore increased state-corporate means to capitalise on the expanding net of border controls and arbitrary (in)justice.

Deathly consequences of structural violence

The most recognisable use of structural violence as a tool for analysis in relation to immigration is evident in Weber and Pickering's meticulously detailed accounts of deaths at global borders (2011). In their critical text, *Globalization and Borders*, Weber and Pickering address the increasing restrictions placed on migrant access to asylum in areas across Europe, North America and Australasia/Oceania. As they point out, over 17,000 migrant deaths had been recorded by UNITED[2] across Fortress Europe between 1993–2010 – a number that increased significantly in the following five years. By the end of 2015, 3,771 deaths were recorded by the International Organisation for Migration in the Mediterranean alone (IOM, 2016).

While recent dominant discourses have focussed on the problem of people smugglers, poorly funded and inadequately actioned rescue missions, and even on the people themselves (see Chapter 7), Weber and Pickering had already highlighted the responsibility of border control measures, and the states who impose them, which facilitate deaths at global borders. Drawing on debates around processes of control as a way to deter immigrants, they highlight the 'fatal consequences of illegalisation' (ibid.: 98), thus turning our focus to the problems in the process, rather than accepting deaths as an unforeseeable by-product of precarious migration. After all, it is mostly those from poorer, non-Western states whose access to Northern regions is structurally limited (Bauman, 1998, 2000). The idea that people fleeing some of the most abject forms of poverty and/or intense instances of sustained conflict would attempt to flee at any cost, even when that may be through desert or sea (Andersson, 2014; Carr, 2012; Sales, 2007; Weber and Pickering, 2011) is not unpredictable. States well know the human cost of fortified borders, and that borders will not stop attempted crossings, yet sovereignty and control prevail. Even as the number of people dying at Europe's borders has increased so dramatically since Weber and Pickering's initial analysis, the response has been to further militarise borders even to the extent of deploying the North Atlantic Treaty Organisation (NATO), which is otherwise reserved for military intervention.

As discussed in Chapter 1, public opinion regarding asylum and immigration moulds, and is moulded to, punitive government policy and legislation that has increasingly restricted the rights of asylum applicants, while simultaneously criminalising more and more aspects of immigration for those entering outside of the EEA (Bowling and Sheptycki, 2015; Sales, 2007). The fine line between denying foresight for border deaths and inadvertently indicating that we simply don't care has arguably been crossed. While deaths at Europe's borders continue to tally in significant numbers, the British state and its corporate allies unwaveringly move further forward to defend and control borders by any possible means. This has included criminalising smugglers, increasing expenditure for patrol ships across the Mediterranean, providing funds for camps outside of Britain, blockading the Channel Tunnel and Calais crossing, and detaining undocumented – or under-documented – immigrants within Britain itself.

Poverty and destitution as structural violence

Three key socio-political conditions within British asylum will now be addressed, as will some of their gendered implications: poverty and destitution, detention, and deportation. Having started with the most extreme outcome of structural violence – death at borders – it is perhaps most fitting to move to the one example of a wholly avoidable social problem which affects almost all people seeking asylum in Britain: poverty. Wealth and poverty form the basis of Britain's approach to immigration. Britain welcomes, in fact often specifically targets, wealthy immigrants from outside of the European Union. Former Prime Minister David Cameron has gone to great lengths to encourage 'the best and brightest' (Cameron, 2013) to come to the United Kingdom, yet simultaneously the Home Office have made it more difficult for foreign students to gain funding or student visas. Likewise, fee increases from 2012 across English universities have made it all but impossible for people seeking asylum to engage in Higher Education. Even prior to this, however, poverty became a staple part of Britain's asylum system through the illegalisation of working (Burnett and Whyte, 2010), removal of access to mainstream welfare benefits and, more recently, reductions in already poor benefit allowances.

Pinpointing poverty in Britain's asylum system is difficult, partially because it has become so fundamental to the process of the dehumanisation and social exclusion of people seeking asylum (Bloch and Schuster, 2005b; Sales, 2002, 2007; Schuster and Solomos, 2004; Tyler, 2006; 2013). As Allsopp *et al.* argue, the definition of poverty provided by the Joseph Rowntree Trust is perhaps most fitting: 'when a person's resources (mainly their material resources) are not sufficient to meet minimum needs (including social participation) (JRT, cited in Allsopp *et al.*, 2014: 7). One relatively easy aspect is to outline poverty in financial terms: at the time of research single asylum seekers receive £36.95 per week for food, clothing, toiletries, travel, phone usage and incidentals. In 2014, the Refugee Council took the Home Office to the High Court to challenge the amount given to people seeking asylum, which at the time equated to £5.23 per day. Refugee Action described the payments as 'cripplingly low' and stated that in their research:

> Half of asylum-seekers surveyed couldn't buy enough food to feed themselves or their families. [Our] research also found that 43% of asylum-seekers miss a meal because they can't afford to eat while a shocking 88% don't have enough money to buy clothes.
>
> (quoted by Bowcott, *The Guardian*, 2014)

The High Court ruled this an insufficient income, particularly since asylum incomes have not been matched with inflation rates but also because this placed asylum seekers' welfare at almost 50 per cent of the resident population's (ibid.). Considering the minimal standard should sit at at least 70 per cent under European Law, this was clearly unacceptable. Nonetheless, and despite the ruling, the British government have so far refused to address the poverty gap.

At first glance this move – or indeed lack of movement – appears financial and perhaps even understandable considering the impacts of austerity measures on the poorest people in Britain. As Theresa May plainly emphasised in her Conservative Party speech of 2015, Britain is not prepared to pay out to non-British nationals who are state dependent. But there are two obvious points to be made here; first, that Britain is economically stable. As outlined in Chapter 1, it ranks highly in global GDP measures. Similarly, as many critical scholars have shown, but which have perhaps been most clearly evidenced by Danny Dorling, the poverty-inducing austerity measures implemented by three successive British governments deliberately deflected from placing accountability on the key sector that was predominantly responsible for the economic downturn of 2008/2009: the financial sector (Dorling, 2014; Tombs, 2016; Whyte, 2015). Second, and importantly, the impacts of unequal financial distribution and the structural imposition of state dependency for people seeking asylum was foreseen. As far back at 2002, Alice Bloch and Liza Schuster had mapped the politicisation of asylum as part of wider debates around the value and maintenance of the British welfare state, which had become privy to dismantlement under Margaret Thatcher's Conservative government. The incremental barriers introduced for people seeking asylum (Bloch, 1997 in Bloch and Schuster, 2002: 395) embedded an exclusionary backbone to the ideals of welfarism. As they would later point out (2005a), the exclusion from the British job market enforces dependency while gaining access to work, which would reduce the levels of destitution faced by some, as well as exposure to the irregular and undocumented labour market. This would in turn remove people from the benefit system, reducing the amount of support paid by National Asylum Support Service (NASS)[3] and thus avoid accusations of 'sponging' (Bloch and Schuster, 2005a, see also Sales, 2002).

This is a fair assessment, however the successive governments have opted to act with an opposite agenda. As Jurado *et al.* point out, 'The UK has pursued the opposite of welfare state policies: asylum seekers are denied chances for social inclusion in order to ensure that the migration process is reversible' (2013: 8). The objective is not to promote conditions of security and inclusion: it is a capitalist, classist system which encourages immigration from third-party countries only when it will benefit from economic advancement though skills or the transferring of capital. Indeed, 'the underlying logic is the same [across European labour markets]: if only governments could find ways of attracting "useful" immigrants to our borders while keeping "unwanted" immigrants out, Europeans conundrum would be solved' (Jurado *et al.*, 2013: 3). As I will argue below, legislative changes moving away from welfare and towards securitisation, easier deportation and the physical Othering through detention have in many ways facilitated this, complemented by the earlier processes of exclusion identified by Bloch and Schuster, Sales and others. As we will also see, there are big benefits for big companies investing in the 'misery of migrants' (see also Bhatia and Canning, 2016).

'I am destitute'

Although the following chapter will address the consequences of structural violence in more depth through case study analysis, it is useful to glimpse the human outcomes of these policies. For example, Freedom from Torture's report *The Poverty Barrier* (2013, see also Keefe, 2014) recently indicated that poverty and poor housing often goes alongside poor nutrition and limited access to other welfare benefits. Out of 85 questionnaire respondents, more than half said they were never or not often able to buy sufficient food; 53 said they never or did not often buy new clothes and had particular problems obtaining warm clothes for winter; and more than half reported not being able to buy hygiene-related items, including sanitary towels for women and nappies for children.

The limited finances afforded to single people seeking asylum can make it all but impossible to eat healthily, particularly for those who cook individually since meat, fresh vegetables and fish are costly items and expensive to buy in small quantities. This issue cuts across a broad demographic in Merseyside as with many poorer regions, and the response has been a resounding increase in foodbanks. However, for some, the foods available through mainstream support are not a regular staple in people's diets, and followers of some religions are limited to non-meat products due to the lack of Halal or Kosher alternatives. Some organisations are left straining to provide food for those who attend – one non-governmental support group provides food for up to 200 people seeking asylum *on a daily basis* as a way to bridge the lack of provision from the state. As their manager told me, 'Destitution is another big thing we deal with here. We have about 230 destitute people working with us', before going on to argue that, as he saw it at least, 'it's that total disconnection of the Home Office and the policies they pursue, and the effect they have on people's lives … it's dreadful. And they just go, "that's the way it is".'

The term destitution is quite specific in the context of asylum. An applicant is deemed to be destitute if:

> They and their dependents do not have adequate accommodation or any means of obtaining it, even if other essential living needs are met, or they or their dependents have adequate accommodation or the means of obtaining it, but cannot meet essential living needs.
>
> (Home Office, 2013: 1)

This threshold is easily met by most people seeking asylum, but those who have been refused and awaiting the outcome of appeal should be able to access Section 4 support, provision of accommodation and an Azure pre-payment card for food and essential toiletries. For this, applicants are asked if they will become destitute or street homeless within 14 days, and if so, on what day they might expect to become homeless. The Asylum Support Application Form (ASF1) is 32 pages in length, and thus difficult to complete if English is not a first language, or indeed if the applicant has difficulty with reading or writing. Perhaps the most degrading aspect of the form comes at Section 26, which requires the applicant to tick a box stating: 'I am Destitute'; the ultimate label at the end of process of poverty and marginalisation.

A fairly common response to asylum and destitution, and a comment which has been put to me more than once, is that living in poverty in the UK is surely better than living in fear of one's life elsewhere – it is better to be poor and alive than persecuted and dead. However, as Kisson pointed out in her study of destitution in British and Canadian asylum, 'Homelessness, hunger, and fear are not confined to warring and unstable regions in the "Third World" but are increasingly faced by asylum seekers arriving to deterrent asylum policies in the West' (2010: find page). Meanwhile, as Chase argued at a recent Parliamentary inquiry into asylum and destitution:

> There is increasing evidence of the impact on children's physical health, their mental health … from not having enough food to eat … not having a warm coat to wear in the winter … ha[s] a long term effect on children and young people's wellbeing.
>
> (quoted in Ghelani, 2014)

What are really at stake here are not only the short-term consequences of destitution, horrendous though they may be, but also the cementing of 'asylum seeker' as the parasitic Other in British consciousness. Poverty is of course relative and definitions are spatially and historically dependent (Lansley and Mack, 2015), but the clear and public division of migrant rights in asylum is manifest in poverty and state dependency. This discourse recently seeped through British news when asylum seekers drew attention to that fact that the front doors of more than half of the accommodation provided by G4S in Stockton and Middlesbrough had been painted red – distinguishing them from non-asylum accommodation and facilitating escalations in targeted abuse against the residents affected. Coverage in the *Daily Mail* in particular gained comments online such as 'GO HOME and hope you still have a door left'; 'when people start paying to live in houses, then they have a say in what colour the door is painted. If they have a problem living for free in the UK, then GO'; and 'looks like a proper dump anyway, let them have it' (Mail Online, 2016). While this echoes Rosemary Sales' concerns around the 'deserving/undeserving' migrant (2002), it is also an indicator of the manipulation of public perceptions on labelling through enforced state dependency, a predictable concern which had been foreseen by Liz Fekete in 2001 when she identified the expansion of xeno-racism based on such state-orchestrated cultures of financial dependence (Fekete, 2001).

Detention and degradation

One of the most controversial and well-recognised aspects of the British asylum system is the use of detention, and specifically the detention of women. Indeed, the landscape of asylum detention allows for clear insight to the levels of toxicity evident in certain immigration policies and procedures. At the time of research, the United Kingdom had a total of 12 IRCs, 11 of which were in Britain (10 in England, one in Scotland) and one in Northern Ireland. Probably one of the fastest-growing aspects of study in border criminologies, the IRC estate echoes many of the concerns inherent to the prison industrial complex as well as the problems of outsourcing and privatisation (Aas and Bosworth, 2013; Bosworth and Turnbull, 2015; Burnett *et al.*, 2010; Canning, 2014b; Canning and Bhatia, 2016; Detention Action, N.D.).

As Bacon (2005) and Bosworth (2014) have documented, the use of IRCs began in 1971, with the opening of IRC Harmondsworth. At that time, and for years after, detention centres were on the whole a 'last stop' for people whose claims for asylum had been rejected, or who were to be deported for reasons related to criminality or overstaying on restricted visas (Bosworth, 2015; Sales, 2007; Webber, 2012). It is difficult to imagine that the exponential increase of IRCs as an almost arbitrary aspect of the asylum process could have been foreseen at this time. Global mobility, for example, was not as technically fluid as it has become, nor could the increases in conflict-related violences and persecution, which would produce conditions leading people to seek sanctuary elsewhere, have necessarily been predicted.

The response to increased capacity for mobility (Bauman, 2000) has therefore been the increasing of state and corporate capacity to capitalise on control (Andersson, 2014). This has been legislative and administrative – with the expansion of immigration policy and law which curtails the ability for asylum seekers to move freely through borders – and through detention expansion. These go hand in hand: 'Detained Fast-Track System', or 'DFT,' was established in 2003 and aimed to process all applications within a short period of time, with some deportations taking place after just 22 days (BBC, 2015a). This resulted in a number of further failures, ranging from increased refusals which then lead to appeals, to increasing the detention of people who are deemed vulnerable (including survivors of torture, see Girma *et al.*, 2014) and as discussed in Chapter 2, people who identified as LGBTQ. Simultaneously, the increased restrictions on work and welfare has meant more laws that facilitate detention or removal if broken, so people (most commonly men – see Bhatia, 2014) can be effectively criminalised and thus illegalised. As with the parasitic identity placed on welfare-dependent people seeking asylum, the 'criminal asylum seeker' which 'somehow embodying illegality and disorder' (Webber, 2012: 136) gains little public sympathy, even if the crimes they commit are more reflective of crimes of the powerless than those of violent criminals (another unenviable label which men seeking asylum are conflated with). As such, the expansion of the IRC becomes justified as a way to manage borders *and* the border criminal.

The following section thus documents the ways in which violence has become manifest in the IRC estate, not only evident through documented physical and sexual abuses, but also in the treatment and handling of the civil liberties and freedoms which should be afforded to people under Article 1 of the Universal Declaration of Human Rights, which advocates innate freedom and equality, and Article 9: freedom from arbitrary detention (also see Webber, 2012: 132). As such, the detention of people seeking asylum has become a cornerstone of structural violence, and one that has also facilitated further forms of violence to be perpetrated.

Violence as manifest

In the past few years, British detention centres have been plagued with reports of easily definable (that is, physical or sexual) forms of violence, as well as corruption. Three damning reports from Women for Refugee Women documented instances of sexual violence, including assault and sexually suggestive interactions. Daily experiences mirror prison-like conditions, such as role-call up to four times a day, regular use of restraint against non-conforming detainees, and a securitised landscape that does not permit inmates to leave (as opposed to immigration detention in other areas – see Canning, 2013). Although guards are expected to knock on women's doors in Yarl's Wood, women (including women I have spoken to in Liverpool who had previously been detained) report male guards entering rooms without awaiting a response or invitation to do so (see Girma *et al.*, 2014).

In 2014, Channel 4 News aired an equally and undeniably powerful account of life in Yarl's Wood, Britain's main centre for detaining women and children (in family units). The 15-minute expose – the first documentary access of its kind, and so difficult to obtain that it had to be recorded undercover – portrayed instances of medical negligence (a G4S practitioner left a pregnant woman for two hours, telling her to 'wait her turn' to see the doctor. She subsequently miscarried); suicide attempts; instances of racist and sexist abuse (Channel 4 News, 2014). Although it gained national coverage and condemnation in Britain, it is worth outlining the specifics of the exchanges that were documented in the footage for anyone who did not watch. To give an insight, one Serco manager refers to detained women as 'beasties' and 'caged animals', suggesting that his colleague 'take a stick in with you and beat them up'. Rather than condemnation, raptures of laughter can be heard from others in the room. In another scene a guard refers to women as 'bastards', while another states nonchalantly that 'these Black women … they're fucking horrible'. The implicit racism and animalisation is clear here, but this is met with sexist objectification when a conversation about women's resistance to the detention regime, which has included the taking off of clothes in protest. One guard states, 'they take their clothes off … it's a very common thing with African ladies', to which another responds, 'They're never slim and petite or pretty'. The ultimate accumulation of race sexualised and denigrated.

Although the language used was perhaps more extreme than one might anticipate, that there could or would be racist or sexist attitudes within Yarl's Wood was surely not unanticipated. As the reports from Women for Refugee Women started to emerge, national concern grew for the conditions that women in Yarl's Wood might be experiencing. This was exacerbated when Rashida Manjoo, the UN's Rapporteur on Violence Against Women, was denied entry to the centre in 2014. Later, in 2015, she stated:

> I can't speculate on the state's reasons since I wasn't given access to discuss the issue. Whether there is something to hide, whether there's a denial or whether there's a lack of accountability I wouldn't be able to comment, because I didn't go.
>
> (Manjoo, quoted by Townsend, 2015b)

This final point – the aspect of denial – will be picked up in more detail in Chapter 7. It is worth saying, however, that to circumvent concerns around the potential for institutional and endemic abuses, and at the public's demand, a number of inquiries were commissioned in 2015. These two inquiries – The Review into the Welfare in Detention of Vulnerable Persons, and the Independent Investigation into Concerns about Yarl's Wood Immigration Removal Centre were published simultaneously in 2016, the former making 64 recommendations for change and the latter resulting in Serco agreeing to make 35 changes in light of the findings (see Bhatia and Canning, 2016). Neither recommended closure, and problems were arguably individualised rather than recognised as institutional.

Structural responsibility

While each of the examples addressed so far vary in terms of the forms of violence which has occurred in IRCs, the landscape of detention is inherently structurally violent. First, Britain – unlike most other countries – has chosen to adopt an approach which rejects a time limit of immigration detention, having refused to join the EU Return Directive's 18-month limit for detention in 2008. Where other countries such as Sweden or France have clear cut-off points for detaining individuals, Britain aims to hold people for a short term, but can detain individuals for more than one year. As Silverman and Hajela pointed out, in 2013, the most recent statistics available:

> about 81% of total immigration detainees leaving detention had been held for less than two months. It is also not uncommon for detention to span two to four months. A small but consistent minority of detainees – about 6% – are held for more than six months, including 1% held for more than a year.
> (The Migration Observatory, 2015)

Second, the inclusion of an asylum system which facilitates the detention of women inherently – and deliberately – overlooks the continuum of violence in many refugee women's lives, thus facilitating secondary trauma or compounding the impacts of previous abuse (see Canning, 2016a, and Chapter 4). As Chapter 2 documented in depth, women seeking asylum might face multiple forms of violence as part of a continuum of gendered violence within her own life (such as child sexual abuse, domestic violence, rape or other forms of structural violence – see Canning, 2014a) or in relation to trajectories of violence during her time fleeing conflict or persecution. The latter of these may take place prior to leaving her country of origin, at border crossings, in camps, or while awaiting asylum and can incorporate sexual violence and rape, sexual torture, so-called 'transactional sex', with perpetrators including traffickers, border smugglers, border guards, port police, government officials, camp protection officers (including United Nations representatives), and partners, husbands or family members. Detention guidelines state that women or men with a history of trauma will not be detained, and yet detention remains a cornerstone of the asylum process, despite the widely recognised levels of disproportionality in surviving violence among refugee groups generally, and in relation to surviving sexual violence, women in particular. Yet as Women for Refugee Women documented, out of 46 female interviewees who had been held in detention in the UK, 33 had been raped in their home country (Girma *et al.*, 2014: 5–6). In their earlier report, *Refused*, 66 per cent of the women in the sample had experienced gender-based violence, and 32 per cent of those women had previously been raped by soldiers, police or prison guards.

Third, and importantly, is the lack of women-only space. Considering that refugee women are disproportionality affected by male violence, it is unfathomable (from a feminist perspective at least) that any women-only spaces for confinement (such as Yarl's Wood) would be guarded predominantly by men. While most men are not perpetrators of sexual violence – as many feminists have pointed out (Kelly, 2011; Wood, 2006; 2009), and while some women officers may be violent, perpetrators of sexual violence (whether physical, emotional, verbal or coercive) are disproportionately male (Bourke, 2007). Neo-liberalised equality agendas increasingly overlook or downplay the significance of structural ine-qualities between women and men in these terms. The idea that men are almost as likely as women to be victims of sexual abuse or domestic violence – although not necessarily new (see Dobash and Dobash, 2004), has arguably become so widely accepted that the opposite recognition is routinely quashed, ignored or understated.

Finally, and for criminologists researching the harms of confinement, perhaps the most signifying element of structural violence is that all of the above are wholly avoidable: because we, as a society, are aware that *confinement causes harm.* Years of critical documentation have shown that holding people in prisons or prison-like conditions can greatly affect people's mental, physical and emotional wellbeing (Prison Reform Trust, 2009; Segrave and Carlton, 2011; Sim, 1990) and increase feelings of suicidality and instances of self-harm (Scott and Codd, 2010). As discussed above, the effects of sexual violence can be greatly exacerbated by confinement, where a loss of sense of self or autonomy impedes longer-term healing or indeed access to support networks or mental health services. While those who demonstrate evidence of trauma or mental health problems cannot legally be detained, a landmark High Court ruling in 2015 found that torture survivors were indeed being held in detention (RT, 2015). As such, the practice of detaining immigrants and asylum seekers directly, deliberately and knowingly puts the health and wellbeing of an individual in jeopardy, yet the state continues to seek no real alternative to the IRC complex.

Custody officer violence in a xeno-racist landscape

Although the conditions of confinement in detention are, as we have seen, structurally violent, questions should still be raised about the perpetration of deliberately violent acts against individuals. The men responsible for acts of sexual violence in Yarl's Wood for example, all of whom were identified and dismissed from their roles (BBC, 2013), were of course accountable for their own actions. Those recorded by Channel 4 News verbally denigrating migrant women are identifiable, and thus also accountable, to their own verbally violent actions.

As such, no attempt can be made to deflect from individual responsibility: not all guards are violent, thus violence cannot be intrinsic to the existence of the role. In fact, as Leanne Weber argued in 2005, some Detention Custody Officers might also engage in acts of disobedience and dissent, refusing to co-operate in mandatory operations in IRCs or finding ways around the implementation of policies which they consider to be inhumane (Weber, 2005). However, there are a number of aspects worth considering in relation to both violence, such as that above, and institutionalised cultures of xeno-racism. The first is from a Trade Unionist perspective: the conditions of work for those on the lowest grade of employment within IRCs (and indeed prisons more generally) are categorically problematic. In 2015, Channel 4 News once again gained footage from an Immigration Removal Centre, this time recorded by a detainee in IRC Harmondsworth, the biggest facility in Britain that detains only men. In the films, different staff members can be heard stating that conditions are 'shit'; that photos and recordings are not allowed as the government 'don't want the bad publicity that would entail'; and one guard claiming that Mitie, the security company which won the contract had 'fucked this place up' and that 'there's only so much people can take' (Corporate Watch, 2015).

To contextualise, those who work face to face with people held in detention are generally employed on shift work, meaning 'flexible' hours requiring night shift and weekend working. Wages are low, ranging from around £14,000–£22,000 depending on the role of the officer. Compounding this, private security companies such as G4S and Serco regularly adopt zero-hour contracts (Inman, 2013), so contractors can decide whether the worker will gain anything between full-time hours per week, to zero hours, regularly with little notice. As Spanjers pointed out in 2013, the 'use of zero hours contracts could impact on the quality of service offered, as casual workers are less likely to feel engaged in the business or valued by the employer and are therefore unwilling to go the extra mile' (2013). Although not an explanation for violent actions or abuse, in accumulation with the broader structures and agendas of immigration detention and control, it seems feasible that poor working conditions might decrease the standards of care given to those held in custody.

The second consideration relates to the expectations of the state and/or companies in terms of competency or experience. Only recently *The Guardian* raised concerns about the employment of gap-year students for making decisions in asylum claims. Such students, who would be deciding the outcome of persecution cases, require five weeks of training (Taylor, 2009). For most researchers in this field this was not surprising, since the practice has been longstanding. However, it did draw attention to the deprofessionaliation of legal work in the context of asylum case work, an issue which reflects the points made above as well as the requirements for certain experience related to working in care or protection environments, which IRCs regularly claim to do. For example, to quote a job advertisement as a Detainee Custody Officer for Mitie at IRC Heathrow, 'This role requires no specific previous experience or qualifications but experience of dealing sensitively with a wide variety of people who have been agitated, confused or angry *would be an advantage*' (Mitie, on Total Jobs, 2016, own emphasis added). This is telling of two points: Mitie here recognise and even publicly advertise that those within its care are likely to be behaving in ways related to experiencing distress, and that experience of handling such fundamentally precarious situations is not an *essential* criteria, but *desirable*. This is questionable practice, not only for the detainee, but also for the person held responsible for the care of those in their custody.

Deportation

The final example of structural violence in Britain's asylum system is in the politics, process and outcome of what has been termed 'the deportation machine' (Fekete, 2005). As Blinder (2015) outlines, there are three key forms of deportation. The first is deportation, which is enforced and seen as conducive to the public good by the Secretary of State, or is ordered by court in relation to a conviction resulting in a prison term. The second is administrative removals, which refers to non-admittance and removal of people attempting to enter the UK illegally or who have been refused legal permission to stay. The third relates to voluntary departures, which are not necessarily voluntary in terms of choosing to leave the UK, but which refer to the person's agreement to leave either through an Assisted Voluntary Returns Scheme, or by leaving on their own accord (for a more in-depth discussion, see Blinder, 2015: 3).

There have been steady increases in the number of deportations across some – although not all – countries in the Global North. Gibney (2008) has argued that the deportation of failed asylum seekers and foreign prisoners has been rising since the early 2000s in countries including the United States, the Netherlands, Germany, Canada and Australia. As Weber (2015) has shown, this varies considerably across the Global North, as does the way in which this increase has been facilitated (i.e. administratively or legislatively), and the demographic background of who is most commonly deported. In Britain specifically, however, the categorisation of deportations can make definitive statistical analysis unclear. As Table 3.1 indicates, Home Office statistics indicate a decline in enforced removals between 2009–2014, while voluntary departures have increased somewhat.

The decrease in enforced removals relates clearly to the reduction in the number of asylum applications, which had dropped substantively during this time, in part because of the restrictions placed on entry for non-EU citizens meant legal routes were all but cut off during this period. However, for lawyers and criminologists, the increased *capacity* to deport has been of particular interest. As Webber indicates, removals *overall* have increased exponentially since the 1990s, largely based on the legislative and administrative capacities to do so:

> In 1997, about 7000 refused asylum seekers and around 3,500 overstayers, illegal entrants and offenders were removed or deported … by 2005, the numbers of refused asylum seekers removed had doubled, and removals of irregular migrants and offenders had quadrupled. The enforcement budget was massively expanded again in 200, and by 2010, while the number of refused asylum seekers had fallen to around 10,000, the number of offenders and irregular migrants had jumped to 31,500 - nearly ten times the 1997.
>
> (Webber, 2012: 162)

Gibney (2008, 2013) documents the legal frameworks under which deportation has been facilitated in Britain over the past five decades, beginning with The Commonwealth Act 1962, which made it possible to deport Commonwealth

Table 3.1 Removals and voluntary departures by type

Year	Total enforced removals	Total refused entry at port and subsequently departed	Total voluntary departures (1)	Assisted voluntary returns (2)	Notified voluntary departures (3)	Other confirmed voluntary departures (1)(4)	Other confirmed voluntary departures as a % of voluntary departures
2009	15,252	29,162	22,800	4944	4317	13,539	59%
2010	14,854	18,276	27,114	4541	5996	16,577	61%
2011	15,063	15,700	26,419	3120	7587	15,712	59%
2012	14,647	13,789	29,663	3706	6749	19,208	65%
2013	13,311	14,396	32,178	4297	8150	19,731	61%
2014(1)	12,460	15,943	24,001	2406	10,609	10,986	46%
Change: latest year (5)	−851	+1547					
Percentage change	−6%	+11%					

Citizens; through to the Nationality, Immigration and Asylum Act 2002 and the Immigration, Asylum and Nationality Act 2006 which allows the state to strip citizenship from UK citizens with a second nationality (Gibney, 2013: 220). The fundamental game-changer in border politics and deportation was, as Gibney (ibid.) and later Bhatia (2015) point out, the UK Borders Act 2007. This introduced mandatory deportation orders for non-EU citizens who were imprisoned for a year or more or had committed certain categories of serious offense' (Gibney, ibid.). As such, legislation has structurally allows for increased deportations overall, even though most offences relate either to minor crimes or crimes related to the criminalisation of immigration (Aas and Bosworth, 2015; Aliverti, 2012, 2013, 2015; Bhatia, 2015).

The increase in immigration deportations more broadly has been interpreted in a number of ways. The issue of sovereignty and control has become central in understanding the deportation drive: a way to govern through migration control, typifying the social outsider and Othering the non-citizen (Bosworth, 2008; Bosworth and Guild, 2008; Grewcock, 2015; Weber, 2015). There is also the aspect of the illegal immigrant as spectacle, and as Carr argues, the political theatre that entrenches deportation and populist punitiveness is crowd-pleasing – 'quotas are presented as evidence of toughness and implacability in the fight against illegal immigration' (Carr, 2012: 136). Webber (2012) draws a number of further conclusions: a lack of requirement for a reserve army of labour in post-industrial Britain; the value that contracts play for global security corporations set to gain financially; and as a 'political virility test' which delights the nationalist Right and the media (2012: 162).

Identifiable acts of violence in removal

The process of removal can be categorically degrading: the physical aspect of deportation can include handcuffing, binding and restraint in public and private areas, leaving individuals powerless and physically vulnerable in ways similar to arrest (for example see Gilmore *et al.*, 2016). However, forced deportations can also be fatal. Since 1991, 17 deaths have been recorded while attempting forced removal (Fekete, 2015). Two of these took place in Britain, namely Joy Gardner in 1993, and Jimmy Mubenga in 2010. These are not vast numbers, but as the families of both individuals have made clear, their deaths caused significant emotional harm and, crucially, were both wholly avoidable. Gardner, a 40-year-old Jamaican woman, had been targeted by police and immigration officers at her home and was bound, sat upon, and gagged with 13 feet of tape around her head. She died of an asphyxia-induced cardiac arrest four days later. Mubenga, a 46-year-old Angolan man, died after being held for over 30 minutes in a restraint position on a British Airways flight bound for Angola while crying out 'I can't breathe' (Webber, 2014) and 'They're killing me, they're killing me' (Grierson, 2015) as three G4S guards held him down. Although cases against officers (three in each case) were brought to court justice went undelivered, with no manslaughter or murder convictions made in either case.

While these are perhaps the most extreme outcomes of deportation, use of force could surely have been foreseen and thus prevented. As Webber points out, reports by the Medical Foundation and the BBC evidenced degrading treatment which drew wider concerns and, astoundingly, even after Mubenga's death Amnesty International found 'continuing use of excessive force, including deportees being dropped down aircraft steps, strangled and beaten, causing broken limbs and other injuries' (cited in Webber, 2012: 178). Indeed, restraint methods continue to be used today. In his 2013 report on deportations to Ghana and Nigeria, Nick Hardwick (then HMP Chief Inspector of Prisons) noted cases that included long-term restraint including one woman who had been placed by Home Office contractors in 'leg restraints for 10 hours 5 minutes and in handcuffs for 14 hours 30 minutes, continuously in each case' (Hardwick, 2013: 12). Overall he emphasised that 'While there were some noticeable improvements, especially in the attitudes and language of escort staff ... The distress of detainees undergoing removal is evident from the behaviours and accounts outlined in this report' (ibid.: 5). This perhaps indicates that even beyond the physical or fatal implications of violent acts, deportation is intrinsically harmful for those leaving a life behind, as we will explore more in the following chapter.

Deportation and structural violence

The majority of people – around 55 per cent – who are deported from Britain are from Asian countries, including Pakistan, India, China and Bangladesh (Blinder and Betts, 2016). Since these countries also reflect the global regions from which many economic migrants move to Britain, the Home Office perhaps finds some justification for refusing stay, particularly considering the illegalisation of work for undocumented migrants. On one hand, this arguably overlooks the significant global disparity in wealth between the North and poorer regions in the South that perhaps warrant global mobility in this context. However, these nationalities are also overlooked in relation to repression and conflict-related violence in certain regions, particularly in parts of Pakistan and India.

Taking Pakistan as an example, the Foreign and Commonwealth Office currently advise against travel to almost all regions, including 'all but essential travel' to six regions. The country is noted for sporadic acts of terror that affect civilian safety and mortality, not to mention lethal US and UK drone strikes across mainly Central and Southern regions of the country (Ackerman, 2015). Simultaneously, however, Pakistan rated as the second highest region for deportations (enforced and voluntary) from the UK in 2014 (Blinder, 2015). While some of these cases may not have been accepted as asylum claims, there remains a colonial undertone of 'us and them' – it is acceptable to return people to Pakistan, but not considered safe for British nationals. Countries deemed 'safe for return' are not always seen as safe to travel to for anyone other than returnees themselves.

As Kelly notes, 'asylum and immigration procedures involve making a distinction between those risks that are acceptable and those that are not, those lives that should be protected and those that should be risked' (2012: 101). The 'acceptable asylum seeker' discourse has become increasingly focussed on countries in conflict that are seen as a threat to Western security, most notably Syria and its bordering areas. As the current crisis in border management across Turkey and Greece ensues, those who are not from that immediate vicinity have been sidelined in global responses to the crisis, particularly Afghani refugees (Connelly, for Al Jazeera, 2016). The British state is thus effectively and knowingly facilitating returns to countries that it has itself – for all intents and purposes – declared unsafe.

Bureaucratic violence

This brings me to a second key aspect of deportation: diplomatic assurances. These relate primarily to execution cases and are non-legally binding agreements made between states to mitigate the possibility of a death penalty or the prospect of torture on return. These have been deemed not credible by some, including the former Council of Europe commissioner for human rights, Thomas Hammarberg (in Kelly, 2012: 107) while Liberty question that, 'if you need ask whether a person will be tortured how can you ever rely on such an assurance?' In 2010, Amnesty International termed the UK:

> the most influential and aggressive promoter in Europe of the use of diplomatic assurances to forcibly return people it considers threats to national security to countries where they would face a real risk of serious human rights violations, including torture or other ill-treatment.
>
> (2010: 28)

and highlighted cases where such assurances were not kept thus resulting in torture on return. The structurally violent aspect of this is not necessarily based on intent on behalf of the British state, but in knowing that the prospect of torture is potential and thus avoidable, and yet still deportations are carried out.

The final point to be made in relation to this is internal relocation: a concept which assumes that if a country is deemed unsafe, but regions within the same country are generally secure, then the person can be returned and internally relocated. As research by Asylum Aid highlighted in 2008, 'Internal relocation is being simplistically applied without sufficient evidence based analysis and scrutiny of risks' (Bennett, 2008: 1). The most recent site of contestation around this is perhaps in Greece and Turkey which, it has emerged, have been returning asylum seekers to Syria as a means of reducing migration to Europe (Amnesty International, 2016b). In Britain however, this process has long been critiqued by rights advocates and NGOs who have highlighted concerns similar to those outlined above, but also in relation to the deportation of women who are internally relocated in countries that have poor women's rights records. In this context, women's fears of familial or male violence and sexual abuse can go unrecognised or blatantly disregarded. Unlike public forms of torture or political violence, there are no such diplomatic assurances for women's protection, and mechanisms to alleviate or mitigate harm are generally not viable once women return (Bennett, 2008). In my experience of reading deportation orders and Home Office responses to appeals against deportation, it has been astounding to see the kinds of assumptions that are made for women fleeing partner violence in particular, and gendered violence overall. Vast differences in language, culture and religion are obscured: claims are made that women could move elsewhere, sometimes with suggestions to move to areas picked from a COI file by someone who has probably been as unlikely to visit the suggested region as the applicant herself.

There are many other such aspects of deportation that could harvest similar critiques. For example, it became evident in 2009 that refused asylum seekers had been tortured on return to the Democratic Republic of Congo, only two years after a suspension on returns to the region had been lifted (Taylor, 2009). More recently, Gladwell *et al.* (2016) released a report based on research investigating the returns of young men to Afghanistan who had lived their formative years in Britain as unaccompanied minors, only to be deported when they were at the legal age limit of 18 for returns. 'After Return' documents the harm, social exclusion, and instances of abuse that the young men faced, as well as the threat to their own security in a region deeply affected by conflict and where young men are disproportionately targeted for involvement in military or paramilitary activities. Ironically, only one month before the publication of the report, former Home Secretary Theresa May (now Prime Minister) won a Court of Appeal bid to resume deportations to Afghanistan (McClenaghan, 2016), a ruling that would facilitate further enforced returns of young people to the country despite the potential risks involved, in an era of mass mobilisation from this critically unstable region.

Chapter conclusion: the banality of structural violence

Galtung argued that problems which are *not avoidable* are *not violence* (1969: 169). This chapter has highlighted ways in which some strategies are not only avoidable, but deliberately and knowingly inflict suffering, thus facilitating scope for a structurally analytical lens in relation to common practices in Britain's asylum system. State-sponsored policies that have embedded poverty and destitution in the lives of women, men and children seeking asylum have been done so knowingly. While the extent to which that could be measured is unquantifiable in some ways, and since individual actors are not always present to be held accountable (and seldom are, even when identified), pinpointing responsibility is complex.

However, the evidence that policies relating to destitution, detention and deportation can inflict serious harm seems overwhelming. The studies reflected upon in this chapter indicate clear examples of illness or death, degradation and – ultimately – human suffering in ways that are not necessary and which do not reflect the humanitarian agenda centralised in the Refugee Convention or other subsequent rights-based acts and legislation ever since. To borrow a phrase from Frances Webber, 'human rights obligations have become *optional*' for some Northern states, including Britain, (Webber, 2016). As we will see in the following chapter, the consequences of this can be grave for individuals seeking asylum, and harms have arguably become intrinsic to the process of seeking asylum in Britain.

Notes

1 This argument has been deconstructed in some depth in David Whyte's *How Corrupt is Britain?*, which analyses ways in which corruption is enacted throughout British politics and within and between corporations and financial institutions. Thus it is not only the typified representation of corruption as a 'Southern' problem (often African or South American) that is of concern to criminologists, but also in Northern states which carry out acts of corruption in less typical – and less identifiable or definable – ways (Whyte, 2015).

2 Full title 'UNITED for Intercultural Action', is a European network against fascism, nationalism and racism. It is made up of over 560 organisations from 46 European countries. For more information, see www.unitedagainstracism.org/about-united/, last accessed 20/10/2014.

3 NASS has since been absorbed into the Home Office.

4 The infliction of social harm

There is a dire need to de-link women's immigration status from their humanity.
Sandhya Sharma, Safety 4 Sisters activist (2016)

Introduction

Processes of criminalisation have become central to the study of borders and, as Wickes and Sydes point out, criminology has a long history of engagement in this area (2015). Keeping pace with shifts and changes in border control practices and the crimmigration aspect of policy and legislation is a complex feat (Aliverti, 2012; Stumpf, 2006). The outcome is that there can be some disconnect between socio-political analyses of asylum systems and the recognition of the impacts they have on the people who live within the confines of them. Thus if structural violence can be understood as the manifestation of macro and meso-level of political decision-making as argued in the previous chapter, then the everyday consequences of such processes are perhaps best viewed from a micro-level lens.

To do this, this chapter and the next focus on a case study region of Britain: Merseyside. Flyyberg's justification of case study research (2006), which challenged the notion of small-scale and in-depth analyses as ungeneralisable, has been central to the studies I have undertaken. As a researcher and activist based in this area for a decade, participation in various asylum support groups, sexual violence advocacy organisations and women's rights movements has facilitated a deep insight into the socio-political landscape of British policy and practice. Most importantly, activist-based involvement has provided glimpses into the ground-level and everyday impacts of deterrence agendas, inadequate funding support and the lack of a gendered lens in asylum application procedures.

While some of the interviews and focus groups I have undertaken since 2008 will be incorporated into this chapter, it is perhaps in seeing the longer-term trajectories of women's lives over years in the British asylum system which has developed the kind of critical reflections that feature more prominently throughout the following pages. The hundreds of conversations I have had with small groups of women have covered resistance, survival, exhaustion, depression, suicidality and hope. To feature these would undermine trust and friendship, and so my own reflections are central in the most part, with the exception of recorded qualitative data.

Addressing social harm

In 2004, Hillyard and Tombs outlined a social harm perspective as an alternative to mainstream perceptions of crime in criminology, arguing that the notion of 'crime' can limit definitions and understandings of harm or wrongdoing (2004). The hierarchal, arguably elitist, nature of the story of crime is entrenched in historical and contemporary focusses on crimes of the powerless. For immigrants generally and asylum seekers specifically, the notion of crime is often a one-way narrative. The militarisation of criminal justice approaches to immigration are embedded at figurative and literal borders (see Wilson, 2015) and in all forms of policy, practice and legislation (Aliverti, 2015; Melossi, 2003; Sales, 2007). As Frances Webber (2012) has shown, the criminalisation of immigrants has been facilitated by the punitive expansion of control measures that can illegalise people before they even reach the UK, due to visa requirements that leave people vulnerable to prosecution without them. Aliverti (2012, 2013), Bosworth (2008), Bosworth and Turnbull (2015), Grewcock (2013) and Silverman and Hejela (2015) among many others have documented the rise in imprisonment, facilitated to a degree by the implementation of policies which have moved the possibility of criminalisation further from the criminal justice process itself, and deeper into administrative policy application. The impacts range from increased imprisonment of foreign offenders, to deportation, to the potential for violence on return to ones' country of origin.

Although arguably similarly limiting, the micro-level impacts of criminalisation, securitisation and deterrence agendas are generally more banal in the daily life of the asylum system. While some harms, such as physical and emotional harms (Hillyard and Tombs, 2004) are fairly easy to define, they can remain difficult to identify. For example, survivors of torture may have evidential scars or trauma-induced mental health problems, but may never speak to the violence which created them. In an era of mental health funding cuts and inadequately reviewed asylum applications, it may be that there is no one to speak of them with. Survivors of sexual violence may experience flashbacks, nightmares, anxiety – all of which are well defined and acknowledged as resultant of harm among practitioners and academics, but as I have argued elsewhere, support for this group is often sparse (Canning, 2011a, 2016a).

Pemberton outlines more structurally determined examples of physical and mental health harms, some of which can be evidenced in the asylum system. These include limitations on accessing healthy diet, access to and time to participate in physical exercise, access to appropriate healthcare systems, adequate shelter and a non-hazardous physical environment to ensure a sufficient level of physical health is maintained (Pemberton, 2015: 28). Further harms include gendered harm (Cain and Howe, 2007) or economic harms (Hillyard and Tombs, 2004), many of which sometimes interlink or entwine. However, Pemberton also addresses two forms of harm which can be difficult to define, yet limit the quality of people's lives: autonomy harms and relational harms.

The first of these, autonomy harms, affect a person's self-worth or esteem, and can result from role deprivation and the absence of available opportunities to engage in productive activities. The second, relational harms, include enforced exclusion from social relationships, and harms of misrecognition (such as mis-representations of particular social groups in society – Pemberton, 2015: 28–31). As this chapter goes on, I will add to these a category of *temporal* harms in the British asylum system.

Physical and emotional harms

In his recent work, Pemberton (2015) combined physical and emotional harms to create one broad category, which is a shift from Hillyard and Tombs' catego-risation that set each separately (2004: 19–20). For this section and for the sake of condensing what are perhaps the most identifiable forms of harm that women face, they will be combined as the examples included draw on aspects from both into them. However, each of these two harms will be more explicitly and individ-ually addressed in the following chapter.

First, physical harms can encompass harms deliberately inflicted by someone else, such as an act of domestic violence or state torture against an individual. Such harms might include death at the hands of another individual or group of people. In both cases physical harm is bodily harm, and these can be resultant of isolated instances of violence. As with the harms outlined above, and as the previous chapter documented in depth, physical harm can also be the outcome or product of structural violence in other ways, such as illness from inadequate housing, death due to corporate negligence in the workplace (Tombs and Whyte, 2015), or malnutrition due to inadequate welfare allowance or poverty more gen-erally. In all cases, these are inextricably linked to macro and meso-level pro-cesses that determine the scope and provision of welfare, support or workplace safety and thus are deeply politicised.

Hillyard and Tombs argued that emotional and psychological harms are 'much more difficult to measure and relate to specific causes' (2004: 20). While this holds some justification, since physical injury or death can often be seen and usually eas-ily identified, both refugee and feminist literatures have provided many examples which might contest this. Although individuals may each respond to harm in dif-ferent ways (see Chapter 6), the spectrum of emotional harms is vast and, on the contrary, easily identified. For example, problems such as sleeplessness, anxiety, de-pression or suicidality can be the outcome of instances of violence or other traumata. What lies at the source of the problem of measuring or relating to specific causes is the lack of capacity or space for these to be drawn out. To relate to specific causes, one must be provided the ability to speak to the causes (Herman, 1992; Kelly, 1988; Smith, 1987). However, those violences that cause most emotional harm – such as sexual violence, domestic terror or torture – remain socially silenced in a multitude of ways (Canning, 2014a, 2015; Jordan, 2012; Kelly, 2012 – see also Chapter 7).

Health and harm

> Health inequalities that could be avoided by reasonable means are not fair.
> Putting them right is a matter of social justice.
>
>   (Marmot et al., 2010 in Feldman, 2012: 14)

Public health is a central aspect of asylum. Immigration Removal Centres and Initial Accommodation Centres often have 'wrap-around' services which include locum or resident doctors, nurse(s) a midwife, counsellors (where possible) and a health visitor. In Liverpool, this has been provided by Urgent Care 24, a social enterprise that provides services for the National Health Service (NHS) and was, according to a practitioner I interviewed at one accommodation centre, 'set up at the request of the GPs because they were just getting swamped'. According to MacPherson (2014), almost 100 per cent of people who are offered initial health assessments at the centres accept.

People seeking asylum can have complex healthcare needs, including anything from minor medical ailments or vitamin deficiencies, to heart problems, a positive HIV status or torture-related traumata. The nature of asylum sets it separately from the general population, in that people applying for refugee status are more likely to have been subjected to some form of persecution, physical or sexual violence, torture, and/or conflict-related trauma/traumata (Arcel, 2003; Peel, 2004; Peel *et al.*, 2000). Without advocating a medicalisation agenda, some people do require intense medical attention or support. This can be greatly affected by three issues: ongoing cuts to mental and physical healthcare services, and to the NHS overall, further reductions and limitations on asylum rights to healthcare, and the impact of dispersal on people, and particularly pregnant women or survivors of violence which affects her ability to engage in support services or networks. As a sexual violence outreach counsellor alluded:

> *I'll go up and do initial support with women. Sometimes it's two or three appointments, but mainly because of dispersal and where the women are depends on how much they get but normally one, possibly two appointments if it gets that far, because sometimes they're dispersed before I get to see them. It's quite sad. And you do get the phone call two days later saying they've disappeared. And my diary, obviously sometimes I can put down for a week or two later, but with Home Office visits and doctor's appointments it's usually a week before I can get to see them, and often then I'll get a phone call saying they've been dispersed to Manchester or London or wherever they go.*

To contextualise the financial aspect of harm, according to *The Guardian*, by 2014 the Coalition government had cut 12 per cent of the social care budget, while demand for services actually grew by 14 per cent during the same period (Brindle, 2015). For NHS staff, this has placed insurmountable pressures on healthcare provision. At the same time, the reduction in doctor/patient time slots can affect any possibility of determining underlying psychological or medical problems, particularly complex mental health issues, and although the general population are advised to visit their pharmacy for minor ailments (NHS, 2014), affording medical products without a free prescription is simply not feasible.

In my experience, people seeking asylum also incur suspicion as to why they seek medical attention. Rather than advocating the well-established recognition that refugee populations can have disproportionately high levels of health problems, a number of women I have spoken with suggest that some practitioners equate medical attention as a way to secure evidence for their asylum claim. Although this might be the case for some (since evidence is so difficult to collate) I recall attending a doctor appointment with a woman who had suffered psychotic episodes, including publically at a support group. When she informed the examining doctor of her forthcoming asylum appeal, he simply replied, 'Ah, that's why you are here. Your case is under review' (Field Notes, March 2015). Instead of being able to focus on the wellbeing of the patient, doctors are increasingly asked to act as guardians to refugee status, and as such the responses to the patient might end up more focussed on their status than their health.

Perinatal care and health

One key gendered differential for women seeking asylum is pregnancy. To move across borders, apply for asylum and await the outcome of a claim can be stressful for any applicant, but pregnancy brings added healthcare needs, and stresses or physical health problems can be exacerbated by precarious status, poor housing and living in poverty.

In researching maternity in asylum, myself and Dr Helen Churchill undertook a small-scale study between 2011–2012 in Merseyside, incorporating interviews with practitioners and focus groups with women who were receiving, or had within the past year received, perinatal care. The outcomes were mixed – essentially we saw that policy and practice did not always combine, and that key issues for this were structural, rather than individual, failures (Churchill and Canning, 2011). These included a lack of funds for interpretation, incapacity to provide in-depth support due to staffing shortages, and the problem of dispersing women who were up to 38 weeks gestation. The latter of these has been documented in depth by Maternity Action and the Refugee Council (2013), who similarly found that dispersal has the ability to affect women's engagement in perinatal care as well as diminish her informal support network if she is moved from friends and family.

Indeed, a number of serious issues can develop for women that incorporate the potential for both physical and emotional harms. For example, Fatima was refused asylum by the Home Office and told Helen Churchill:

> *I went through without money, with the child and they didn't even write to me and they was about to ask me to leave the house, make me go, not knowing where I will live with my child. Was very painful for me. I wanted to go and kill myself with my child, I was walking out of the door but I didn't know where I was going after hospital, no money, no house.*

Manifest here is poverty, isolation, fear of homelessness and a fundamental lack in communication – women in this position should not knowingly be sent home after giving birth, but rather contact made to relevant support services. Similar disconnects have been evident for other women. Lem, for example, walked to a maternity ward while in labour and was informed by the midwife that she was not ready for birthing but should return when she is more fully dilated. A breakdown in communication ensued, with Lem not knowing how she might do that and the midwife presumably not realising she had no transport. Having only recently arrived in Liverpool at the time Lem walked home to the L15 district of the city and walked back in agony, not knowing she was entitled to call for an ambulance.

The potential for serious harm to have been incurred by either mother or baby is clear here, but less obvious harms can result in other aspects of communication breakdowns. The formally medicalised nature of much maternity care in Britain can be a fairly new phenomenon for women who otherwise might receive more holistic or community-based perinatal care. Routine procedures can be daunting, particularly if there is a lack of interpretation. For example, through an interpreter, Ali told me of the anxieties she felt when, '*The nurse come and just give me two injections in my tummy, I don't know why. I had three children before and never received injections on my tummy*'. As a trypanophobe, any prospect of injection is anxiety inducing. Ali's experience is certainly at the worst end of a needle phobe's nightmare – an injection at her most vulnerable, but without knowing why or what it is for or what impacts it could have on baby during birth. While the physical implications of this might not be reduced, the trauma of not knowing could be, had an appropriate interpreter been on hand to assure her about the procedure.

The harms of poverty

As outlined in the previous chapter, housing is regularly inadequate with some inspections concluding asylum accommodation to be inhabitable. In 2013 Liverpool became a City of Sanctuary, but by 2015 Mayor Joe Anderson had raised concerns that the city was taking more of its fair share of asylum seekers than other similar regions. To give credit to part of this concern, as demonstrated above, Liverpool is recognised as an area of deprivation. As of 2015, the Local Authority registered fourth for highest proportion of their neighbourhoods being in the most deprived nationally on the English Index of Multiple Deprivation (Department for Communities and Local Government, 2015). Compounding this, and perhaps acting as a reminder that deprivation relates to political decision-making and wealth distribution, Liverpool was identified as one of five areas with most severe council cuts in 2016 (those with the least were all based in Southern England, all of which were constituencies with the lowest levels of deprivation, and which were represented by high-profile Conservative cabinet ministers – see Boffey, 2016). Mayor Anderson went as far as to call the disproportionality of asylum dispersal – whereby some areas reportedly received 300 times the expected ratio – a form of 'asylum apartheid' (BBC, 2015b).

This is an interesting claim, not least in its use of a politically super-loaded term such as *apartheid*. However, although Anderson draws the phrase to compare the impacts of asylum on Liverpool City Council (contrary to the Home Office's statistics) the term is not altogether undue in a different capacity. The areas that asylum seekers – predominantly Eritrean, Ethiopian, Pakistani, Indian, Somali, Afghani, Syrian and Sudanese nationals – are dispersed to are amongst the poorest in England[1] (Canning, 2014a). In one interview, a GP went so far as to argue:

> *People are housed where no one else want to be housed in British society, in areas which are very deprived, which have a high prevalence of people with British Nationalist Party [a far-right nationalist party] views, and they are subject to harassment and abuse on a daily basis. They live in a very poor environment and their access to healthcare is not very good.*

In some ways, this view attends to the oft-played narrative that areas with predominantly White British working-class people are in and of themselves problematic, as though racism does not play out in the middle classes. This is of course not the case – racism simply plays out in different ways, including structurally violent law and policy formation developed and implemented by political elites. That said, the increased policing of hate crime in predominantly inner-urban areas of Liverpool indicates that some sectors of the city are more affected by racist hate crimes than others, and overall recorded a 22 per cent rise in racist hate crimes from 2014–2016 (n: 1653), with a trebling of religious hate crimes in the same period (n: 119, see Paget, 2015). Perhaps predictably, these are also areas that are most affected by deprivation and 'austerity' measures and have faced social and economic turbulence since at least the 1980s, when Thatcher moved to deindustrialise the North of England, Scotland, Wales and Northern Ireland, and certainly since the more recent government cuts. These are also predominantly the areas that serve as key dispersal zones across the city, thus the council areas with the least financial resources are disproportionately expected to stretch social welfare the farthest.

In 2014, Liverpool's local newspaper – *The Liverpool Echo* – ran a timely expose of the state of housing for people seeking asylum in the city. At a time of increasingly negative representations of immigrants, Oliver Duggan's article offered one of very few insights into the standard of facilities in some parts of the city. The journalistic piece highlighted the prevalence of substandard accommodation including damp, overcrowding, and with high rates of racist attacks against property (Duggan, 2014). Some observations were remarkably similar to the experiences of women I have spoken to, as well as accommodation I have visited myself. For example, a woman who had two children told me repeatedly about anxieties related to her flat that had become infested with rats. A second woman told me of cockroach infestation; a third woman about the impact of her struggle to get up her stairs. Living on the top floor of a block of flats, heavily pregnant and with a toddler in tow, everyday tasks such as shopping or taking her child to the park were made almost impossible. Another woman with two young children told me how her ceiling fell in while they were out, thanking God throughout the conversation that she had been away at the time.

I use these examples, not because they are specifically unique to the experiences of people seeking asylum or indeed Merseyside (as critical welfare commentators can clearly evidence for poorer areas more generally – see Cooper, 2015), but precisely because they are *avoidable* scenarios. The falling in of a ceiling is usually the outcome of a longer process of decay or damage. Cockroach and rat *infestation* – not occasional habitation – takes escalation and lack of intervention. The decision to provide a pregnant woman with a toddler a top-storey apartment suggests not only a lack of alleviation of struggle, but the overlooking of potential injury or death: in 2011 alone, 693 people died in stair-related accidents deaths in the UK (Rogers, 2012). To contextualise, the same period from 2010–2011 saw 619 people murdered (Travis, 2011), but as Dorling (2007) and later Pemberton (2015) have pointed out, everyday harms do not make headlines even when they cause greater statistical harm and could – like this case – be avoided.

So we can see quite clearly the violence in structurally avoidable problems, even the potential for death or indeed self-inflicted death. But what of women's experiences of life and 'normality'? In interviews and focus groups with women over the past decade, two things are often most evident: anxiety, often about the impending or longer-term future for themselves and/or their families; and the impact of temporal confinement, the lack of capacity to plan for the future, today included. In conversation with the woman who faced rat infestation, for example, her ultimate fear was the ingestion of rat faeces by one of her two children (the youngest, who had just learned to crawl). While not an altogether unimaginable scenario, and one with real potential for illness, the same woman was (at the time) challenging the threat of deportation back to Syria for the whole family. However, the already manifest harm was the fear of her children's potential illness and the impact that this fear had on the child's mother. By now she had called the responsible housing provider numerous times and subsequently suffered nightmares, all while obsessively cleaning to avoid her worst imaginable outcome.

Across other areas of the UK, similar stories appear, including of overcrowding and dilapidated conditions. Like Merseyside, the running of asylum housing is often outsourced by the government to private agencies, including G4S and Serco, which ironically also cover much of the asylum detention estate. People dispersed to areas outside of London might begin their experience of a new area in a reception centre with wrap-around services, such as an onsite GP and outreach support from agencies such as the British Red Cross, the Refugee Council or localised psychological and emotional services. Time in these facilities is understandably short lived, as people are processed quickly and moved on to other areas in cities while awaiting a decision on their refugee status. As in Merseyside, however, these are often some of the poorest and most economically deprived places in the city (Canning, 2014a).

Inadequate responses from the Home Office

For well over a decade now, the length of time that many asylum claims take to process has been highly criticised by commentators on both the left and right of the political spectrum. Before the dissolution of the UKBA in 2013, the expense of the asylum process, alongside the mishandling of cases (Smith, 2004a) led to various reviews and influenced the establishment of DFT. As highlighted in the previous chapter, DFT is now suspended. However, the original objectives of it have been presented as a process that would facilitate speedy case reviews so that people were not left suspended in the system, and indeed welfare dependent, for long periods of time. This objective might have been welcome had the practice not been one that facilitated inadequate investigations into cases, and thus quick rejections and increased detention. Nonetheless, despite the aims of DFT to undertake asylum reviews more efficiently, many aspects of the asylum system actually take a very long time. By the end of June 2015, the Home Office indicated that 21,604 cases received since April 2006 were still pending: a period of almost a decade (Home Office, 2015a). Case decisions are often flawed or highly problematic and thus result in lengthy reviews, leaving women and men suspended in a kind of temporal limbo for years at a time. To give an illustration, in one focus group with five women from four countries in 2014, I asked how long each had been awaiting a final asylum decision. One had been in the asylum system since 2013, one since 2012, one since 2009, one since 2010 and one since 2002. In just one small group, that is an accumulation of 24 years of waiting – hardly conducive to their time, or anyone else's.

The physical and emotional cost of this time takes its toll. Friendships, skills and relationships can break down or become affected. As the Refugee Women's Strategy Group (2014) have also shown, women can lose their sense of self-worth in a system that renders them incapacitated. For some women, the micro-level impacts of these failures can be disastrous. Some years ago in one of the now defunct activist groups I worked with, one woman who had been refused asylum and was receiving Section 4 support for herself and her child, was diagnosed with cancer. Technically, since the support she received entitled her to urgent medical care, she should have gained treatment for her aggressive form of cancer. Misinterpreting her rights, and with little guidance, support or access to language interpretation, her health deteriorated rapidly. She died of cancer around three weeks after her diagnosis.

The impact of having an asylum application rejected can be one of the lowest points of an individual's experience of the process. Support organisations often try to find ways to prepare people for refusal in the first instance, for example I have even seen one poster stating, 'Only one in four asylum seekers will receive refugee status. Prepare for an alternative.' As a refugee services manager indicated, the impacts of such decisions can also be grave, since 'people's mental health is very much tied up with their asylum claim, and if they go through the whole process thinking they're going to be successful and then they fail, that is a tremendous blow', and considering the flaws highlighted so far, sometimes erroneous. Discussing the impact of incorrect information distribution, a women's HIV support officer relayed one such example:

> *I have had experiences with case owners who have known the system and have made mistakes and haven't dealt with it ... I had someone who tried to commit suicide a couple of months ago who was pregnant, because the discontinuation letter, she didn't get it in time ... her case owner said she needed to leave her accommodation, but NASS (National Asylum Support Service[2]) was saying 'no you don't have to leave your accommodation'. She was being pulled back and forth, back and forth. And it was actually the case owner's mistake for not sending the discontinuation letter to her in the first place that got her in the mess that she was in. It resulted in this woman trying to commit suicide. She was eight months pregnant.*

Autonomy harm

There are many forms of autonomy harm evident in the British asylum, some of which are mirrored in other regions of Europe, North America and Australasia/Oceania. Poverty – a form of economic harm which relates to unequal or inadequate distribution – often acts as a controlling factor for how people eat or where they might spend time. Some activities across Europe have been shut down to people based on their asylum status (for example, in Bremgarten, Switzerland, refugees were banned from swimming in public baths – see Murray and Abu-Heyyeh, 2014) while the offshoring of detention in Australia has limited practically all avenues of activity involvement.

In Britain however, the limitations are comparatively insidious and bureaucratised, whereby policies or legislations have been developed and implemented in ways which are not directed at people seeking asylum, but disproportionately (arguably deliberately) impact on them. The three examples here are: work and education; fear of detention; and surveillance and control, although this no more than a snapshot of such autonomy harms.

Structural limitations on personal opportunities and social engagement

To begin with, people seeking asylum are structurally limited on what they can do with their lives for the period of time in which they seek asylum. As a case in point, working is legally prohibited up until the applicant has been in the UK awaiting an asylum decision for at least one year, and even then access to employment may only be granted on request and under special conditions. Further Education may be available depending on the applicant's age, entry requirements and welfare claimant status. This is of course assuming the applicant would have the financial capacity to physically attend, since bus or train travel can be expensive considering the amount of money an individual receives per week. Applicants may also access Higher Education classed either as an overseas student (which is generally significantly more expensive than resident students) or – where concessions are made at the discretion of a university – a home rate tuition fee. Seeing that in 2012, the Conservative/Liberal Democrat Coalition introduced fee caps of between £6000–9000 per academic year, this is a diminished opportunity for almost all people seeking asylum in England. In Scotland and Wales, where the fee is significantly lower (around £1800 per academic year for those without Scottish or Welsh nationality) this remains an unlikely feat for anyone receiving less than £6 per day, and with limited or zero access to external financial support.

What has effectively happened in the lives of people seeking asylum in Britain is a gradual increase in restrictions on relatively normative ways to participate in society. While working or studying are in no way the only way lives might be lived, the current socio-economic climate is one of restriction and austerity – a kind of 'class war' (Jones, 2011) in which those who do not or cannot participate in these aspects of liberal capitalism are regularly vilified as state scroungers or as grossly uneducated. Simultaneously, asylum seekers, refugees and economic migrants have faced further barriers to learning English. Since 2009, there has been a reduction of more than 50 per cent of English for Speakers of Other Languages (ESOL) funds (Migrant Rights Network, 2015), limiting people's capacity to learn the language as a way to engage with resident English speakers, but also reducing acts as a form of relational deprivation since opportunities to interact with people in similar positions are removed.

In some ways those seeking asylum sit between a rock and a hard place: some women may wish to study, but are dependent on spouses or cannot access childcare. Others might wish to gain employment, but are not legally allowed to do so. A university lecturer who had been in the system for over 18 months stated, '*What do I do? I am not like all these people. I can't just sit here and do nothing*' (see also Bosworth, 2014: 89). This may seem (to some degree) a manifestation of hierarchal class identity – that some people are shaped to sit and wait, while others must find ways to fill their time. Precisely the same argument has facilitated the very sets of categories which render one set of immigrants 'worthy' of work, of welfare, or of education, while others are legislatively excluded or even criminally targeted if they participate in illegalised employment (Bhatia, 2015). Nonetheless, her sentiment remains understandable in that she has been structurally excluded from what is perhaps the key limitation here: personal autonomy. Those awaiting asylum decisions may do so for years at a time, their weekly or monthly schedules determined by Home Office interviews, solicitor appointments or other legal support meetings. Geographical autonomy is reduced by the lack of funds one may have to actually move around, since even a bus fare can consume almost all of a daily budget. A lack of access to educational resources or other stimuli can leave people feeling detached, depressed or simply disengaged. To quote one focus group participant, there is a feeling that '*an empty mind is the devil's playground*' – participation is replaced with isolation. As I have seen with a number of women over the years, even those engaged in Further or Higher Education do so with many priorities to consider, many of which link to their short-term futures in asylum, or long-term futures in – or out of – Britain. In either case, uncertainty strains autonomy in both futures.

Fear of detention

Perhaps the most literal form of autonomy harm within the British asylum system is detention. The various harms and violences of detention have been detailed in some depth in Chapter 3 with reference to confinement, abuse and sexual violence. While these are clearly identifiable, they still remain socially silenced through shut-down mechanisms and public denial, including Yarl's Wood's refusal to grant entry Rashida Manjoo (discussed earlier). However, as well as being an apparatus of deterrence for would be asylum seekers in Britain, the use of detention arguably results in two forms of autonomy harm: role deprivation, and fear of detention among people seeking asylum.

If we look first at the role deprivation of immigration detention, there are obvious aspects of confinement that aim to remove both the person from society, and society from the person thus maintaining a function of Othering and control (Ugelvik, 2013). Although there are many differences between prisons and IRCs, not least the fact that prisons are generally the end result of a criminal justice process, the physical and psychological containment of detainees reflects those of prisoners of criminal justice. On recounting IRC fieldwork, Mary Bosworth described the process as 'painful', that its 'purpose and impact is far less clear' than prisons, and that 'its ethics is rather more murky' (Bosworth, 2015). People who are detained or have been detained often reflect on the impacts of indefinite detention on their own well-being as worse than prison, since people in prison at least know their sentence (ibid.).

Yet detention is expensive, costing around £97 per detainee per day (Silverman and Hajela, 2015) and its purpose unclear. However, as Mary Bosworth argues:

> For its proponents, immigration detention is a necessary part of border control, both a right and an obligation of the British sovereign state. Those without visas and immigration status are not entitled to stay and, if they will not go voluntarily, they must be detained to prompt their deportation. For critics, however, immigration removal centres should be abolished. They cause long term psychological distress, are used in an arbitrary fashion, and are expensive and inefficient.
>
> (Bosworth, 2014: 5)

From this angle, there are clear roles for the use of immigration detention in responding to asylum seekers. IRCs are physical manifestations of a sovereign ideology that has created space for those who do not belong (Bosworth and Guild, 2008; Bowling and Sheptycki, 2015; Zedner, 2013). They limit individual autonomy and participation in British life. If, as Joe Sim argues, the backbone of imprisonment is the infliction of pain, then those seeking asylum are evidentially punished (Sim, 2009). Considering the gradual illegalisation of seeking asylum (Dauvergne, 2013; Stumpf, 2006), the infliction of psychological pain through imprisonment is increasingly legitimated and justified.

However, as Stephen Box argued in the context of prisons specifically, they are 'used to serve as a warning to those not deserving imprisonment *this time round'* (1983: 207, own emphasis added). This strategy has been recognised as a form of immigration deterrence for those considering travelling to the UK to seek asylum. If we look at the detention of asylum seekers from a social harm perspective, and specifically in the light of autonomy harms, we can see that it is not only the act of detention, but also the threat of detention that inflicts fear on asylum communities already living in the UK. In Merseyside, for example, one group I work with faced two detentions and one short-term holding within the space of around two months. All had been detained or informed they may be detained when attending their Home Office interview for appeals in Liverpool City Centre. The consequences of this were increased anxiety for the whole group, particularly women who shared nationalities with the detainees, who feared they may be targeted for a charter flight departure. Two women who were released (the third was deported) became anxious when their appointments were approaching again, one even beginning to avoid her interviews that would of course increase, rather than decrease, the likelihood of detention or even deportation.

The objective of harming one's autonomy is arguably the production of an informal, invisible culture of control that can therefore work across groups of people with shared identities, in this case asylum status and gender identity. Furthermore, increasing the number of reasons one can be detained induces fear not only of detention, but also of being actively involved in political resistance or dissent. Asylum seekers can be detained when the 'decision has been reached' on the basis of one or more of 13 reasons. On reviewing a detention case, I was surprised to find that the thirteenth included 'your unacceptable character, conduct or associations' (in Canning, 2014b: 11). This is an astounding feat for the state's control of immigrant autonomy. Few categories for any form of detention are as subjective or open to interpretation as deciding what is or is not 'unacceptable character, conduct or associations'. At a time in Britain when no-platforming has become the new norm, when measures against so-called extremism have been dispersed into the responsibility of non-state actors ranging from teachers to hospital staff, this is indeed a worrying advancement in the control of a specific group's political autonomy.

Surveillance and social control

As has been outlined above, and as is well established in the social sciences (particularly in border studies) state responses to asylum applications over at least the past 50 years[3] have been to increase controls for people travelling into Britain. Although freer movement has been possible for European Union citizens (at least up until Brexit), non-European Union citizens face substantial layers of surveillance and control, often even before arriving in Britain. Like many Western and Northern European countries, Britain has restricted entry without a visa. This was, according to Frances Webber, an opportunity seized by the British government who capitalised on the need for refugees to have left their country of origin according to the Refugee Convention. Thus Webber argues:

> Visa requirements were imposed on citizens of countries from which many
> people were fleeing, preventing many from reaching safety. The catch-22
> was (and still is) that until they leave their own country they are not refugees
> (and so are ineligible for visas).
>
> (Webber, 2012: 20)

Many of the controls that people seeking asylum face in Britain are well
documented – finger printing is undertaken at the point of entry; applicants are
expected to re-register with the Home Office fortnightly or monthly; and those
who are seen to be a 'flight risk' may be electronically tagged (Tyler, 2013). Since
April 2015, the British border with France by Eurotunnel and the English Channel
have seen increased controls (termed Exit Checks) in surveilling *emigration* in
response to high-profile cases whereby British-born citizens have left the UK
with the intention of joining organisations such as Islamic State in Syria, Iran
and Iraq. Similar to detention, however, the limits of border control stretch well
beyond the objective divide. In discussing biometric controls at the Australian
border, Wilson and Weber argue that risk thinking (or pre-emptive strategies
to control asylum seekers) 'in relation to border control therefore leads inexo-
rably to temporal, and hence spatial, displacement of the border' (2008: 127).
The where and when of borders is increasingly fluid to a point where some seem
almost invisible.

Researching and campaigning with women seeking asylum in Merseyside has
facilitated insight into some of these more banal, insidious and racialised forms
of everyday surveillance and control that people regularly face. As well as the autonomy harms addressed so far, some women have pointed to less formal forms
of control such as warning signs in asylum accommodation. To give an example,
after some disagreements among residents about leaving room doors open in
shared accommodation, the private housing provider (in this case, Serco) placed
a warning that 'anyone who leaves their door open will be reported to the Home
Office' (see Figure 4.1). As with other aspects of the British asylum system, this
kind of veiled threat effectively eludes to punitive measures as a consequence of
any level of disobedience or dissent. Considering the thirteenth reason for detention discussed earlier, who is to say how far controlling this portrayal of deviance
(Cohen, 1985) may be taken.

Moving on from domestic controls to geopolitical spatial controls, it is worth
looking to the relatively under-reported phenomena of border enforcement within
and between major cities. In separate discussions with a number of women, three
occasions came to light within the space of one month. In the first (chronologi-
cally), one woman had been travelling from London to Liverpool when Border
Force agents and police officers stopped the bus and requested passports. From
the woman's account, everyone – not only asylum seekers – were requested to
show identification. Although this is not actually a formal legal necessity, the
woman did so and was not reprimanded presumably, she thought, because her
asylum appeal was ongoing. According to my informant, the Border Force agent
carried a handheld scanning device (similar to those developed by Sagem to scan

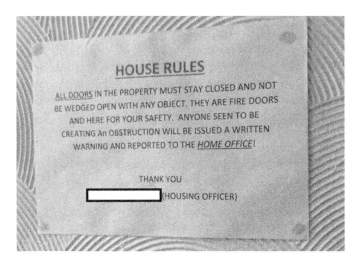

Figure 4.1 Social control as border control at the everyday level.

their Application Registration Cards, or ARC, which read biometric information alongside immigration status). One woman was removed from the bus. The other examples follow similar narratives, although neither resulted in the removal of people from the buses. The second took place *within* Liverpool. Interestingly, the bus was travelling towards one of the most deprived areas of the city which also counts as a key dispersal area for people seeking asylum. The third was between London and Liverpool, when a woman had been visiting her family who lived in the South of England.

While this kind of informal spatial control can be difficult to pinpoint – since the borders are not officially those between states – it is actually fairly easily defined. From preliminary consideration, I interpreted these borders and boundaries as invisible and undefinable. They are not guarded as airports or ferry ports are. No passport or visa is required or essential. Instead the temporal and spatial boundary has shifted to specific *kinds of people* and passengers, and the spaces that they might use as throughways to internal migration. That is, people who move through and between dispersal zones, and to poorer areas where they – or their friends and family – reside or have been moved to. What this does, effectively, is restricts support networks, people's opportunities to engage with organisations (such as a torture support organisation outside of Liverpool, which some women depend upon) or even illegalised work opportunities, thus further reducing individual autonomy, bringing us to consider relational harm.

Relational harm and its gendered implications

There are clear overlaps between some of the above illustrations of autonomy harm in this chapter, and the relational harms that they embed. When women,

men or unaccompanied minors leave their countries of origin, many of their relationships and friendships are affected or dissolved completely. Other relational harms are, however, directly the result of policy and practice. Within Britain and the UK more generally, the impact of spatialised controls outlined above is perhaps the most obvious form of relational harm, since the climate of such controls has the capacity to limit individual's relationships, friendships or support networks outside of their immediate living vicinity. Relational harms are also strongly connected to emotional harms: support networks, friendships and activist involvement are impeded by some of the many barriers women seeking asylum face and yet each of these can be particularly important for women's mental and emotional wellbeing (Refugee Women's Strategy Group, 2014). The issues raised outlining poverty and lack of social opportunities here and in the previous chapter are relationally harmful. However, two examples will be developed here to bring to life Pemberton's definitions of harms of misrecognition and enforced exclusion: racism and Islamophobia, and the micro-level impacts of deportation.

Misrecognition

The current Islamophobic climate embedded in pockets of British culture have also arguably affected relations between Muslim immigrants and communities broadly, as well as settled non-Muslim populations who have increasingly been targeted in attacks since the Terror attacks in Paris in 2015. A recent report by Tell Mama, an organisation which measures Islamophobic violence, showed more than a 300 per cent increase in attacks in the following week in Britain. These were significantly gendered: as *The Independent* synopsised, 'Most victims of the UK hate crimes were Muslim girls and women aged from 14 to 45 in traditional Islamic dress. The perpetrators were mainly White males aged from 15 to 35' (Wright, 2015).

Women in three groups I have worked with have raised similar issues. As a White Irish woman, I arguably have an innate lack of consciousness regarding everyday racism and Islamophobia, as I would argue men do with regard to everyday sexism. That is, I might have friends or spend time with women who are not White, who wear the Hijab or Burqa, or who are seeking asylum, but I do not have to negotiate racist barriers or abuse in my own daily interactions. I might be responsive to or proactive against racism and Islamophobia, but it is not part of an externally defined and socially constructed identity. And yet, as Black feminists such as Patricia Hill Collins, Audre Lorde, Angela Davis and Nira Yuval-Davis have long pointed out, it is the banality and everydayness of racism and (increasingly) Islamophobia which can be most socially restricting.

The limits of understanding these through a criminal justice lens have been illustrated on everyday levels – the times I've seen men mutter at Darfuri women wearing Burqas I have been walking with in Liverpool; the woman who arrived at one of our groups asking for a safety alarm because she had been chased from the bus stop and spat at; or even the general feeling of suspicion when driving with women in Hijabs and Burqas and being stared at on every traffic light we stopped at. These processes of Othering are not all criminal, nor are they necessarily violent. However, they are potentially *harmful* in inducing feelings of exclusion, and the extended norm of these forms of Othering is violence and the fear of violence.

The most recent example I was made aware of is the informal barriers set for women leaving their homes after dusk in some areas of Liverpool. On one occasion when we attended an evening fundraiser, only a handful of the group turned up as most women did not feel that they could leave their homes after dark. When I later asked how else this fear might affect the women involved, four women, all of whom are Muslim, told me they did not socialise in the evening in winter, that they only go to shops during the day, and that the three who had children did not allow them to leave the house out of daylight hours. The verbal abuse they had each experienced had incurred fear of further victimisation, raising barriers to participation in ways that are spatially controlled outside of the direct responsibility of the state, but within ways that are an extension of the normative processes of structural exclusion which are embedded in a post-9/11 landscape.

Enforced exclusion from social relationships

The legal and policy landscape of deportation has been addressed in some depth in Chapter 3, but the emotional and relational harms attached to deportation go much further than this. When Pemberton refers to enforced exclusion, it is not in the literal sense of bordered exclusion, but rather closer to the structural limitations placed on people through social isolation (Pemberton, 2015: 30). These examples – such as limits on emotional security and supportive networks – are likewise relevant to people seeking asylum. However, the threat of deportation is arguably the greatest cause for anxiety for this group, not only due to the potential for harm on return, but because relationships and attachments can be torn or lost in similar ways to a persons' original experience of migration. As we have seen so far, the length of time that people can be in the immigration system can mean solid relationships are formed with friends, organisational networks or religious groups, and these are compromised with removal. The way in which deportation – or bordered exclusion – is detailed in criminology literature is often through quantification of bodies, and in looking at percentage margins and shifts, such as in Chapter 1. But the human aspect is much more than this, not only for the deportee but also for the people that deportees have relations with.

One way of looking at this is the through the case of a woman – whose family has requested anonymity – and who was deported to her country of origin after spending 13 years living in Liverpool. She has British children, British grandchildren and had been heavily involved in church support networks and a number of activist collectives which spoke out about the harms of asylum. The last time she spoke out was at a public event attended by Home Office staff. Within days, she had been detained in Yarl's Wood. Within weeks after that, she had been deported. To raise awareness, one group member wrote for Right to Remain:

> *She was refused and detained simultaneously. We could not get her adequate legal representation. There were horrible panicked calls from the detention centre. She successfully resisted her first removal. While waiting for transport back to Yarls Wood somebody called her on the phone in the waiting room. A guard handed her the phone. A person told her she would be bailed for £800. Her family gave this person the money. They were not heard from again. Her family went to the police. They asked to file a report. The police did not allow them to file a report. The detention centre admitted that this has happened before. Her family asked the detention centre to call the police so that she could make a report. She never made a police report. They removed her suddenly. She called me. She told the guard she wanted to pray.*
>
> *The guard told her that God wanted her to get on the plane. I heard this because I was on the phone. We don't know what to do with her stuff. There is a lot of stuff. The fake solicitor was finally apprehended. It is over a year and her things are still in our office. We do not know what to do.*

I had been involved in one call where the group sang and chatted and filled this woman in on local events she had since missed while in Yarl's Wood. She told us she was fine and looking forward to seeing everyone soon. When the likelihood of her deportation became clearer, group members did all they could to contact the flight attendants and inform them that this deportation was against her will, and the will of her family.

In the aftermath of this deportation, we tried to send on what might be the most important belongings, but as Figure 4.2 indicates, there were many. Thirteen years of living as part of new communities, and with family and friends, is a substantive history to take away. Her daughter told me of the impact it had: she had given birth to another child and her mother, who would have come to live with her for some weeks as part of cultural tradition, had not even met her new born.

Figure 4.2 Belongings of a woman who was deported after 13 years in the asylum system, and who had not been given the opportunity to collect her own bags and boxes.

Beyond this, other women in the group had heightened concerns that this might affect their own status and as such some were temporarily reluctant to speak out in public forums after this but, as we will see as this book moves on, such acts of control also spur resistance and organised dissent.

Rationalising the deliberate infliction of harm

There are many ways to understand the incorporation of structural violence and social harms into Britain's asylum system, and certainly too many on the political spectrum to incorporate into one chapter so I will focus on two. The first is a kind of liberal 'managed migration' justification (see Somerville, 2007) – the borders should not be closed but we do nonetheless need to manage the number, and importantly, the kinds of people entering Britain (Morris, 2010; Somerville, ibid.). To do this, we need management strategies, and this includes deterrence strategies. Such strategies might include the forms of restrictions outlined by Aliverti (2012) or Webber (2006; 2012) and be based on the creation of 'buffer zones' (Webber, 2004: 138) outside of the UK, and technologised visa and passport restrictions within.

The second, more conservative justification, is akin to the example highlighted by Bosworth: a political opinion that there are people who simply should not be here, they have broken laws by entering illegally and we, as a nation, have the sovereign right to exclude them at any length. This perspective stands more comfortably with nationalistic preservation of White British identity, although considering that Britain hasn't been monocultural for at least a millennium it might be apt to highlight this as something of an imagined community (Anderson, 1991; Gilroy, 1987). Nonetheless, this racialised undertone dominates the justification for the infliction of harm on people who are not White, and especially those who have broken laws to be here.

In 2002, then Home Secretary David Blunkett highlighted to Parliament the problem that integration can cause for removing immigrant families, since children often attend school and become part of a community. Reflecting on this, Webber points out that there is another clear rationale 'for making asylum seekers live in a limbo away from society ... they become too well integrated to be easily removed, and they must be removed in the interests of "managed migration"' (Webber, 2012). Similar sentiments periodically raise their heads through the Human Rights Act, or more specifically Article 8, the Right to a Private and Family Life. This Article, which incorporates the European Convention on Human Rights has been under threat of revoke by the Conservative Party since 2010. Adamant to remove the right to claim on these grounds, the then Home Secretary Theresa May (again, currently Prime Minister) even went as far as to claim, 'We all know the stories about the Human Rights Act ... about the illegal immigrant who cannot be deported because, and I am not making this up, he had a pet cat' (BBC, 2011).

By all accounts, *she* was not making this up – the speech and its inaccurate claim[4] had been copied almost word for word from Nigel Farage, the leader of right-wing UKIP, who used almost the exact turns of phrase months earlier (Wagner, 2011). The binding objectives of such discourses has been to remove people's capacity to build relations, to have autonomy over their own lives, or to live free from structural violence or restriction. What has been dissolved, along-side autonomy, is not just the right to a private or family life but access to civil liberties, an aspect often eroded from the debates around asylum, liberties which facilitate not only general freedoms reflected in human rights, but also freedom of movement and association.

Chapter conclusion

The harms outlined within this chapter fall into two broad categories: those that are direct consequences of immigration policy, such as the harms of con-finement or deportation, and those that are by-products of structurally violent policies and legislation, such as increased anxiety or reduced relational in-teraction. Those first are significantly easier to campaign against, to protest or write articles around. They are visible, and when significant harms occur they may be in violation of laws. The second, however, is banal, dull, almost boring to address. It is the unspoken 'everydaynesss' that resonates well with liberal feminist discussions about domesticity (Friedan, 1963) – all who expe-rience its confines see its problems, but those who do not, see little of it. Rather than central to migration management agendas, it is a by-product of them on a micro-level.

Many of the above examples have the potential for serious harm. Some, such as pest infestations or poor access to adequate healthcare, have the potential to lead to illness or even death. The emotional impacts that are repercussive of inadequately slow decision-making processes evidently affect people's mental wellbeing, and as we have seen, can even induce or exacerbate suicidal feel-ings. These issues, coupled with the looming fear of deportation, dispersal or detention, are all either deliberate or avoidable outcomes of policies developed to control the lives of asylum seekers. The latter problems echo the sentiments laid out by Weber and Pickering (2011) in the previous chapter – that the imple-mentation of toxic policies can have long-lasting, even life-threatening, conse-quences. The earlier examples, however, reflect a kind of decrepit banality – one that sprawls into the private and domestic sphere, to the everyday lives of women seeking asylum. Rather than ameliorating life changing problems or scenarios – such as detention – these chip at the daily existence of women's lives, with the outcomes being that of temporal confinement and restrictions that can affect the physical and emotional wellbeing of women awaiting refu-gee status.

Notes

1 Similar can be said for other dispersal areas in the UK, for example Glasgow in Scotland.
2 Note that some practitioners and people seeking asylum might still refer to 'NASS' as asylum support, even though the system itself has been changed.
3 Although controls date back to at least the 1905 Aliens Act, the expansion of illegalisation as we know it today emerged more clearly in the 1960s, with the 1962 Commonwealth Immigrants Act.
4 The appellant – a former student in Britain and Bolivian national – had appealed against deportation on Article 8 grounds of the ECHR, based on a long-term relationship which included the joint ownership of a cat (see Wagner, *The Guardian*, 2011).

5 Hawwi

Violence, resistance and survival

They are single testimonies, and one of the dangers of that is that sometimes you will read a very moving testimony from a woman, and everyone will be moved by that. They won't think, 'so is that the women who come into this country seeking protection with their children and their families?' There isn't a way of helping the public see that this is actually that most of the people who come to the UK have histories of this type, and all are in fear of that

(Interview Participant, Trauma Counsellor)

Recognising the limits of finding voice and speaking out need not result in an unwillingness to deal with the risks associated with such efforts

(Naples, 2003: 166)

Introduction

The implications of political decision-making on a macro level, and the outcomes of punitive policy implementation, are clearly evidenced so far. The micro or everyday impacts of these can be seen in the concerns raised by those working closely with refugee groups and people seeking asylum, as well as with women seeking asylum. It is therefore within this chapter that we will more fully and explicitly unpack the lived experience of asylum through the voice and reflections of woman who survived sexual violence at an international border. As the following section argues, the aim of this is to give due recognition to the complexity of individuals' lives and to facilitate an understanding of the intersectional continuum of violence that women can face not only across identities, but within and throughout lived experiences.

The politics of oral history

Oral history has long been tied with feminist epistimologies; debates around the intrinsic domination of the social sciences by quantitative research proliferated throughout the 1980s and 1990s (Chase, 2008; Harding, 1986, 1987; Kelly, 1990; Kelly *et al.*, 1994), an era within which the value of subjective voice was drawn further into the centre of knowledge production. Subsequently, feminist research has supported the development of qualitative analyses of social phenomena in a way that meshes together the personal and political, the everyday and the extraordinary, so that we might better challenge these concepts as simply binary (Oakley, 2010; Ramazanoglu and Holland, 2002). This has been important in drawing out the lived experience of violence, inequality and oppression in the lives of women.

However, the value of this has arguably become hostage to its own fate, particularly in relation to asylum and immigration. The prevalence of personal history narratives throughout refugee support communities, NGOs and international fund-raising initiatives has become a key avenue for drawing attention to the precarious experiences of women, men and children making their way to a 'better life', running from persecution and toward safety and normality. This is particularly the case in the representation of survivors of trafficking, sexual abuse, and domestic slavery or servitude. In some ways, this can be highly voyeuristic and the value of individuals' voices is undermined by the constant attempt to engage a sometimes apathetic and disconcerting public in responding in some way to the suffering of certain groups of people (Butler, 2004, 2009; see also, Fisk, 2016).

As such, engaging in personal narratives is open to criticism in a way that other methods are not. First, a lot is required of personal history emotionally. The speaker relaying their experiences and memories depends on the trust of another person who interprets and analyses their 'story'. Second, although all efforts might be made to ensure clarity, accuracy and anonymity, the informant and the researcher can never know who will read the narrative and thus can never truly control what becomes of one's own history in the mind of readers. Third, memory and objectivity is contested. While other methods may allow for subjective discussion, oral history is all-immersive and depends largely on the ability for one person to relay historical information from their own perspective (Atkinson, 1998; Chase, 2008; Ramazanoglu and Holland, 2002; Thompson, 2000). Lastly is the *intention* of the use of oral histories and the way in which personal narrative is often represented through stories to evoke emotional responses such as sympathy, empathy or even pity. As Salazar argued, 'The attempt to place some of these testimonies and autobiographies into larger contexts (both material and textual) of relations of power is not without problems' (1991: 93). Perhaps most problematic is that these are commonly undertaken by White researchers, evoking an almost colonial gaze on the 'ethnic Other' (hooks, 1990, Rice, 1990).

It is therefore not without pause that I undertook oral history as part of my PhD research in 2011. The limitations are clear, and the potential for creating a kind of research voyeurism is highly problematic: who has the right to speak, and whose narrative becomes a story (Mauther and Doucet, 1998). These have been serious concerns for me and mitigating them has not been easy. However, from a critical criminological perspective, a book that levies mostly on my own interpretations and analyses has the capacity to reiterate dominant ideologies when subjugated voices are obscured (Chase, 2008; Harding, 1987; hooks, 1984, 1990). I am clear to make women who are accessing services aware that I am a researcher, and that discussions they have with me will not be included unless they agree to a formal interview. A woman, who has chosen to be known as *Hawwi*, contacted me through a mutual friend and asked to contribute to any research I was doing, having been interested in research and academia herself. On agreeing to meet, I asked how she would like to contribute, and oral history ensued. The key to creating an understanding of the structural implications of violence in Hawwi's life has been dual analysis. On completion of transcription, analysis and writing up the key aspects of tens of thousands of words, we discussed the content, the representation of her history, and the way in which I observed cultural or patriarchal practices as oppressive from a potentially limiting Western perspective.

The objectives of this chapter are thus to incorporate the experiences of a woman who I met within a research capacity over a six-week period. Although more oral histories would provide broader insight, I deliberately chose to include one oral history to avoid comparative discussions and instead draw in-depth analysis of multiple structures of oppression throughout the life of one woman. Rather than necessarily focussing on acts of violence in isolation, I was interested to understand how the *impacts* of specific subjections to patriarchal violence can manifest and arguably ultimately be compounded by further structural and personal oppressions in seeking asylum. Oral history encompasses the opposite of Home Office interviews in that defining or understanding violence is not restricted to legal definitions or conventions, but instead reflexively engages with narratives of experiences, survival and resistance. It is built on trust and belief rather than adversary and prodding inquiry: I only ever asked Hawwi to tell me how she came to be living in asylum in Liverpool, with few questions in between. As is pivotal to feminist work, the conditions for disclosure of experiences centred on what Hawwi wanted to tell me. This, she stated, was in some way cathartic: *For me it is like a healing that I express my emotion like that.*

Alongside the importance of subjugated knowledge, my own justification for focussing on Hawwi's oral history is that the macro and micro are drawn together in a way that emphasises the lived impacts of experience, in this case of state violence, sexual violence, and life awaiting asylum in Liverpool. It personifies the theoretical implications of the intersectional continuum of violence outlined in Chapter 2 in a way that does not aim to make assumptions or cast dominant narratives of what seeking asylum is, or who women seeking asylum are, but the opposite: to challenge the assumption that people's experiences are monolithic or prescriptive. Instead it considers the complexities of personal realities that are affected by the structural decisions and policy implementations that have real and substantial effects on the lives of women, men and children seeking asylum.

History and identity

When we first met, Hawwi was in her thirties. Almost two years before, she had fled her country of origin – a country in the Horn of Africa – alone due to political victimisation by the state. Although we met many times, the oral history used in this chapter was recorded in three meetings that accumulated almost six hours of narrative. This began with her early life.

For the most part of her childhood Hawwi lived with her parents in a rural village. One of many children, three of her siblings died while she was young and the family overall experienced drought and periods of hunger, recalling, '*My childhood, there is no place to sleep in the night, there is no clothes to wear. And because there are a lot of childrens we are fighting and starving for food*'. In the domestic sphere, Hawwi identified her mother as holding all responsibility for the household and experiencing domestic violence at the hands of her father. Hawwi remembers this as there being '*no peace at home*' and that '*he is just bringing huge stick and he's just beating her. He is making her bleed*'. This culminated in her mother leaving for varied periods of time and her sister adopting the role of 'mother'.

Although most girls are removed from school in Grade Eight (13 years old), Hawwi's father allowed her the opportunity to continue schooling for one year in return for living as a domestic servant for her brother, and then further afield to her aunt where she would continue education beyond 13. At that point, Hawwi began to be subjected to physical abuse – beatings and starvation – at the hands of her aunt and uncle while replacing '*the job of a servant*'. Hawwi disclosed this to her father and family, who ignored the claims. This led her to cut ties with her family and move to live as a servant with an unrelated woman where again she was denied breakfast, lunch and dinner. While completing high school, moving in with friends and starting her first job in a factory, the government changed and guerilla fighters occupied the country for several years, when '*military power is everywhere*'. Hawwi recalls this period stating '*wherever you are going you are in fear of rape of the soldiers, not rape of the society … if they see a woman there is no question, they are just taking her from the street for rape*'.

Political opposition

By 21, Hawwi had completed a diploma and moved from her home to work. Here, she contracted Tuberculosis and, due to the lack of a hospital, moved nearer the capital city for hospital treatment. Here she volunteered for a public service and spoke out against advertisements encouraging men to join the military for an ongoing conflict because '*if you are going to the military, you are dying*'. This is the first point at which she was accused of having '*hidden objectives*' against the government and military, this time by the people she worked with and local state actors.

On losing her voluntary role, Hawwi moved in to the capital and applied for a job in journalism. Due to her education and ability to speak multiple languages, this application was successful and she began work as a journalist. Hawwi highlights the first stages of this conflict, stating, '*there is tribe conflict starting now … after this transitional government … this tribe issue arises from every corner of the city*'. She goes on to argue that '*[her country] is a country with a very huge military power. At the ground, people are starving and dying of hunger*'. At this point of her career, Hawwi covered demonstrations that led to the death of students at the hands of the government. Hawwi stated that she, along with other journalists who reported on the shooting, was accused of '*provoking society'* by showing the force military used against students. An investigation ensued by Parliament to examine the role of the media and specifically, Hawwi argues, the role of some ethnicities in journalism. She continued to report on the issue and as a result was fired from her role. As a response to government actions, including the imprisonment of journalists and students from the protest, Hawwi decided to flee to a neighbouring country. As there were no flights due to conflict, this was an overland trip hiding in the back of a car.

It is here between borders that Hawwi was raped. After two *'safe nights'* staying with one woman and three men, Hawwi was woken by one of the smuggling agents. She recalled:

> *He come and sat by me. I pushed him, he resisted, he start pushing me and start doing like that. "Please leave me". He can't hear me. "Leave me". He can't hear me. He said, "are you a virgin?" or something, some word which was broken Amharic. "Why, you are not a virgin, why you are not doing this? Shut your mouth" or something. As much as I am trying, pushing him, he is just pretending and just pushing me and pushing me. In the middle of the night, he beat me. And he start doing sex. Just, he put some dirty cloths in my mouth and he just done everything he likes and I will not tell you the situation, it is a very big shame.*

She went on to state that *'He told me that "we will play on you, three of us will play on you".* She remembers, *'I cried a lot, I cried a lot, I cried a lot, oh',* feeling as though, *'I have to go to my house and I have to die there',* and *'there is pain all the day. He struggled, he beat me as much as he can. Every pain is on my body'.* Once he left, she travelled to an organisation in the same area where she was taken back to the country's capital city. At this point, she remembers, *'I took my shame in my mind. I didn't speak to anyone.'*

Hawwi experienced constant vaginal discharge and itching, and was diagnosed with having contracted a venereal disease, which subsequently was not effectively treated until she later arrived in Merseyside. On realising she had missed a period, Hawwi undertook a pregnancy test that confirmed she had become pregnant from rape. She stated, *'Now there is no way I have a child. I don't have home, I don't have job, by any means, whether I die of it, I have to discard it, I have to remove it I decided.'* Hawwi was then able to obtain an abortion at one of the few abortion clinics in the country, but suffered 12 days of continuous bleeding as a result. On receiving treatment she was advised to undertake an HIV test, which she did. Hawwi recalled the test proving positive:

> *Finally the doctor is White Russian and interpreter said, "it's for you", and they told me, "sorry, we are very sorry. You got HIV" they said. I don't know what to do, really. All the heaven comes to me and I don't know what to do.*

For the following weeks, Hawwi blamed the transmission on the religious belief that *'God didn't observe me in society and didn't forgive my sins'* and that God could cure her if she repented, including reunifying with her family.

After some months Hawwi applied for and was appointed a new job as a journalist. She recalled this particular appointment as '*the first happiest year of my life. One phase of my life is switched off and the other is open*'. After this point, the political position in Hawwi's country of origin began. An election ensued, which the government was accused of rigging. Again, demonstrations took place in the capital that Hawwi was required to report. She stated, '*I am a reporter. I am independent. I have to interview the victim's families ... I will get information from non-government organisations and the civil society.*' As a response to this, the government again accused her of '*provoking society*' and, because of her contact with guerrilla fighters as a reporter, forms of collusion. As part of reporting, Hawwi followed the story of the detention of members of the government opposition, three of whom Hawwi states were tortured and killed in prison. She reported this through monthly visits to court. Finally, on one occasion, the police opened a pack to find radio equipment she carried to record the trials. Although she openly declared herself as a journalist before entering the court through security and to the police, Hawwi was detained, kicked and beaten before being released. They took her equipment, but she recalled, '*I am OK, I can walk.*' After this, and despite attempted protection by her international employers, the government revoked Hawwi's licence to report. This once again left her unemployed.

At the same time, Hawwi had begun a relationship with a man, who was also HIV positive. This partially developed from a friendship with him, and he was able to obtain anti-retroviral drugs to support Hawwi's immune system. As a result of her popularity, Hawwi felt unable to attend clinics to acquire HIV-related medications, as:

> *I have fear of the society and I need to get an informal way without exposing my HIV... people need to see it, I don't know why, They say "at the back of the clinic is a corner, the HIV positive peoples are there". The other patients are hearing that ... as if they must gossip they want to see who ... are sitting there.*

Hawwi's relationship changed gradually to become steady. However, after some time, Hawwi's partner informed her he had one daughter from another girlfriend, but that they now live in another country. Hawwi acknowledged that '*he is treating me well because I have got a lot of money*' and that, although she was religious, after six months they started '*doing sex together*' and she soon became pregnant. She referred to buying him food and clothes and paying rent, and that '*I am loving him too much*'. It was during her pregnancy that Hawwi's journalism licence was revoked. To challenge this, Hawwi contacted an international NGO who invited her to speak about her treatment by the government at a conference held by a human rights organisation in a nearby country. Despite being far along in pregnancy, Hawwi attended but could not convince her husband to accompany her. She also acknowledged this point as a reason for refusal from the UK Home Office as they questioned '*How is it possible for you to travel by airport if you are eight months pregnant?'* and that this was even though *'I gave the days and pregnancy months and even the pictures with the pregnancy. Everything. Even the pictures with the human rights organisation in [says country].'*

Later that year, Hawwi gave birth. Hawwi's partner *'is evaluating me ... Now there is no dollar, there is nothing'.* After one and a half years in a relationship, her partner disclosed having a wife and children in another corner of the city. Instead of looking for jobs during the day, as he had said, he had been spending time with his *'other family'.* Hawwi states at this point that her partner had become aggressive towards her and would not interact with their child.

Having had little support from national organisations, Hawwi contacted an international independent NGO for political support as a result of her incarceration and abuse by the government. They granted Hawwi money to travel back to the same country to meet with an African human rights organisation. Hawwi planned to seek political asylum there, which encouraged her partner to return to his family to support their child and travel as a family unit but only if they got married. Hawwi agreed to this, and reflects *'he started loving me'.* However, after two hours of marriage:

> *he discussed with things how he will claim my property and that he has house with me, he has money in account with me ... I gave the chance to share my house, to share the money in the account [bangs table] by that marriage certificate [bangs table]. I killed myself without knowing.*

After a short time, Hawwi filed for divorce. By this stage, her husband had a claim on the house.

In response, Hawwi's husband disclosed that she was a member as part of opposition to the government, in a report to local police. She was subsequently arrested, recalling, *'everything that we shared as husband and wife he completely told the police. The police come and caught me without any court decision ... when police come to you, they start by beating or insulting you'.* Hawwi was detained for a short while, questioned about why she was planning to leave the country and eventually beaten. Hawwi stated:

> *he will beat me on my face, he is kicking me on the wall. Now I am just standing like this [gets up to show she is standing still]... sometimes he is beating me, sometimes he is trying to put something in my eyes, I am crying. Sometimes he is kicking me, he is saying, "give her slump", he is ordering him.*

Eventually the police released her, and Hawwi recognised her husband's involvement in her arrest; *'I just completely understand that ... he gave them money to frighten me and to leave anything for him. Because if the court says give them order to arrest me they will not say "don't tell anybody".'*

Once released, Hawwi stayed on the street in a bus station where she began to experience the first effects of breakdown. She recalled:

I am trying to speak but I can't activate it, I tried to speak to someone ... nothing. If something, if anger or something happened to me I don't know. I just can't speak at all really. Crying all the night, I just completely lost my mind.

Once found by her brother, who had contacted the police, Hawwi was admitted to hospital where she was medicated, injected and remembered, '*when they gave me injection I don't know, something completely happens to me. I start shouting, extremely shouting ... I remember some of it ... I tried to beat every person who approaches me*'. When her brother took her to the toilet, Hawwi threw herself into a river, '*the purpose is to kill myself*'. She was rescued by a number of people, and admitted to a psychiatric hospital. She remained here as an inpatient for some months. On release, she remembered '*I will see visions and I will hear some voices in my mind ... I can't control myself.*' At this point, Hawwi began to publicly disclose her HIV status in shops and on the street, and to her family, with whom she was now living. In response, her brothers would not allow Hawwi to use shared cutlery, plates or cups because of her HIV status. She stated, '*if they touch me they will wash their hands with many things ... [they] are just putting some paint on their cups, not to mix by any means*'.

After a fall out with family, Hawwi began state-funded anti-retroviral medication (ARVs), as well as medication for newly diagnosed bipolar disorder, suffering at this point from being '*extremely depressed*'. HIV combination therapy impacted on her overall health, reducing her appetite and resulting in weight loss. Hawwi decided that '*I can't take this child anymore, I can't hold my mind, my attention is completely diverse in everything*'. As a result of this, Hawwi left her child in the care of her mother.

Migration and asylum

During discussion with opposition party offices with the party leader, Hawwi was informed of a course for political members funded by a British organisation. Although uncertain if her HIV status would prevent membership, Hawwi applied and was accepted to the course. Her status did not affect her application, and three months later she was granted an opportunity to travel to the United Kingdom as part of a collaborative country scheme. She went on to inform her family, collected paper documents and left her mobile phone to allow her to contact her son.

Hawwi arrived in the UK, recalling, '*the weather is cold, it is completely different, it is icy and I am shivering*'. As part of a number of focus groups within the scheme, Hawwi was asked about her political experiences and affiliations in Hawwi's home country, which led to disagreements with members of oppositional government groups during the event.

To ensure she would receive ARVs, Hawwi was sent to an NHS clinic, where blood samples were taken which showed problems with her liver and that she had a highly detectable HIV viral load. Tests also found that her heart had become enlarged as a result of inadequate and incorrect ARVs in her country of origin. At this point, Hawwi began to consider claiming asylum, again writing to an organisation for a support letter. Hawwi did not yet know how to apply for asylum in the UK, but was informed by another woman that this could be done in Liverpool (since changed) or Croydon. Again, on investigating, Hawwi found out how to get to offices, left the compound and took a bus to Liverpool. On applying for asylum at Liverpool's UKBA screening unit, Hawwi was finger printed and had her picture taken, but that she was not given any documentation before being sent to a hostel. Hawwi remembers arriving here, '*my mind is not active like other people's is active, people are studying me, staring ... I don't know what they are really staring*'.

Hawwi was then asked for details of her solicitor and for her asylum card, neither of which she had. The Home Office took another picture and gave her an asylum identity card, but she was not allocated an asylum case owner. Eventually she was given the address of a solicitor where she was informed of the process and chose to proceed. She waited for six months initially in the UK asylum system to be allocated a case owner while living in Home Office NASS accommodation and receiving the standard £5 per day for food (for that time), clothes and travel. Eventually, after six months, UKBA staff interviewed Hawwi. This was undertaken on a Friday, four days after surgery in Liverpool to improve her enlarged heart, the result of inadequate ARVs. Half was done on the same day and, due to recognition of her illness, half one week later. After one month, another interviewer was sent to Hawwi, again not her case owner, to clarify the previous interview. Hawwi's solicitor informed the Home Office that 'this lady is a victim of torture, victim of rape, and she was a journalist. Many things she told them'. Hawwi's solicitor included letters of support in her application from numerous local, national and international charities and NGOs that she had been in touch with, including support agencies in Merseyside that Hawwi had accessed on request of her solicitor through one national organisation.

Hawwi's solicitor requested that the Home Office did not grant a decision in the case while waiting for a final medical report. However, the Home Office sent a refusal letter during this time, over a year after her first application, stating discrepancies in her documentation. This included questioning her relationship with the organisation that had supported her, and arguing that there are sufficient anti-retrovirals in her country of origin for HIV treatment. The refusal stated that most of the government activity that had taken place against Hawwi had happened before 2007, while she applied for asylum in 2009. Furthermore, as she had come by air using her own passport, it was deemed unlikely that the government would have any interest in her. They stated that they believed what job she claimed to have and which 'tribe' she was a part of, but questioned why she had not claimed asylum at the airport. To this, Hawwi stated, '*I don't know the asylum process and even after I claimed, I stayed for a long time without card, without solicitor. And who believes you? It's very hard.*'

Hawwi moved towards appealing against the refusal based on a set of interviews she had given while with the British Council in Birmingham. These had been recorded and displayed on television, where she had highlighted human rights abuses by the government of her country. Tapes and newspaper articles were disclosed in court and, although translated into English, were again rejected until they were supplied in their original format to the courts. Although she has since been granted leave to remain, at the time of exploring Hawwi's oral history, she was still waiting for final decision on her second appeal. During this time, the court date was also moved back by over two weeks.

Life in asylum

As the final part of the overall oral history, I asked Hawwi to describe life in the asylum system in Merseyside. She stated, '*for me, asylum is a new process ... I entered into it and learned all the process by myself through the system*', one which she struggled with. Her anxieties include having a '*restless mind*' whereby, '*I don't know whether I can join that little child, I don't know whether we are just disappearing forever, I don't know if I can have an ability to raise him. I don't know what will happen*'. She went on to say that '*when I just tried to gain a little relief in my health situation, the result of my asylum become negative and all my thinking and hope become darkened at a time and I don't know what I am going to do*'. She questioned why no one believed her asylum claim, and argued, '*the suffrage that I came through, no one will understand that. I am not a thief; I am not like a criminal*'.

On her fear of being returned, Hawwi stated, '*There is no way I am going to escape the eyes of the government, and there is no means of surviving there ... Deciding to turn me there is killing me.*' She identified problems in her country of origin at the time including:

> the human rights abuses, look at the life of women, look at the rape of women ... if you are a female you can't have your own property alone, you have to have a bodyguard, or a good relationship with the government

and went on to argue, '*you can't tell any media that we are suffering, people cannot speak to medias, medias are controlled by the government. You cannot expose anything. International organisations cannot function in that country*'. This also led to questioning of COI at the (now dissolved) UKBA, about which Hawwi argued:

> the reality in [country name] and the country report, or what the government can speak to the world, is very, very different ... the government denies the reality in this country and tried to negotiate with other governments and he is doing well.

Hawwi acknowledged positive elements about her asylum claim at various points, most significantly, '*I am thanking and I will give them thanks always because they treated me well ... I have good accommodation and I get good health treatment, shower, good type of food*', referring specifically to her heart operation. However, there were other elements of life as an asylum seeker that she found difficult, for example, '*I can't control my time, I am losing my way all the* day', and at times had problems recognising her environment, for example, '*I lost myself twice and reported to the police ... and I can't cross the traffic light properly. Every time the drivers are shouting at me and just I am, it was very, very devastating*'. She also continued to have problems with her mental health, including, '*I have great depression ... sometimes I need to kill myself and some-times I need to kills someone*'. She referred to '*remembering the past. Always the past is in my mind*'. She continued to struggle with side effects from ARVs, including nausea and sickness.

In terms of support, Hawwi spoke positively of one particular local organisation who have provided counselling and where she was able to network with people living with HIV in the asylum system. She received one-to-one peer discussion and has been allocated a clinical psychologist. These have, she said, led her to reduce the number of tablets she takes on a daily basis, and that most times, '*the idea of killing myself, all the idea of drinking poison, or doing something to others is completely released in my mind, and I am controlling every emotions of my life*'.

Although her mental health had improved since receiving counselling and sup-port, Hawwi referred constantly to feeling restless, losing sleep and not eating while waiting for a response from the UKBA. She questions why asylum seekers cannot work in the UK, as this has left her with empty time which she spent '*dreaming about that people, about the court and the response of the court*' while she waits for her appeal to go through the Home Office. She argued, '*there is plenty of things that we can work. Not by depending on the government and not always by being benefit claimants or just by not doing anything. There is many things we can do*'.

In the concluding part of her story, Hawwi questioned the Geneva Convention, and whether it is sufficient to protect '*vulnerable ladies, childrens and peoples who exposed to many different diseases*'. She questioned her own protection un-der the convention in the UK, adding:

> *I don't have very sufficient years to live in this world, and I don't need to finish the rest of my life my struggling and by conflicts and by disturbing my mind. I need rest, I need peace of mind, so I need this protection to protect my life from danger.*

Structural inequalities, marginalisation and exclusion

Hawwi's history interprets and relays whole discourses of power that impact on her individually, as well as on wider individuals and social actors related to the historical moments that she discusses. Notable social inequalities include poverty and malnutrition, such as in her reflection of there being little food as a child and at varying stages of her adulthood. These can, for example, relate to global distributions of wealth, state crime and corruption, and ecological regions in terms of farming and crop development. They are clearly important points for concern, however this section will focus more specifically on conflict, state power, migration, impacts of sexual violence, gender inequality and the UK asylum system.

As the synopsis of her oral history indicates, Hawwi had actively engaged in challenging state power and, as she identified it, social inequalities in her ethnic identity through her role as a journalist. Wider governmental problems manifested in conflict often include corruption and state violence. As Hawwi indicated, her country of origin is one of Africa's poorest countries and currently sits fairly close to the poorest country in the world (Pasquali, 2016). There are regular shortages in food and as UNICEF highlights, almost two-thirds of the country are illiterate, with women holding just over half the literacy rate of men (United Nations High Commissioner for Refugees, 2013). Hawwi identifies these as reasons for her involvement in political opposition, for example arguing, '*My country is the most poor country in the world, it will get grant from everyone. That grant will go specifically to the government region,*' The way in which individuals experience forms of state control are identified by Hawwi in stating:

> *They [police] are coming to you not in a polite way, without knowing anything just in a harsh ... Everything is warning, there is no way of saying like in this country, with regard, with kind, with sincerity. You can't hear like this from any [states country] organisation. Everything is warning, everything is harsh. When the police come to you, they start by beating you or insulting you.*

Hawwi also highlighted the fear of '*rape of [by] the soldiers*' when outlining militarisation of rural and urban areas. While Hawwi did not experience sexual violence at the hands of government militia, sexual violence by the military had been widespread during various points of civil unrest (Arieff, 2009). The fear of rape is a very real concern for women during conflict and civil unrest, and soldiers and militia groups are often one of the most prominent perpetrators of sexual violence (Bastick *et al.*, 2007; Brownmiller, 1975; Canning, 2010; Leatherman, 2011; Wood, 2006). This gendered fear of crime is echoed globally, and develops elements of self-regulation in women and, if subjected to sexual violence, can increase internalisation of shame for not 'protecting' herself from rape.

Gendered inequalities

Referring to countries in the Horn of Africa, Kedir and Admasachew argued, 'there is widespread tolerance of violence perpetrated against women at individual, family, community, peer-groups, school, religion and state levels' (2010: 438). Certainly, elements of violence as perpetrated by most of these groups are evident in Hawwi's accounts, whether she had experienced them herself or is relaying details from other women, or broader systems and structures. Indeed, many of these are evident in Hawwi's story and experience. As standpoint and Southern feminists have argued, the domestic sphere can be a place of violence and intimidation for women (Copelon, 1994; Devessa *et al.*, 1998; Jewkes *et al.*, 2009; Nesabai, 2005). There are various points in

Hawwi's oral history where this was evident, experienced by her mother, her sister and herself:

> *'I don't know any days that my mother is sitting and speaking good things with my father. I just know that all the time she is terrified of my father'; 'my sister becomes like a mother. My elder sister became my mother and she became like a wife for my father ... She suffered a lot a lot a lot and finally my sister become mentally ill'; 'My brothers, one of them will beat me, my younger brothers they are beating me'.*

While the contexts of these change in relation to who is perpetrating and who is experiencing violence, the element of gendered inequality remains static in that it is in the most part male violence against women. This is relatable to all but one instance that Hawwi disclosed, namely that she was physically abused by her aunt while at school.

Various inequalities relatable to patriarchy are weaved into other elements of Hawwi's life history. These included, for example, education and legal entitlement. Although Hawwi was able to obtain an education and while her own father encouraged it beyond the state regulation, her study was transactional, in that she had to supply domestic labour in return for it. Hawwi stated:

> *My father send all of us to the school. He sent all of us whether the girls or the mens but when we reached grade 8 he told us to stop education, it is enough for you. Now more than this you will get a husband, it is not good for you, what are you bringing more than sons?*

The oral history also demonstrated other elements of cultural social control based on gendered spatiality, for example while Hawwi was struggling to get food while living with her brother, she found:

> *I can't eat outside, which is culturally very bad, and you can't eat on the street as a married girl ... even if you are married it is cultural very, very shameful for a lady to eat outside. But still, because of the shame of the society I will not go somewhere and I will not eat anything.*

Furthermore, cultural power binaries include women's access to legal rights, education and property (Alemu And Mengitsu, 2009). Hawwi stated:

> *As a female, if I don't need anything from that government, and if I need to live by my own thing, if I got my own money, I can't build something and then leave. Death can happen to me, anything can happen to me.*

This questions the level of autonomy some women may have in regard to their own lives, finances and futures and in some ways sets up a pathway for further violations of civil liberties and human rights. Hence violence against women does not remain only in the physical and emotional sphere, but can relate to institutional sexism and patriarchal cultural codes that can lead to further harms (Edley and Weatherell, 1995). This includes, for example, Hawwi's experience of being denied food as a result of gendered cultural restrictions rather than physical, economic or ecological factors.

The impacts of sexual violence

Physical implications

As the outline of Hawwi's history illustrates above, there were various physical implications that developed from rape. Sexual violence can have varying consequences physically, some short term and others significantly longer term or permanent. This can include different levels of fistulae (some irreparable), sexually transmitted diseases and infections (STD/STIs) and damage to internal organs. These may be particularly common in conflict situations due to high levels of rapes and multiple rapes experienced by individual women, as well as multiple perpetrator rapes that can increase the likelihood of STD/STI transmission or internal damage (Elbe, 2002; Mills and Nachega, 2006).

The physical consequences of rape were, for Hawwi, vast. Hawwi gradually disclosed numerous effects, all in the initial part of the oral history but with implications of each effect transcending to wider problems and decisions in other parts of the history. Except for the physical pain she experienced due to rape and being beaten, the first instance of recognition of any further implication began with a venereal disease, from which she suffered until she arrived in Liverpool:

> *On the fourth day I got itching. itching, itching. I am like my, my legs itch me like, how can I tell you [scratches thighs]. I have a lot of itching ... There is liquid, discharges. Oh my God, there is some venereal disease I have got and what can I do I said.*

After this, Hawwi realised firstly that she was pregnant and then that she would have an abortion, which consequently led to blood loss. She recalled that, '*I waited for my period, there is no period. I convinced that this pregnancy, again I went to check my pregnancy test. It is positive*' and that, '*after that abortion my blood count stop. I have bleeding, I have bleeding, I have bleeding. 12 days continuous bleeding*'.

The most permanent physical consequence of Hawwi's rape was the transmission of HIV, which had significant knock-on effects for her health more generally, many of which she continued to experience during the collection of her oral history. Remembering back to her diagnoses, Hawwi relayed the way in which she was told, '*Finally the doctor is White Russian and interpreter said it's for you,* and they told me that *"sorry, we are very sorry. You got HIV"* they said.' Her reactions were clear:

> *'Physically I am completely devastated'; 'I am struggling with side effects of my anti-retrovirals. I am nauseous; always I am taking anti-sickness tablets with my medication. That is always a big challenge at that moment for me'; 'My previous medication systems I started in [names country] ... my liver and kidneys and my heart, most of my organs were damaged, but I got treatment now and I become very, very well after that. And because of this I am always give thanking'.*

It is this particular effect that other elements of this section will focus on, as many of Hawwi's experiences are directly relatable to this. This included stigma, further physical problems and, Hawwi's oral history suggests, contributed to the development of mental health problems.

Psychological and Emotional Effects

Hawwi first identified experiencing feelings of shame directly after rape, and decided not to tell anyone about her ordeal. This response can be common among women who survive rape, due to the social stigmatisation of sexual victimistion, and in victim blaming attitudes in many areas:

> *'I took my shame in my mind, I didn't speak to anyone'; 'But my life is completely damaged, I lose weight, I am not eating, keeping my hair, I am not brushing my teeth. Completely I become rubbish thing. I become rubbish'.*

It was in the diagnosis of HIV after being raped that she first recognised emotional and psychological changes in her mental health, as she said:

> *Now I have some sort of depression. I need to stay without reason on the bed, or I will not be very eager to do as I used to do in the past, but there is no very complicated health issue in my mind, and I can't control my mind, I can't think what I have to do.*

Depression is a common emotional and psychological response to HIV diagnosis, and is associated with 'increased disability, lower quality of life, shorter survival and greater probability of dying' (Sambamoorthi *et al.*, 2001: 33). A fear of these elements may also contribute to depression on initial diagnosis, which Hawwi refers to at the point of diagnosis and later in discussing her asylum claim.

Suicidal Feelings and Mental Health

Throughout the oral history transcripts, Hawwi repetitively disclosed suicidal feelings after contracting HIV, and attempted suicide on a number of occasions, as has been indicated in the outline of her oral history above. She recalled her first response to waking up after being raped as feeling like, '*I have to go back to my house and I have to die there. I planned that.*' This later included an attempt at suicide soon after she began to experience a breakdown after an arrest:

> *My brother took me to the toilet. I left the toilet and run and put myself in the river. It is very, very bad and it was full of you know every toilet in that. I tried to sink myself; the purpose is to kill myself. It broke bits of my legs and I am bleeding and I sink and some of it entered my body.*

Following on from this, Hawwi remembered that:

> *They washed me and again they took me to the mental hospital. Then they said I have to stay there. I stayed in the mental hospital and they gave me injection and they gave me injection. They gave me injection; they will tied my hands, my family members, my brothers. And for medication they do by forcing me and forcing me and putting water in my mouth. For one week I struggled like that. I struggled with them a lot. They left me there; I stayed until three months in that as inpatient.*

As well as evidencing the psychological impacts, this section of history also points to further problems in terms of mental healthcare. While Hawwi was suffering psychological trauma, the forms of treatment she received are arguably less effective than the kinds of support that she has since received in Liverpool, which she says herself have helped her to move away from depression. Forms of support or 'medicine' vary from country to country, and through cultures, however Hawwi's use of the words 'forcing', 'struggled' and 'left me there' indicate inadequate care and medicalisation against her will. She was later to consider suicide again, further questioning the effectiveness of her 'treatment'.

Rape, HIV contraction and stigma

As with sexual violence, survivors of HIV can be subjected to stigmatisation and ostracism for a number of reasons, including fear of HIV and the social stigma of some transmission routes. Hawwi pinpointed this at various stages:

> *Because they heard about my HIV. If I drink something in house, they will check, 'did she drink in this cup? Did she sit here?' My own brothers. They discriminate me'; 'my family is ashamed of me. If anyone comes to the home they want to hide me. It was very, very horrible'; 'they have a very big fear of HIV, even the doctors of the hospital or the place where you are rented. If I am giving the other peoples who rented me house, the peoples will start to abandon me from house.*

The physical effects, then, of sexual violence may not be limited to the individual, but can transcend to wider groups. This was also clear in the emotional effects of sexual violence and HIV contraction, as Hawwi's family had also struggled with her breakdown and admittance to a psychiatric hospital, issues which continued after her release:

> *'you know the sadness comes to all family members. Some of them ... she is the one who brought this whole disaster. I become like they tell things to each other and all the credit is by me'; 'one day even my brother cried a lot because he suffered from me.'*

Again, these factors indicate that the effects of rape have serious consequences for the victim or survivor, but also for their family and community. As argued elsewhere, 'when a woman is raped, the effects are seldom experienced by either a society or an individual. Society and the individual are interlocked in a complex web of consequences' (Canning, 2010: 852). These consequences range in severity, but can include familial breakdown or social isolation and for Hawwi, like many others, may eventually end in influencing her decision to flee her community and country of origin.

'Now I am Floating': Hawwi and asylum in Merseyside

First, although asylum seekers are in theory to be allocated a solicitor at the time of application, when they are finger printed, photographed and given an asylum card, Hawwi did not receive either a card or solicitor before being relocated to a hostel in Liverpool. Furthermore, she claimed that, '*I don't know how to study or why solicitor is needed. I don't have any solicitor.*' During her asylum review, Hawwi experienced disbelief, where she felt that, '*The judge didn't consider anything about my case, about my suffrage, about my file. The judge only wanted to approve the decision of the Home Office and I disqualified.*' This was coupled with inadequacies in the legal system. At the time the Home Office had stated: 'Your case owner is the person who will deal with every aspect of your application for asylum, from beginning to end. You will be allocated to your case owner within a few days of making your application for asylum' (Home Office, 2011). Hawwi's case owner was changed on numerous occasions, resulting in repetitive questioning, as she stated:

> *We concluded with my case owner and I submitted all my document but I don't know, that case owner is not my case owner, and the other case owner changed for me after a month. And the new case owner when she saw my file she called me for another interview, and again I attended another interview, and that is like 125 questions.*

More concerning, during her appeal for leave to remain, Hawwi's male representative was not fully aware of her history when presenting her case in court, which we can see here:

The man from the Home Office he said, "to be honest I didn't know the whole story of this file and I didn't get decision, but the Home Office send me to represent and I don't know most of what she is claiming about, I don't know, I didn't see it". So the judge want to give him again to check the file and the judge will compare that radio show.

Considering that the decision to be made at this point of the legal process will determine the future life process of an individual, as well as her family, this response seriously undermined the then UKBA's claim to assess all applications individually and on their own merits. The fact that her representative was male is also questionable under the current Gender Guidelines (Home Office, 2010b). The issue of subject knowledge was further questioned by Hawwi, who challenged the appeal judgment regarding their COI. She argued:

They say even the very remotest area in [names country], in the dry regions, they get medication there. But they don't know about [names country], and about my tribe's conflict, and the government don't do any development in that area. It is very hard to convince the truth, and if especially a person like me.

Generally letters of support, evidence and documentation are expected to strengthen an asylum applicant's claim and yet Hawwi's application was still initially rejected, further undermining the legitimacy of the official asylum process in terms of 'merit'. Beyond this, Asylum Aid (2011) found that cases were viewed unfavourably if applicants *did not* have written materials, which exposes the unpredictability of the outcomes of a case either way. Hawwi recalled:

I have support letters and I have my IDs and everything I have I submitted for the Home Office, I positively waited for the result issue which was I will get Refugee Status. But when the result comes, really, I was disappointed really.

Furthermore, the reasons given for her refusal were not unique, indicating that Hawwi's claim may not have been assessed on individual merits as according the UKBA's guidelines. Smith (2004a) suggests that refusal letters appear to be recycled in some instances, sometimes even across Countries of Origin. Hawwi's rejection reasons reflect those found by Asylum Aid (2011) and Smith (ibid.) and included questioning her government's interest in her politically, as she was able to leave by plane, and that she had been safe for a period of time before leaving her country (see also Smith, ibid.). She recalled the UK state's response and her feeling towards it as:

We didn't believe that the government revoked your job licence. If the government didn't revoke my job licence, if I didn't suffer, why is my intention by leaving my small child and just sitting and waiting for asylum. What am I doing in this country? What pleasure does my mind give me?

This feeling of being disbelieved was later a point Hawwi expressively reflected upon, stating:

> *The reality really, to tell someone your reality, to tell someone the truth, it is very hard if you don't have any acceptance, if there is nobody else that believes you, that accepts you, there is nothing that you can do. Like speaking on an air, no one will reply to you like that. Your suffering, your pain, no-one will understand you.*

This statement questions acceptance and belief, reflecting feminist arguments around the disclosure of women's experiences of domestic or sexual violence in the criminal justice systems in the UK, and the effects of being cross-examined and disbelieved by patriarchal forces (Lees, 1996; Temkin, 1997).

As I have also heard from other women and men, Hawwi struggled with the criminalisation aspect of seeking asylum, reflecting that, '*The suffrage that I came through, no one will understand that. I am not a thief; I am not like a criminal.*'

Asylum, mental health and human rights

Hawwi's feeling toward accessing rights in the UK asylum system waver from good, in terms of provision, to poor in terms of autonomy and social rights. Her experience of the Right to Health, Article 25 in the Human Rights Declaration (1948) was substantially better in the UK. As discussed earlier, Hawwi received inadequate anti-retrovirals in her country of origin, which had a lasting effect on her health overall, and still suffered symptoms from the venereal disease she contracted from being raped. In the UK she was able to access food and accommodation, as well necessary operations:

> *I can't live until now if I am not getting that good treatment in this country. The way they managed me, the good accommodation and the amount of money that they will give to me as a single person is enough for me. It is very interesting, because of that, because I have a good accommodation and I will get good health treatment, shower, good type of food. That's why I recover with that illness, I was very weak and my immune system was very low, because of the treatment really I recovered.*

However, as argued so far, the British system can still cause inadvertent implications for the mental health of asylum seekers. As Burnett and Whyte (2010) found, and as also discussed earlier, denying the right to work can leave individuals feeling under-valued or useless, and can effect self-worth, wellbeing and personal purpose. A general loss of autonomy also appears evident, where Hawwi had been kept dependent against her will on the UK state with little opportunity to make her own decisions, '*At this moment we are not entitled to buy anything of our own, all the things we are using is from the hostel. We will take £5 in a day and [Asylum and Refugee Service] will fill a form for us.*'

Further problems can be experienced in terms of feelings of loss and changes, evident in Hawwi's reflection of her migration overall:

> *leaving your country and claiming asylum is denying you mother you know, no-one needs to leave his country. For myself, my country is like my mother because I born there, I grow up there. I need to help my society, I need to do something good for that society. But it comes to the time that I can't tolerate anymore, because it is only if my life is with me that I can do something for that country, or it is only if I saved my life that I will proceed something more.*

These are problematic issues generally, but may be more harmful for people already living with wider mental and physical health issues, as Hawwi had been. If women demonstrate degrees of Post-Traumatic Stress Disorder (PTSD), which may be experienced by survivors of sexual violence, wider problems of disassociation can result in severe breakdowns in mental health, as has been documented by Freedom from Torture (2009). On her experience of asylum generally, Hawwi indicated adverse effects on her mental health on numerous occasions:

> *'I am floating, my mind is floating and restless, after I received that decision, and I don't have sleep'; 'Every time I try to think about the situation and all the passes that I came through, it is really very, very devastating and very big headache – I prefer not to remind it at all. Whenever I try to remind it I will be very sick. It is very bad, by any means. If it rains gold, really in [names country], if God even created some miracles for that country, I promised myself not to see any good things in that country'; 'Now what remains? And I don't know what will happen really, it is very, very hard. [pause] Asylum is not really, it's not, not, not at all an acceptable thing for anyone for anyone, it will not give for anyone pleasure'; 'There is no way we are coping with life, and it is very, very hard really. It's very hard'.*

In all, Hawwi's experiences within the British asylum system were personal but not wholly unique. Aspects reflect wider findings from research undertaken in the fields of asylum support, health and human rights (Asylum Aid, 2011; Freedom from Torture, 2009; Refugee Council, 2009; Smith, 2004a, 2004b). As we have seen, women can be subjected to forms of double victimisation (Temkin, 1997) through ongoing emotional harms perpetuated through disbelief, inaccurate decision-making under the Geneva Convention, and inadequate protection from further state crimes if women are wrongly returned to their country of origin. Hawwi's experiences within this system also ignite further questions regarding the viability and time-cost of the UK asylum system as it stands. As Hawwi recalled, *'I interviewed and I waited for a long time, for more than a year for response. And my response become negative. This is very, very, something which very disappointed me.'*

Chapter conclusion

Sometime after we first met, the decision to reject Hawwi's claim was overturned and she was granted leave to remain. Similar to the points raised in the previous two chapters, the process had been arduous, exhausting and arguably unnecessarily time-consuming: the decisions made had not been adequately reviewed. What is also clear throughout Hawwi's experience of seeking asylum is that some processes heightened anxieties and affected her emotional and at times physical health, but were arguably wholly avoidable.

It is worth highlighting that these last issues increasingly resonate with the landscape of asylum in Britain today, since reductions in legal aid for immigration cases – specifically appeals – seriously affects the quality of representation in asylum cases and since 'deport now, appeal later' has been firmly established in recent Immigration Acts (2014; 2016). There is so much else that we can see, however: the long-term impacts of sexual violence on one woman's life, and the serious outcomes that violent men can have on women they abuse; forms of oppression and persecution regularly inflicted by states in conflict or unrest; and the value and limitations of support responses if and when people seek asylum. What we can also see is the extent to which Hawwi has embedded resistance and survival in her life, and in her own response to violent subjections. It becomes even more important that immigration and asylum statistics are seen for what they are: lives, and not just numbers. This last point is perhaps particularly poignant considering the contemporary experiences of so many others who have not reached Britain or indeed Europe when fleeing North Africa, and whose lives instead have been lost in the Mediterranean.

Having now seen the value of sanctuary and the challenges of gaining it, we will move to consider ways in which survival and wellbeing are hampered by the process of seeking asylum, and consider whose responsibility it is to appropriately and sustainably support women, men and children seeking refuge in Britain.

6 Compounding trauma

Women asylum seekers are entitled to have their rights under the Convention respected; they are entitled to be treated in a non-discriminatory manner and with respect and dignity at all times during the asylum procedure and thereafter, including through the process of finding durable solutions once asylum status has been recognized by the receiving State.

(CEDAW recommendation no. 32, point 24)

They [immigration officers] speak to you, not like you should not be in the country, but that you should not be on the planet.

(Fozia, focus group participant, 2014)

Introduction

As we have seen so far, there are contentions between what the British state has responsibility for and has agreed to in international law, and what is actually carried out at ground level. Perhaps the contradictions set between CEDAW and Fozia in the two statements above shed light on how legislators see recommendations, and how women feel the lack of their implementation. The impacts of this disjuncture have been considered in some depth, across groups of women as well as in the context of Hawwi's individual lived experience. However, as with defining violence, defining the *impacts* of violence (structural, physical or emotional) is arguably contentious. Since experience is intersectional and transcends trajectories and personal identities, so too are the impacts for an individual. There are commonalities that can be disproportionately experienced by survivors of certain violences, such as sexual violence or torture; nightmares, flashbacks, anxiety attacks, depression or intense sadness (DIGNITY, 2012; Kastrup and Arcel, 2004) but there is 'no such thing as a uniform response to highly stressful events' (Summerfield, 2000: cited in Ward *et al.*, 2008: 16).

Throughout the duration of this research, there have been three ways in which women engage in or identify support in the aftermath of violence and while awaiting a decision on refugee status. The first of these is the more formal therapy-based scenario that incorporates one-to-one interaction or group-based sessions with a counsellor, psychologist or other therapist. The second is the use of formal and informal spaces, networks and organisations within which women are enabled to build friendships or gain social support in ways that facilitate knowledge sharing or legal assistance. It can be this form of network that effectively helps resist the kinds of social death that can otherwise be imposed through the debilitating aspects of the asylum process discussed in Chapters 2 and 3. The third is more akin to political resistance: the involvement with groups or organsiations that outwardly challenge the problematic policies and procedures that inflict harm or reduce refugees' capacity to live autonomously. It is the first and second of these that I will predominately focus on for the remainder of this chapter, and will move further toward the second and third points in the overall conclusion.

This chapter will then focus on findings regarding the process of seeking asylum and specifically barriers which can prevent women being enabled to participate in either violence or trauma-related support, as well as social networks. Reflecting on interview findings and broader literature, I will draw out aspects of harm mitigation and non-mitigation: what ameliorates the effects of previous traumatic experiences, what barriers might there be to engaging in such services or networks which do this, and what has the capacity to worsen the mental and emotional health of women seeking asylum.

Part one: support in the aftermath of violence

As I have argued so far, there are aspects of the British asylum system which are inherently harmful. Some of these, such as destitution, detention and deportation, are politically charged and relate to successive governmental agendas that aim to control or reduce immigration while profiting from some aspects of this control. As pointed out in Chapter 4, these harms can be alleviated but would require a combination of reform, dismantlement and overhaul. That said, the nature of historic subjections to violence and persecution can also mean that individual survivors may benefit from access to mental and physical health support services as a means to alleviate suffering which can otherwise be a 'pervasive presence' (Jefferson, 2014: 236).

While the barriers to these will be explored later on it is worth outlining some of the key ways that supporting survivors of violence – and specifically women survivors of sexual violence – can be insured. The first of these relate to the availability of multiple forms of support. In discussing women survivors of violence, Ussher argued that:

> We need to acknowledge the complexity of women's responses to sexual abuse and violence - the ways in which the consequences of abuse can be highly individualised, located in a woman's socio-historical context, her negotiation of distress, and *the availability of options open to her to cope.*
>
> (2011: 128, own emphasis added)

The long-standing debate regarding Western-centric models of trauma counselling and psychological intervention among refugees arguably instigated shifts in dominant perceptions of counselling. Rather than ascribing one form of support, as Ussher addresses here, many organisations advocate multiple forms of interaction. As Hawwi indicated, these can encompass social support, physical pain alleviation, and counselling or psychotherapy as a means of facilitating a process whereby women can manage or address physical pain or emotional distress.

Building trust

With regard to sexual violence, Peel argued that for a process of support to develop, trust is fundamental: 'In any psychological intervention with refugee clients who have been raped, trust and safety must first be established before therapeutic work can proceed' (2004: 33). As I will discuss later in terms of uncertainty, there are key challenges in providing a sense of safety since the process of seeking asylum is so precarious. However, the significance of trust is central: for people who have been subjected to sexual violence or torture, the need for a safe environment with a trusted counsellor is probably the primary factor in working through trauma-related problems. This can be affected by the use of shared space as the manager of an asylum support organisation indicated: '*Confidentiality is not high in this place because we couldn't get through the volume of people if we said it was one person to one room.*'

There are two key resources which building trust requires: funding and time. For trust to be centralised in a counselling or support relationship, space and a place of safety is required, and the use of an interpreter may be needed. As Rape Crisis has long argued, developing a relationship within which a survivor of sexual violence can begin to discuss their experiences can take a lot of time – some women may not refer to their subjections to abuse until after multiple meetings (Jones and Cook, 2008; London Rape Crisis Centre, 1984). This can be affected by restrictive budgets or counselling allowances, such as the standard 6–12 sessions of counselling that is statutory through the NHS (NHS, 2016). Organisations such as Rape Crisis therefore generally try to avoid statutory limits, allowing survivors to determine their own length of involvement in counselling or group support sessions. As we will see below, this can be significantly affected by cuts to funding for support services across the women's sector, as well as dispersal for women seeking asylum.

The value of effective counselling

Counselling or therapy is not necessarily appropriate for everyone, and it is important that engaging in such a process is self-elective rather than ascribed. However, if and when survivors of sexual violence or torture have the opportunity to engage in counselling or trauma support, it is not only the mental health impacts of violence which are opened to alleviation, but the internalisation of social and external attitudes. To echo the sentiments of a rape support outreach worker:

> *You notice the change, you do. A couple of weeks ... when someone accesses counselling and you see them after a month, it does have a change [sic]. It really, really does. Cause it's a way for them to express themselves.*

> *Release that emotion, the anger the fear, the frustration, whatever they had. And then they do also become more open about networking or being referred to other organisations and then maybe starting to become active.*

For some women and men engaging with sexual violence support, they may be speaking to the first person they ever tell of their experience. A central contributor to trust is thus belief in the story that a person tells. The stigmatisation inherent to sexual violence or torture can leave survivors internalising a sense of shame, self-loathing or self-blame (Jones and Cook, 2008; Jordan, 2012; Kelly, 1988). The opportunity to be believed and listened to seems simple, but it really is crucial. The prospect of disbelief has long been challenged by feminist campaigners across the globe and yet, as we will see, is still a serious issue in Home Office responses to asylum claims.

Even if the first form of support that a woman engages with is not the most appropriate for her, it does open doors to other forms of social and emotional assistance. As a Detective Inspector working in a dedicated sexual violence unit stated, '*once someone is engaged with services, it does tend to follow that they would get support*'. The kinds of 'wrap-around' services increasingly provided at asylum accommodation centres are one way to promote this, but there can be an understandable scepticism for people engaging in these. The concept of trying to 'treat' all forms of problems among a group with such diverse experiential histories and languages takes time, which is one key aspect of initial accommodation that people seldom have, since they are usually dispersed or detained within the period of around one month. Certain elements are also financially costly, including long-term treatment for physical ailments, and for interpreters which are often either expensive, or inadequate (Crack, 2013).

Four key organisations I worked with had gone some way in developing outreach services to women who were seeking asylum. As I have argued elsewhere (Canning, 2011b; 2014a; 2014b), and as might be expected at a time of substantial funding cuts, some of these had geographic or identity-based limits. For example, one organisation worked predominantly with pregnant women and/ or women with children; one with survivors of sexual violence; one with a mostly male uptake. Whether or not women were able to attend might depend on whether they could afford the bus ticket to get there, as some are dispersed across Merseyside. The most positive aspect of organisational development was that there *were* services – mixed in capacity though they might be – which responded directly to intersectional identities. That is not to say that there are not challenges, particularly for people identifying as LGBTQ and who can face secondary layers of oppression and exclusion, as discussed in Chapter 2. However, a number of organisations had nonetheless fought hard for specifically inclusionary space for LGBTQ people, as well as for women survivors of domestic or conflict-related violence.

As an example, a number of women involved in activist circles and research have highlighted the positive impact that HIV support groups have had in their lives since moving to Merseyside. The region has a dedicated HIV support service that holds women-only and men-only support sessions, asylum support groups and LGBTQ asylum advocacy groups. The significance of individual identities is placed centrally in the scope of their support delivery. Recalling her time in counselling, Hawwi told me:

> *many peoples are living in the same situation with me and I saw them, I am happy there ... all the week I am passing my time by treatment and support-ing my mind ... there is some minor depression, not like before. I don't need to kill myself, I need to take care of my life.*

Broadly, 'there is a general consensus that "good practices" constitute an action or series of actions that, resulting from the identification of needs, are system-atic, effective, efficient, sustainable, and flexible' (Asociación EXIL, Comissió Catalana d'Ajuda al Refugiat, 2016: 14–15). Each of these aspects are challenged by the process of seeking asylum, but at least self-elective interaction with groups or organisations can facilitate further support in the future.

Gaps in mental and emotional support

Considering the value that social support networks and/or counselling can have for some women and men who engage in them, organisations that facilitate them face significant barriers to providing them. Perhaps the most fundamental to these is funding. As Finnegan notes:

> Government income to the voluntary sector fell by £1.9bn in real terms bet-ween 2009/10 and 2012/13 and was not compensated for by a proportionate increase in funding from other sources such as public donations. Reduc-tions in public spending had also led to the withdrawal of provision of some non-statutory services by local authorities, creating gaps in provision that charities were sometimes expected or felt obliged to fill.
>
> (Finnegan, 2016: 6)

Welfare spending cuts in Britain and the UK more broadly have affected a whole spectrum of the public sector, including housing, healthcare, financial welfare provision and fuel provision. For poorer people in society, post 2008/09 austerity measures have literally been lethal. 2380 people who had been deemed 'fit to work' under new welfare measures died between December 2011–February 2014 alone (Butler, 2015), while suicide among men grew by an extra 1000 per year after the economic crash (McVeigh, 2015).

Like the problems raised regarding the British asylum system, many of the decisions taken to incur cuts to the public sector have been conscious, deliberate and politically driven (Cooper, 2015). Where funds might have been managed in ways that drew tax from banks who had been responsible for the crash (Tombs, 2016) or indeed richer groups in society, Britain approached its financial deficit by reducing welfare for the poorest sectors in society (Dorling, 2014). As such, the financial landscape has been one of crisis across much of the public sector and specifically smaller or vocational organisations and projects.

I have already outlined the general effects of legal aid cuts, poverty and, more explicitly, destitution in Chapters 3 and 4. For women or men attempting to engage in trauma-related support services, further restrictions on funding budgets have clear implications for the quality of support available or the time that a practitioner can afford to spend with individuals. This affects aspects such as language and communication, since many organisations cannot afford (or lack the consciousness to request funding for) interpreters, an issue that effectively stems the capacity for some people to engage in any support services at all. For most people seeking asylum, private mental or even physical healthcare is not an option, and so organisational limitations are wholly limiting.

For those working within organisations themselves, similar issues lead to serious problems. Frustrations can be felt in terms of resources, and the limitations put on staff and volunteers:

> *Because of our financial difficulties at the moment we cannot set up any project so we need partners so we can involve more fully in women's activities in the near future.*
>
> (Medical Doctor and African community group leader)

> *When you're under resourced to just try and squeeze in more, get more volunteers to fill resources, then you're not able to supervise and train them properly to see more people. I don't want to dip the quality of what we do, which I believe in, so we struggle with resources.*
>
> (Psychologist specialising in torture-related trauma)

> *Almost everything that's done feels under resourced. And you just struggle ... Sometimes we have to turn destitute people away because we've got no food, no accommodation, no money, and I cringe when we have to do that.*
>
> (Asylum support organisation manager)

In my experience of engaging with over 10 organisations in the past decade, conditions that many groups meet in can be less than adequate for their purpose. Unheated church halls providing fruit, tea and where possible foodbanks; small Sunday school rooms with boxes of clothes donated by the public; damp inner city community centres that are held together by the will of local activists or empathic community leaders. I have even seen asylum case support offices with windows barred by the legs of sawn down chairs as a crime prevention measure against further burglaries. It seems incomprehensible that these are the conditions that those seeking asylum are met with in contemporary Britain, and that those supporting people must work within. To my mind, the spaces many groups can afford or are donated are beyond the consciousness of those making structural decisions on behalf of funding deficits or immigration policy. In early 2016, for example, the then Home Secretary Theresa

May admitted that, 'I have visited a range of Home Office facilities. But I have not visited asylum accommodation, no.'

The importance of gendered responses

Organisations that support survivors of sexual or domestic violence have long advocated women-only spaces for counselling or group therapy (Jones and Cook, 2008; London Rape Crisis Centre, 1984; Women's Resource Centre, 2010). This issue has re-emerged with force recently. Even from the beginning of this period of research, since 2008, the landscape within which women-only space is made possible has been shrunk significantly in some sectors. To an extent, this relates to the way in which sexual and domestic violence funding is distributed, and the way in which gendered power relations are being eroded from this.

To use a local example, in 2015, statutory funds for sexual violence support from the Police and Crime Commissioner and Merseyside Police specifically released an invitation for regional organisations to tender for funds for the 'Provision of Sexual Offences Services for a 12 Month Period'. Although the issue of minimalised financial investment has been addressed earlier, a key specification required services to provide: *An ageless support service for all victims of sexual offences (including Female Genital Mutilation), offering counselling, advocacy and bespoke care packages* (page 16 of call specification). Apart from the breadth of what is expected from a short-term contract, and that the call effectively erases the term 'violence' in favour of 'offences',[1] this language deliberately silences the gendered disparity of who most commonly experiences sexual or domestic violence.

Gender-specific space is increasingly represented as an unnecessary anomaly in a world of 'equality'. Police and the Home Office put increasingly significant resources into advertising gender-neutral campaigns, implying that men are as likely to be subjected to sexual or domestic violence as women. *Disproportionality* is the key here (Dobash and Dobash, 2004; Lewis *et al.*, 2015). Some men *are* subjected to sexual violence.[2] As discussed in Chapter 2, this is a particular area of concern with regard to torture in detention, where sexually torturous abuses are commonly perpetrated in some areas. The long-term impacts of this can be profound for men. From a feminist perspective, challenging sexual or domestic violence is central to countering hegemony and patriarchy, and thus such violence against men should also be challenged, mitigated and eradicated. What this objective should not do, however, is distract from the experiences of women or reduce space in which some women, including trans women, feel safe to speak about violence in their lives.

This brings me directly to the use of space within and among asylum organisations. As I argued in 2011 and again in 2014, spatial negotiation is complex for women seeking asylum. Different women do of course use space in different ways: some are happy to attend asylum support organisations that are male-dominated where activities or casework support are concerned. Some altogether avoid these scenarios. As I argued then, practitioner respondents who worked with women-centred organisations were forthcoming in identifying the need for women and people identifying as transgender to be able to access sexual or domestic violence support services. Even when women did access general support (such as language classes, foodbanks, or access to computers) it was often male-dominated. Respondents pointed out that '*we don't have many women come in. We used to but now it's become more male dominated, and women[3] feel vulnerable here*', while another stated, '*We've had people who won't come back to the English classes because young men have said things to them.*'

In response to such concerns, a number of organisations developed specifically as women-only groups or group meetings, and some developed women-only organisations altogether. Although funding remains a struggle (most Black, Asian, Minority Ethnic and Refugee organisations receive no statutory funding in Merseyside, see James and Patiniotis, 2013), there have been some attempts made to develop a less formal sector that women engage in. This has been a positive move, but it does not detract from the responsibility of the state (be that central or local government) to ensure *provision of funding* for adequate support for all survivors of domestic and sexual violence generally, and women specifically. I emphasise the terms provision of funding here because I say this with caution: there are limits to coalitions between non-governmental organisations and the state. Apart from the propensity for co-option (Mathiesen, 2004) into state agendas, mantras and (in my experience) even the depoliticisation of language,[4] associations between non-statutory groups and the state can mean that 'their strategies tend to be state friendly: hire more police, give longer sentences to rapists, pass mandatory arrest laws etc.' (Smith, 2005: 139). Apart from the capacity to deflect from longer-term feminist agendas, that is, *to prevent, reduce and eradicate sexual violence*, there are contemporary and historic fractures between the state and Black and Minority Ethnic communities generally in terms of over policing – particularly for young men (Patel and Tyrer, 2011; Williams, 2015) as well as disproportionate levels of imprisonment. For immigrant, refugee and asylum populations, the expansion of immigration controls into the wider social sector adds further problems.

As Andrea Smith argued in the context of sexual violence against Native American women:

> Many state coalitions on domestic/sexual violence have refused to take stands against the anti-immigration backlash and its violent impact on immigrant women, arguing that it is not a sexual/domestic violence issue. Yet as the immigration backlash intensifies, many immigrant women do not report abuse for fear of deportation. Mainstream anti-violence advocates have increasingly demanded longer prison sentences for batterers and sex offenders as a frontline approach to stopping violence against women. However, the criminal justice system has always been brutally oppressive toward communities of colour.
>
> (Smith, 2005: 155)

The last point to make with regards to my cautious approach to state/NGO coalitions relates directly to the role of criminal justice agencies. Survivors of long-term domestic abuse or childhood sexual violence are often encouraged to make a case for prosecution. The nature of asylum or migration means that previous subjections may have been perpetrated in other countries and regions. Prosecution is not an option, so the increasing focus on criminal justice in responses to rape and sexual violence has potential to become increasingly restrictive, thus less geared towards the needs of women who want support rather than justice.

In the context of refugee women and women seeking asylum, the extensive documentation which indicates highly prevalent experiences of sexual and gen-dered violence should emphasise the urgency with which women seeking asy-lum should be provided sustained and quality support. Despite the developments in policy highlighted above, ground-level application of gendered approaches is variable across European states (Ali *et al.*, 2012). According to the Gender Guidelines, applicants should be asked whether they would prefer a male or fe-male interviewer, and this should 'normally' be provided accordingly (Home Office, 2010b, see also Home Office 2015b). According to the UKBA Director mentioned in Chapter 2, '*When they [women] claim asylum at the screening interview and at the substantive interview they will be asked whether they would like to be interviewed by a woman or a man, and we will endeavour to provide accordingly.*' From my experience of speaking with women, this is not always made so clear. In contrast, there seems to be a culture of waiting for women to ask, and then providing where possible. This might seem reasonable, but women seldom know or understand the legal process of seeking asylum until they have been part of the system for some time, so knowing ones' rights is not universal. This was perhaps best encapsulated by the manager of a refugee agency: '*If a woman requested a female caseworker, we would always endeavour to meet that request ... it's very rare that that happens, but occasionally it does.*' Considering the complexity of the system and the other issues I have raised so far, it is little surprise that women may not know they have a right to ask for this or do not feel confident enough to ask.

Alongside this, the lack of time for in-depth consideration of asylum appli-cations, and limited access to women interpreters and/or women-centred space impacts on women's capacity to disclose forms of violence that may be relevant to their asylum claim, such as sexual violence, torture, marital violence or long-term abuse (Canning, 2011a, 2014a, 2014b, 2016a). This is particularly the case for sexual violence and torture, which is often socially silenced and overlooked or not disclosed in asylum applications. Women's asylum applications may not be recognised in relation to the Refugee Convention (1951), while subjections to certain forms of violence may not be disclosed by women due to social and self-silencing. As we will see, this can impact on women's access to sexual vio-lence support, or indeed even impact on access to refugee status (Asylum Aid, 2011; Canning, 2011a, 2014a; 2016; Smith, 2004).

Part two: making things worse?

I think it plays a big part of depression. It's the uncertainty. The unknowing, just being moved from place to place
(Women's asylum advocacy co-ordinator, Merseyside)

The consequences of uncertainty

As discussed so far in this chapter, and as the Refugee Women's Strategy Group (2014) point out, mental health support is a central concern in responding to migrant populations generally, and people seeking asylum specifically. The likelihood of having been subjected to violence or persecution is disproportionately high in comparison to non-refugee groups (Freedom from Torture, 2009), and this can be even greater for women seeking asylum. However, and as has been demonstrated so far, the process of seeking asylum is in and of itself stressful, from complex application regimes to the lack of entitlement that people have in owning any form of autonomy for the present or the future. In a study of 87 women's experiences of asylum, the Refugee Women's Strategy Group for the Scottish Refugee Council found that:

> Overwhelmingly, the asylum process itself and the subsequent impact on mental health was raised by nearly all the women who took part in Speak for Yourself. Women described memory loss, depression, lack of concentration and stress all caused by the asylum process itself. Women felt that a lack of control and lack of choice contributed to their poor mental health.
>
> (Refugee Women's Strategy Group, 2014: 3)

This is an important point that reiterates the fundamental findings drawn out in this book, as well as the real significance of temporal confinement that is inherent in the suspended nature of asylum universally. As Kastrup and Arcel argue, 'Persons who are seeking asylum live under particular stress due to, amongst other things, the uncertainty of their destiny, the fear of repatriation, and frequently the lack of access to adequate care while awaiting asylum' (Kastrup and Arcel: 548; see Keefe, 2014).

An innate feeling of personal insecurity is a recurring consequence of life in asylum, as it can also be in border camps and Internally Displaced Persons' camps (Turner, 2010), Immigration Processing Centres globally (Pickering and Ham, 2015), and Immigration Removal Centres in the UK (Turnbull, 2016). This insecurity does not only impact on people's feeling of safety, but also the kinds of care or support they can engage in. According to an interview participant who worked as a trauma and torture counsellor in the North West of England, *'there's so much about the asylum process that makes women feel under threat, and that's all consuming. And often that's a distraction from some of the deeper difficulties that affect them'*. This is remarkably similar to a claim made by a psychologist I later interviewed in Denmark, who worked with refugee women,

men and children survivors of torture. I had asked what barriers there might be for people accessing psychological or emotional support who are seeking asylum. She responded that:

> *The main thing is that they are not secure, they don't have a secure place. So much of their daily worry is attached to whether they can stay or not, so there is very little room for working on trauma or working on other problems because this is the main problem.*

This is telling of three aspects: that the length of time people spend in asylum systems can affect people's mental wellbeing in the short term; that this is further affected by a lack of access to support services; and that even taking a step to engage in processes of healing or support are potentially diminished by the plethora of other social problems which are tied in with exclusionary elements of waiting for refugee status. This can be frustrating for people who aim to support women seeking asylum and who otherwise feel limited by the many social problems that women and men face. In the context of sexual violence support, one exasperated asylum outreach counsellor told me:

> *Nothing happens. You often see the woman looking at you as if to say, 'why are you here? What you doing? What's going on?' Cause nine times out of ten they've got tooth ache, they've got stomach ache, they've got gynae problems, they've got sandals and beautiful, beautiful African clothes in the depths of Winter. You know, they don't know where they're being moved to, they don't know where their house is. And that's the issue that I'm being bombarded with.*

The feelings implied above are not limited to the British asylum system. In 2013, an interview participant in Denmark – a physiotherapist specialising in torture responses – echoed similar sentiments in arguing:

> *How can we do therapy concentrated on that [torture] if the whole thing is, "where am I going to sleep tonight?" If you don't know where you can sleep at night, even if you have horrible flashbacks, invading memories, you have very much pain, still survival is on your agenda and other things have to come later.*

As psychological and counselling literatures have elsewhere pointed out, these issues are acutely important in developing appropriate support services or networks and incur significant debate on whether it is appropriate to begin psychotherapy or trauma or rape counselling, since it may be harmful to draw out memory as part of a process of recovery, only to have someone dispersed, detained or even deported and no longer able to engage in support. Memories of violence and harm have potential to come to the fore and instigate re-traumatisation (DIGNITY, 2012). However, the temporal complexity of asylum means that people can be left in limbo for years at a time and this drew further concern from the psychologist working in the North West of England, who argued that *'[some psychologists argue]* you can't do trauma work until somebody is safe. Well, I'm sorry, but women can be in the process for five or six years, you can't put off support'.

There are many populations that currently face poverty and exclusion: as recent research shows, there are currently over one million people living in destitution in the UK (Fitzpatrick *et al.*, 2016). The mental, and indeed physical, health impacts of poverty are profound and echo Kastrup and Arcel's arguments regarding asylum seeking in terms of care. However, the key difference[5] in asylum is the unknowing of where the long-term future will be held on a global and regional scale and, for those who are under threat of state violence in their country of origin, if this might have fatal or life altering consequences. The temporal element that this alludes to is central, not peripheral, to people's emotional wellbeing.

Measures of truth and 'the burden of proof'

Drawing back to the role of the state, the Home Office claim that, 'Properly considering claims and making well-reasoned decisions is one of the UK's fundamental responsibilities under the Refugee Convention' (2015b: 4). As outlined in Chapter 1, this consideration begins with the screening interview and then substantive interview, which are undertaken by asylum caseworkers and reviewed in accordance with relevant conventions, statements made to immigration officers, and other supporting evidence (such as medical reports or other files). The Home Office goes on to argue that:

> The level of proof needed to establish the material facts is a relatively low one – a reasonable degree of likelihood – and must be borne in mind throughout the process. It is low because of what is potentially at stake – the individual's life or liberty - and because asylum seekers are unlikely to be able to compile and carry dossiers of evidence out of the country of persecution.
>
> (2015: 11)

This claim is perhaps undermined by the number of applications that are initially refused (59 per cent in 2104) and go on to appeal (76 per cent), evidencing fairly high levels of initial refusal. One-quarter of those who appeal have their appeal upheld (Blinder, 2015). Furthermore, although a 'burden of proof' approach might seem appropriate on the surface, research undertaken by Montgomery and Foldsprang (2005) and later at the Centre for the Study of Emotion and Law (Bögner *et al.*, 2007) have demonstrated that 'credibility' as it is often used in the context of asylum claims is incredibly problematic, as we will go on to see.

The discussion around a xeno-racist culture drawn out in Chapters 3 and 4 are not at a complete disconnect from the internal landscape of the Home Office application process, where border control has arguably long overtaken the state's centralised obligations to provide refugee status to persecuted people, or people who fear persecution (Webber, 2012). The figurative and literal militarisation of the border arguably promotes a culture of disbelief and exclusion, exacerbated by the threat of 'global terror' that has become so heavily embraced by successive Home Secretaries and Immigration Ministers. As one GP questioned:

> *I wonder sometimes if they see immigration as people just trying to get into the country and having to battle them back, and you're not supposed to let them in, like this Border Force type stuff. Rather than seeing the underlying issues. They see it as guilty until proven innocent, this type of attitude.*

The problems that arise from inconsistent asylum review and the application of credibility is manifest in Hawwi's account of asylum in the previous chapter. However, it also arguably reflects three broader issues: the problem of memory in recalling traumatic accounts; the gap between recounting a history, and openly disclosing instances of violence to a stranger, particularly in the case of sexual violence; and disbelief in the stories that are told.

Memory and concentration impairment

First, as Green and Ward point out, 'memory and concentration impairment' can be symptoms of post-torture suffering (2004: 139). Lapses in memory, and inconsistent story-telling can greatly affect the claims of people seeking asylum, and can lead to refusal (Kelly, 2012). This is the case even despite wider evidence that memory can be greatly affected in its linearity for survivors of torture and sexual abuse and that dissociation or repression can be both symptoms of trauma and survival tactics for survivors of violence (Herman, 1992; Bögner *et al.* 2010; DIGNITY, 2012; Masmas *et al.*, 2008; Montgomery and Foldsprang, 2005). Over two decades ago, Judith Herman argued that, 'People who have survived atrocities often tell their stories in a highly emotional, contradictory, and fragmented manner which undermines their credibility and thereby serves the twin imperatives of truth-telling and secrecy' (Herman, 1992: 1). As I have argued elsewhere (Canning, 2016a) this can affect consistency in the stories that women, men or children might tell about their histories or their journeys during migration.

However, aspects that might seem trivial at the time can become more significant as initial and substantive interviews are compared, and completeness in memory is expected. As the UKBA Director I interviewed indicates here:

> *considering the merits, it's a question of the completeness of the information, the genuineness of the information, is it consistent with itself ... If they flew into UK, what countries did the change planes on, what was the colour of the interior of the planes ... any and all information. So we expect somebody to give us some information on the routing.*

In a later interview in Denmark, this reference to detail – specifically colours – seemed almost ironic when I interviewed a psychologist working in immigration detention:

> *the problem with the Danish asylum system is that you have to tell one version of your story. You have to tell it so the details are the same, and you have to tell it 4 or 5 times b... When you work with people in the asylum system, you know their memory is fucked up. [For example] they can't remember if it was a blue car or a red car.*

As with any individuals' response to stress, and to reiterate the point made by Summerfield (2000), there are no ascribed impacts of trauma. Some people may remember detail, some may not, but a system that expects such clarity seems at odds with what evidence around memory seems to show. Although not all people seeking asylum have been subjected to torture or sexual abuse, for those who have this remains a serious issue and barrier to gaining refugee status. Despite the well-documented impacts of trauma on memory linearity, credibility in the context of 'burden of truth' remains the central aspect of the asylum application procedure.

Disclosing sexual or domestic violence

Second, and as feminists have long argued in relation to criminal justice cases regarding rape and sexual abuse (Smart, 1989; Temkin, 1997), there is a clear disjoint in the way in which the asylum system inherently functions and the concept of disclosing instances of sexual violence. As many counsellors I have interviewed or spoken with over the years have consistently indicated, and as discussed above in relation to trust, sexual violence is socially silenced. Most people who do relay experiences of sexual violence and abuse do so on their own terms: in their own time, and with someone they feel they can speak with. This is the opposite scenario of how Home Office interviews function, which is to collate as much relevant information as possible and consider it in line with the Refugee Convention and other relevant policies or legislation (Home Office, 2015b).

If and when women or men do not discuss sexual abuse or torture in the screening interview, they are expected to do so in the substantive interview, but the claim can still be seen as lacking credibility as the two accounts are inconsistent. As Singer (2016) has recently pointed out, this is in contravention of the UK's own recognition of responding to conflict-related sexual violence through the Global Sexual Violence Initiative. Using this example, Asylum Aid argued that:

> Disbelief of disclosures of sexual violence if these are made at a late stage in the asylum process – even though the Protocol recognises that memory and the timing of disclosure are impacted by the trauma of sexual violence and the stigma attached to it. This means that, especially in women's

cases, the decision not to grant asylum is too often wrong in the first instance and is later overturned by the courts.

(Asylum Aid, 2016, message to Lords Select Committee
on Sexual Violence in Conflict)

This is a sentiment felt by many women I have spoken with, particularly women who have been experiencing domestic violence at the time of their substantive interview. In one focus group which explored women's experiences of the process of seeking asylum, Nazreen told me that '*Women are not believed. They want to see your corpse. Until then they won't believe it.*' In the same group, Deb relayed her surprise at Home Office attempts to disperse her as a way to help Deb separate from her abusive husband when she had first arrived: '*They will send YOU, instead of your HUSBAND, to live somewhere else!*' This case was particularly interesting in itself, since the Home Office caseworker had initially asked Deb's husband to act as her interpreter during their substantive interview.

In a similar field, recognitions of the impacts of sexual violence on women are sometimes limited to physical implications, rather than psychological or emotional problems. According to one medical doctor who worked with asylum seekers in Merseyside, and had formerly worked with Medecin San Frontiers:

Unfortunately the Home Secretary does not take psychological effects as evidence of rape. They often only focus on the physical consequences of rape in terms of scars, tears ... any physical evidence to prove the rape took place ... I strongly see that people look at rape as the whole consequences other than just concentrating on the physical evidence of the medical report.

This claim reflects historical discrepancies between women's experiences of gendered violence, and the way in which impacts were outwardly understood, i.e. physically. The statement might be representative for some women's claims, but not in fundamental practice; the Home Office accept medico-legal evidence from two organisations, The Helen Bamber Trust and Freedom from Torture. However, as was discussed in Chapter 3 in relation to LGBTQ people seeking asylum, the threshold in some claims is exceptionally high. This statement perhaps encompasses the frustrations of wider organisations that have also pointed out the Home Office's (and previously UKBA's) inconsistent acceptance or rejection of claims based on psychological or emotional effects (Freedom from Torture, 2009; Kelly, 2012; Singer, 2016; Smith, 2004). As sexual violence does not always leave visible scars, there is no simplistic way to physically evidence its occurrence (with the exception of introducing draconian measures to 'prove' abuse). As a women's asylum support worker indicated, this can prove problematic in even more ways:

the evidence from the medical examination that was done to her was confirmed by the doctor that she had had this degrading and inhumane treatment. But then unfortunately you have other women who haven't got the physical scarring, but yet again mentally they are scarred.

In any case, there is generally around a five-month wait to receive medico-legal evidence from either of the stipulated organisations due to long and ever expanding waiting lists and as Tobias Kelly notes, these are not consistently handled (2012).

'It's the culture of disbelief'

Third, and aligning with concerns within refugee studies and border criminologies more generally, is the culture of disbelief that is arguably prominent within Home Office approaches to asylum claims. Since Ellie Smith meticulously documented the limitations in Home Office interviewing and 'credibility' in 2004, some steps have been taken to address the issues she raised and which have been highlighted in this section. The implementation of Gender Guidelines in 2007 and updated in 2010 (in policy if not wholly in practice) was one such step. As we can see, there are clear limitations in its implementation, but it was indeed a landmark development.

However, participants in interviews and focus groups have indicated that disbelief is still embedded in the attitudes of caseworkers and immigration officers. As Smith (2004) and later Asylum Aid (2011) argued, this can be structural and cultural. As the facilitator of a women's group indicated:

> It's the culture of disbelief [within the Home Office] and for a lot of women, having to claim asylum and go through the process of what happened to them, and to tell someone who's their case owner about what happened and then disbelieving. I mean, the Home Office disbelieve everything. They disbelieve documents, medical documents that come from victims of torture. They don't believe them. They won't.

The respondents' role in working with women seeking asylum might contribute to the exasperated tone of her claim here. She had also highlighted the impacts of funding cuts and the securitisation of borders as impacting on the capacity to effectively run a women's support group (which has since ceased to exist due to the lack of funding for space to meet twice a week). However, this claim is not isolated in its sentiments, as an HIV support worker indicated:

> It's the case owner or the caseworker who chooses to believe whether the story is convincing enough and whether it has consistency. And that's the part that always gets me, because I've had cases which are very similar, and one has had leave to remain, and the other one hasn't because there's been no consistency in the case.

Consistency is contentious: as with most civil or criminal cases in any court of law, the consistent interpretation or application of guidelines or conventions can be all but impossible. For women seeking asylum specifically, this has long affected the quality of decision-making in women's claims (Asylum Aid, 2011).

In summation of the points raised in this section I will draw back to concerns raised by the UKBA Director, who claimed that, '*it is not uncommon for a series of applicants from a certain country to give similar accounts, so we're always looking out for people who are trying to abuse the system*'. Although the whole interview reflected similar levels of suspicion (the interview itself was claused, so any quotes I used had to be approved before use in related publications) I find this claim to be particularly interesting. Correlations in accounts within any other social context are usually taken as a sign that there are common forms of violence being perpetrated against certain groups or within certain regions. For immigrants, it means the opposite: that people who have similar stories or experience similar kinds of violence are less likely to be being honest. This perhaps encapsulates the concerns raised by practitioners throughout this chapter, and by Hawwi: that asylum applicants can be viewed with disbelief from the offset.

Recognising the limits of individualisation

As we have seen throughout this chapter, for survivors of torture or sexual abuse support is often trauma-related, a point which itself has a long history of critique. As Herman argued, serious emotional, social and psychological impacts of violence can at times be presented as reductionist, strongly associated with discourses of neuroses (Herman, 1992) rather than placed within a framing of harm. If we look back to Hawwi's history, we can clearly see that certain decisions were made by others that are otherwise not uncommon in society or during unrest. Police chose to beat her, a man chose to rape her, her family disowned her, the UKBA chose to interview while she was ill. All of these were stressful events, each of which could have been avoided but linked with wider social, patriarchal or military cultures. The impacts have been profound for Hawwi, yet the process is inherently linked to social inequalities and oppression rather than based only on individual choices.

It is perhaps Herman's documentation of women's subjections to violence across domestic and political spheres which cemented the concept of trauma as strongly social rather than intrinsically psychological: the outcome of interpersonal forms of violence which are produced and enacted through physical manifestations of patriarchal abuses. Similar arguments have been aired towards diagnoses of Post-Traumatic Stress Disorder which can have a tendency to individualise otherwise socially inflicted harms.[6] The symptoms of PTSD – which can include anxiety, sleeplessness, nightmares or night-terrors, memory lapse, dissociation and flashbacks (see DIGNITY, 2012) – are of course individual responses. As Ussher has shown, however, 'This apparent normalisation of women's distress is at odds with the definition of PTSD as a psychiatric disorder, which acts to pathologise and stigmatise women subjected to sexual and physical violence, medicalising women's reasonable response' (Ussher, 2011: 127). This argument was reiterated by a respondent who specialised in trauma support for tortured refugees and asylum seekers: '*I struggle with anything that's named as a disorder ... I think it's a very normal and understandable response to a huge violation.*' Thus rather than identifying such manifestations as disorder, they are rational responses to unacceptable and irrational abuses and subjections.

The politics of victimhood

The objective of this chapter has been to focus on aspects of survival rather than only on dominant discourses of victimhood often ascribed to women, and which has been deconstructed in depth across feminist literatures (Walklate, 2014). It does not aim to deny victimisation, but recognises that the ascription of a status of inherent vulnerability is problematic. Imposing hierarchies of vulnerability on refugees – or survivors of violence or torture more broadly – can undermine aspects of strength in survival, transitioning ones' identity from subject to object (Jensen and Rønsbo, 2014; Ussher, 2011), a status that has historically affected women through gendered medicalisation of hysteria, depression and psychosis (Herman, 1992; Showalter, 1985; Ussher, 1989, 2011).

I have aimed to avoid this throughout, although to an extent the inclusion of practitioner voices makes that task difficult, since most work within the confines of 'regimes of knowledge' which are developed and produced within and beyond psychological and psychiatric disciplines (Rose, 1996 in Ussher, 2011: 7). Jensen and Rønsbo argue that, 'we need to distinguish between victims and victimhood. Whereas the presence of victim implies experiential suffering, victimhood is a political construction' (2014: 1). The disjoint between these two aspects are clear throughout: while women might identify as victims of varying forms of violence, the issues raised are inherently political constructions. The first is gendered violences and their consequences: the personal as political, tied to aspects of power, patriarchy and violence. The second is the micro nature of structurally violent policy and practice. Rather than reducing stress or emotional distress, *the British asylum system is geared toward compounding it.*

Chapter conclusion: mitigating harm, and harming mitigation

> The primary needs of traumatised clients are physical and emotional safety, predictability of relationships, reduction of symptoms and the reestablishment of social relationships.
>
> (Kastrup and Arcel, 2004: 556)

As we can see, there are clear indicators of what mitigates harm for people seeking asylum, particularly survivors of sexual violence, conflict-related sexual abuse, and/or torture. Many studies have come to similar conclusions: the autonomous creation of women-only spaces for female survivors of sexual violence; availability of sexual violence and torture support for women, men, trans and non-binary people, as well as specialist LGB-centric support; access to quality interpretation; and one-to-one counselling where appropriate.

As a researcher, perhaps the greatest frustration in the British asylum system is that similar recommendations for support have been made to the Home Office across every administration in my lifetime without much real uptake: Conservative, Labour/New Labour, Conservative/Liberal Democrat Coalition, and back to Conservative. As an activist, however, the greatest frustration in the system is seeing what it does to people after months or years: witnessing women disengage from social circles or college; the cessation of political activism because there seems little point in expending so much energy with such little outcome; hearing self-blame and guilt because children are poorly dressed or inadequately fed; throwaway remarks about suicidal feelings. Rather than progressive movement in the issues raised as recommendations for responding to women seeking asylum, the current state of affairs seems to roll back, rather than roll forward, in improving the deficit in support services for survivors of conflict-related violence, persecution and torture. Considering that Europe has recently entered the most significant refugee crisis since the Second World War, the long-term consequences of this will be profound for survivors of violence and torture.

Towards the end of this chapter, I was clear to highlight the limits of trauma-based models or the practice of counselling as the main focus of survival. They have potential to individualise problems that people face or have faced, and I remain cautious of a therapy industry that has proliferated (and in the private sector, profited) on the basis of the emotional suffering of people. Despite my own contentions in this area, this research does demonstrate the value and importance that counselling or individual and group support can have for survivors of sexual and gendered violence. Although not without faults, the dedication of some voluntary sector organisations can be the key driver to this, rather than the dedication of governmental agendas. As this chapter emphasises, that is particularly the case for the violence against women sector, and refugee or asylum support.

This leads in to the key argument of this chapter, and perhaps the book: it is not only the impacts of previous or ongoing violence that cause women distress and emotional harm, but the systems and structures around women which compound these harms. It cannot be that voluntary or even statutory mental health or crisis support agencies and organisations are forever left to pick up the pieces of this harm. The fundamental systems that impose and ingrain harm require at the least radical transformation, and at the most dismantlement and rebuilding. This brings me to the focus of the following chapters that will explore why such a shift has not occurred, and how individuals and groups resist and challenge these harmful structures.

Notes

1 This might be understandable, considering that the call is from the Police and Crime Commissioner. However, most people who are subjected to sexual abuse or violence do not report to the police, with only around 15 per cent of survivors choosing to report (ONS, 2013). As Ballinger had argued in 2009, statutory funding for sexual violence often attempts to mitigate feminist politics. Support has become increasingly

absorbed by local councils and Police and Crime Commissioners, neither of which are woman centred, in Merseyside at least.

2 In one organisation I worked with over an eight-year period, we developed a model whereby one sexual violence support centre would be women-only, and another would have dedicated times per week that men could use the services. All counsellors who were willing to work with men could, any that did not, did not have to. Men who preferred to speak to a male counsellor (for example, men who had been abused by women) were referred to a partner organisation that specialised in male support.

3 The fact that trans women were not seldom addressed in answers on gendered uses of spaces suggests a potential lack in accessing services more broadly. Considering that trans people can regularly be subjected to transphobic comments, abuses or violence, it is possible that this group would experience further or multiple exclusions from support services.

4 I worked with an organisation for almost a decade that increasingly developed formal links with police, the Police and Crime Commissioner (PCC) as well as a Sexual Assault Referral Centres. My primary insight, which eventually led me to leave, was the gradual co-option and absorption of the organisation into short-term criminal justice agendas: higher conviction rates, more counselling through the courts, longer prison sentences. To me, this deflects from the long-term aims of reducing, mitigating and eradicating sexual violence in society. Even the use of language changed. Child sex abuse became 'CSE' (Child Sexual Exploitation), which was a key focus criminal justice agencies in the North West of England at the time, due to evidenced failures in responses to child sex abuse and so-called grooming. 'Survivors' were increasingly termed 'victims' to align with the PCC's victim support agenda, and gendered language around sexual violence was neutralised. This was so gradual that it went unnoticed among many frontline staff and volunteers who had previously held feminist politics dear.

5 There are some aspects that do mirror this among settled populations, namely people leaving prison. In this case, people regularly face a form of 'geography of punishment' through dispersal that regularly moves people, often women, away from the areas they lived in before or wish to live in again. For further discussion, see Cooper (2014).

6 This might include the kinds of structural violences addressed so far, but also physical and emotional abuse which, in the cases of sexual violence or state violence, can be an extension of normative attitudes rather than a deviation from them.

7 Silence and denial in Britain

No, I don't care. Show me pictures of coffins, show me bodies floating in water, play violins and show me skinny people looking sad. I still don't care.

Katie Hopkins, *The Sun* newspaper columnist, April 2015

You are well aware of the emerging reality, but you vocally deny this because you support the policy, or are not bothered by what is going on. You are oblivious to what is happening; you simply don't care.

Stanley Cohen, 2001: 24

Introduction

So far this book mainly responds to three kinds of question: why, what and who. Why do people seek asylum, and what are the gendered experiences? What processes are there to seek asylum, and in what ways are they harmful? Who seeks asylum, and who loses and who gains from the structures around asylum in the context of border controls? In considering these, the previous chapters have documented aspects of suffering, harm and violence that are individually experienced and simultaneously structurally embedded in the British asylum system. The kinds of questions not fully explored yet relate to *how* or *where*. How have border controls expanded in a way that enables border-related deaths and harm? How can we account for knowing that people – in the case of this research, specifically women – continue to experience harm and yet, rather than overhaul the systems in place, we allow them to continue or even grow? How is it that the harms inflicted on people seeking asylum still remain on the periphery of consciousness? Where do we go from here?

The continuously developing field of border studies has harvested many responses to similar questions (Aas and Bosworth; 2013; Bacon, 2005; Bosworth, 2008; Crawley *et al.*, 2011; Dauvergne, 2013; Fekete, 2005; Gibney, 2008; Melossi, 2003; Pickering and Cochrane, 2013; Webber, 2006, 2012, 2016; Weber and Pickering, 2001). Perhaps one central concern has related to media representation of immigrants, and the way in which this can influence public knowledge and attitudes. Many critical scholars and activists have provided in-depth documentation of news coverage of immigration generally, and the criminalisation and demonisation of immigrants specifically (Berry *et al.*, 2015; Coole, 2002; Moore, 2013; Moore and Clifford, 2007; Pickering, 2005). These evidence long histories of sensationalism and inaccuracy, misrepresentation and even outright untruths. As the crisis across Europe's borders has continued to unfold, so too have stories of illegal immigration, human trafficking and border smuggling, and ISIS/Da'esh terrorists entering Europe freely under the guise of 'asylum seeker'.[1] These no doubt contribute to the ways in which immigration and asylum are perceived by the public: the UN High Commissioner for Human Rights, Zeid Ra'ad Al Hussein, recently went as far as to argue that, 'This vicious verbal assault on migrants and asylum seekers in the UK tabloid press has continued unchallenged under the law for far too long' (Jones, 2015). This was in response to Katie Hopkins' now infamous likening of migrants to 'cockroaches' in one of Britain's most read newspapers, *The Sun* (April 2015). Indeed, many commentators in global and national media have their fair share of blame to carry in the misrepresentation of asylum and immigration.

Although I recognise these as integral to answering the questions set out above, this chapter will not reiterate work done in the area of mediated imagery, discourse analysis or representation. As the above references suggest, other scholars have done this well, and indeed to a better degree and in more depth than I can here. Although some aspects around public attitudes will be considered, what primarily concerns me here is how the British state – the government and specifically Home Office and other border control agents – have managed to simultaneously deny, reconstruct and silence many truths around the processes and practices that cause harm in the British asylum system. From this, the following chapter and conclusion will then address forms of resistance, and consider where we go from here. Two key concepts will be explored, Stanley Cohen's definition of 'Denial' and 'bystander states' (2001), and aspects of Thomas Mathiesen's analysis of 'silent silencing' (2004). This thus allows us to 'look up' rather than 'look down' in terms of responsibility and accountability for the ongoing harms of asylum.

Silencing voices, silencing violence

As a precursor, it is worth addressing the significance of both denial and social silencing from a feminist perspective. With the exception of considering domestic violence at some points of *States of Denial* (2004), neither Cohen nor Mathiesen fully engage in gendered aspects of denial or silence. In some ways, this is surprising: sexual violence in particular is perhaps one of the most silenced forms of violence that exists across societies (Ahrens, 2006). Scholars studying methods of torture have highlighted social silencing: Darius Rejali in particular has meticulously documented ways in which torturers have developed methods of pain infliction that cannot (easily) be proven on the body, and which leave no scars (Rejali, 2007; see also Kelly, 2012). Interestingly, little was documented relating to sexual violence, even though such violence can be torturous and also does not always leave physical scars (Canning, 2016a).

The pervasiveness of sexual violence in most societies – in or out of conflict (Wood, 2009) – remains silenced beyond surface level. Significant social movements have challenged this, and online forums that had not previously existed might facilitate avenues to discuss or disclose sexual abuses. However, both perpetration and survival remain peripheral to social consciousness – to quote Jan Jordan, 'that which may no longer be unspeakable but is still too often unspoken' (2012: 277). So in some ways, the fact that there is so little consideration of such a socially denied and silenced problem is not so surprising, since the social sciences have not always incorporated women's voices or experiences into the realms of everyday violence (Canning, 2010; Oakley, 2010; Smart, 1989). From the case studies which have been drawn from so far – women's focus groups, interviews, and Hawwi's history – it is clear that silence in embedded across the spectrum of survival. I will briefly address three examples here before moving to document processes of denial and *silent* silencing. These are social silencing, structural silencing and self-silencing.

Social silencing

The first of these, social silencing, has been inherent to ways in which some survivors of sexual violence feel that they cannot speak of subjections to interpersonal violence. There are long fought resistances against the stigmatisation of being subject to sexual violence or abuse, but still the projected embodiment of 'victimhood' (Smart, 1989) can leave women and men feeling unable to speak of their experiences. For some, the fear of social ostracism is a serious reality. In varying global regions including countries that women seeking asylum in Britain predominantly flee from, women can face marginalisation from their communities and families, or can be accused of adultery. Sexual violence may even have been a contributor to their reason for fleeing in the first place, and some women might see change as an opportunity to leave this in her past. Some survivors do not feel they can speak of violence, as Hawwi eloquently conveyed when she stated, '*I took my shame in my mind. I didn't speak to anyone.*'

For men, being subjected to sexual violence or sexual torture can affect their sense of self, sense of sexual identity or socially ascribed masculinity. As a clinical psychologist working in torture rehabilitation in Denmark reflected:

I think those [sexual violence] are the worst traumas for many of the people ... they tend not to tell anyone about them. You tend to be the first person they tell about them, even though some of them might have happened lots and lots of years ago. They question their sexuality a lot afterward. Also if you stick an object up a man's rectum, you can get an erection, an involuntary erection. That confuses men a lot. They wonder why they got an erection, you know, 'did I like that?' So for people torturing and trying to break a person down it is very useful to do these things, because they want to destroy the person's mental health. And of course that creates a lot of thoughts that they can't share with their wives because that's so shameful, then they won't be a man any longer. So they wouldn't tell their community, that would be a big no no. A lot of people in those prisons have been subjected to it, but because they don't talk about it they feel very much alone. So it's a very difficult subject. Also the body can, they often are very scared of people touching them, they have problems in certain areas of the body, because memory also sticks on the body.

This 'not telling' is often felt by women and men, and although both these examples focus on heterosexual experiences of silencing, there is nothing to suggest that women or men in single sex relationships would necessarily speak of violence to their own family or partners, nor for people identifying as trans or queer. The fundamental issue remains stigmatisation, a clear barrier to speaking out in any social context.

Structural silencing

This brings me to the more context specific issue of structural silencing in seeking asylum, not only in Britain but in many comparative systems where people are expected to disclose violence as part of an application process. As I have highlighted in some depth in Chapter 6, the way in which survivors of violence are expected to relay instances of abuse or torture when applying for asylum is, in effect, the complete opposite environment within which women or men would otherwise disclose violence, if they do speak out about it at all. There are whole layers that do not reflect examples of best practice drafted and recommended by psychologists or rape support organisations over decades. The initial interview with a complete stranger; the formal setting of initial or substantive interviews; the presence of children at times; the rushed nature of relaying complex histories which are documented by someone that the applicant has no real reason to trust. All of these set a barrier to disclosing sexual violence or sexual torture, thus structurally silencing survivors, and in a way that has potential to affect their claim and credibility in the future. As an asylum caseworker in Liverpool put it:

Some women don't speak about it, 'cos they're ashamed, they're ashamed. I say "why didn't you tell them?" and they say "I feel ashamed. I feel dirty". And you know, sometimes there's men there, or very, very bolshie women. Like army generals. It's not sort of relaxed enough for them to trust them to tell them what's happened.

Self-silencing

The final aspect of silencing to address before looking at denial is self-silencing. Although inherent to the above two examples in some ways, self-silencing relates not only to sexual violence, but also to torture or persecution more broadly. Self-silencing is politically strategic, a simultaneous act of resistance and survival, and alludes to measures that people seeking asylum take to avoid describing state violence in a way that might leave them open to identification if they were to be returned or deported. As discussed in Chapter 3, there have been instances of 'torture on return' when people have been refused asylum in Britain or other countries, and the limits of diplomatic assurances are surely easily recognisable for a politically active person fearing execution on return (which is largely what such assurances are used in the case of). It seems reasonable that someone who has been targeted by the state and fears further persecution would avoid relaying information that might jeopardise their wellbeing or safety in the future. For survivors of sexual violence who have not told family or partners of their subjections, once disclosed their story cannot be untold. Thus avoiding discussing experiences of violence, which can carry shame or stigma, is another way to ensure personal survival. In all, these strategies have the potential to significantly affect an individual's claim for asylum, either by never speaking of violence or by speaking too late and once other aspects of the claim are made. For now though, let's briefly move away from the focus on experiences of seeking asylum and towards strategies of denial that allow the state to rewrite the way in which it responds to asylum.

Denying existence, denying responsibility

I chose the opening sentence of this chapter – the quote from Katie Hopkins – very deliberately. The article that she wrote containing this, in *The Sun* newspaper, gained a high level of criticism to the point of public outrage. Indeed, this is a particularly grotesque portrayal of denial and one that most people would be likely to condemn openly and vehemently. The implied references to dying and starving migrants in a year that over 3500 drowned in the Mediterranean should be enough to have made you feel saddened at best, possibly (like me) very uncomfortable, maybe even angered or upset. It is indeed a strong example of utter disregard for human life, and one that was compared at the time to holocaustal propaganda (Williams, 2015).

This denouncing response is heartening to a degree – reading and listening to news reports challenging these attitudes publically or speaking to fellow outraged activists and colleagues made me feel that at least this was not reflective of most people's views. As the next chapter assures, there is still humanity left; we can see it in localised resistance and campaign groups, relief missions across Calais and Lesvos, and other border areas or camps that have had increased support from campaign and relief organisations. Likewise, the increasing resistance to certain forms of border control (in particular detention) challenges the abject disregard for the lives of migrants.

If, however, we look at Hopkins' quote from a different angle – if we interpret it literally, not just as something of malice from a controversial commentator – the sentiments are actually fairly reflective of much of the British states' outwardly harsh response to people seeking asylum. As I will now argue, this is not only in relation to the current and widely documented refugee crisis, but in the disconnect between recognising survivors of persecution as something far away rather than here, and the consciousness gap between the outcomes of border controls, punitive policy implementation and the lived experiences identified thus far.

Denial as a form of bordering, physically and emotionally

In the key critical text *States of Denial*, Stanley Cohen asked how atrocities are able to take place at the hands of powerful states, at times with complicity from citizens, and how suffering so often goes seen but ignored (2001). Through considering conscious and unconscious awareness of catastrophes and atrocities, Cohen argued that 'Denial ... includes *cognition* (not acknowledging the facts); *emotion* (not feeling); *morality* (not recognising wrongness or responsibility) and *action* (not taking active steps in response to knowledge)' (2004: 9). He highlighted three broad categories of denial: literal, interpretive and implicatory (ibid., 7–9).

The first of these, literal denial, is quite straightforward. It is the way in which we find ways to avoid acknowledging reality. This can be done deliberately; lies are told or false truths are developed to reconstruct reality and alleviate responsibility on knowing parties, and it can be through 'genuine ignorance' (2001: 7) which itself might be constructed by individuals or states as a way to protect themselves from acknowledging truth. The second, interpretive denial, develops through more conscious processes of reconstructing truth or knowledge as a way of renaming or reframing a social problem or issue. As Cohen argues, officials do not claim that "nothing happened", but that what happened is not what you think it is, not what it looks like, not what you call it' (ibid.). The third category, implicatory denial, allows people – individually or collectively – to 'wash our hands' of a problem by downgrading its significance or separating ourselves from it as *not our problem*. This is a little like Katie Hopkins' claim that she simply doesn't care; these are not people she knows or has to worry about, there is little she could do even if she did care, *they are not her problem*. Each of these resonates with various aspects of Britain's responses to the harms of Britain's borders and the kinds of controls they inflict on people within them and spatially external to them.

As Cohen suggested, literal denial can be quite difficult to construct in an age of contemporary global knowledge exchanges. The public saturation of technologies relaying streams of news allow us to know that migrant lives are being lost before the body count has properly begun. The proliferation of research reports and investigations that are openly available to both the public and to state actors means we can seldom literally deny knowledge of suffering – there are simply too many pressure groups and watchdogs informing us to be able to get away with literal denial. What we can see instead is prevalence of discourses that allow for us to deny that the outcome has been deliberate or foreseeable. As Weber and Pickering argued (2011), and Crawley and Sigona recently reiterated (2016), various global regions including the Australia and countries across the EU have refused to systematically respond to border deaths as something related to policy and illegalisation of migration. Other issues are pointed to: the sheer numbers of refugees crossing borders (over one million in 2015); Turkey, Greece and Italy's inability to effectively stop people crossing, i.e. borders are not secured enough; inadequate funds to provide temporary accommodation in border countries. Even though we know that walls and fences only force people to find ever more precarious routes into Europe (Andersson, 2014; Crawley and Sigona, 2016; Weber and Pickering, 2011) we still persevere in denial of this reality.

In Britain, the current most prevalent reconstruction of knowledge seems to be a kind of inadvertent humanitarian protection. Borders must be secured elsewhere in Europe so that fewer people try and cross them. Britain cannot possibly home all the refugees who want to reach it, so it is in their best interests that we stop giving false hope to people who might wish to make it here and drown or fall off a lorry on their way. This discourse has long been in train but is certainly cementing itself into the consciousness of British elites. During her time as Home Secretary, Theresa May placed great emphasis on tackling smugglers (which she and others often conflate with traffickers) who knowingly target people trying to cross Europe's increasingly militarised barriers. For example, if we look at May's statement in the government's 2011 strategy set out against human trafficking, the conflation of trafficking and border control is clear:

> Human trafficking destroys lives and its effects damage communities. The transport and exploitation of vulnerable men, women and children by **predatory** organised criminal groups is something that **no civilised country** should tolerate. We need to do more to stop this horrific crime. The UK has a **good record in tackling human trafficking**. That is something we must build on. Our new strategy for tackling human trafficking has four key aims: international action to stop trafficking happening in the first place; a **stronger border** at home to **stop victims being brought** into the UK; tougher law enforcement action to tackle the **criminal gangs that orchestrate the crime**; and improved identification and care for the victims of trafficking.
>
> (2011, own emphasis added)

What we can see here is the reframing of a serious social problem – that is, the abuse of people through trafficking – with the objectives of stringent border controls. Thus the only way to eradicate a social ill becomes through criminalisation, securitisation and border expansion ('stop victims being brought into the UK'). If we take a leap forward into May 2015, when the EU had begun to wholly grasp the scale of the refugee crisis unfolding on its doorstep, the emphasis on trafficking as a means to deny responsibility becomes clearer. By then, the Home Secretary had fully entrenched border control agendas with humanitarian ones. Statements and interviews had become wholly entangled in discourses of support, of financial aid and personnel power to rescue migrants. In one interview, for example, Theresa May was asked why she did not want to join other EU states in resettling migrants coming across the Mediterranean. She argued that 'we need to deal in this trade in human beings ... callous criminals who are trading on people's aspiration and who are profiting from trying to move across Africa and into Europe' (May, quoted in Price, 2015). She then continued to use the terms 'terrible trade in human beings' and 'organised criminals' again, as she has done in numerous interviews and statements.

This is not simply the rhetoric of one individual; it is a strategy for denial on literal, implicatory and interpretive levels. The social and legal landscape around border controls has arguably shifted to reflect this agenda in light of the escalating refugee crisis. Britain increased spending on naval patrols[2] between Libya and Italy, sending HMS Bulwark and later HMS Enterprise to rescue migrants and deliver them to Libya or Italy thus simultaneously rescuing and removing. This approach shifted in 2016 when David Cameron announced UK deployment for a NATO mission in the Aegean Sea around Greece to help stop people making a 'perilous journey' and join other European countries trying to 'break the business model of the people smuggling criminal gangs which are exploiting people and putting lives at risk every day' (Prime Minister's Office, 2016). The same discourse played out in the political arena when predominantly Conservative MPs voted against an amendment in the Immigration Bill (now Immigration Act 2016) that would have facilitated the intake of 3000 child refugees from across Europe (Waugh, 2016). The key argument was, again, to avoid setting a precedent that might develop a 'pull factor' that would encourage more children to make dangerous journeys, or traffickers to exploit them. The fact that safe passage would reduce the likelihood of deaths at borders anyway, and would eradicate the need for traffickers or smugglers, does not fit this discourse or the UK's dominant political agenda on border securitisation. As Cohen states in reference to interpretive denial, controls are given a different meaning, a humanitarian agenda. It challenges illegal trafficking and thus exploitation, and saves women, men and children. It deters would-be migrants from risking their own lives to enter a continent that doesn't want them and has developed limited means to support them. We can all live with a clear conscious in the knowledge that the country or indeed continent that we live in is doing its bit to prevent migrant deaths. We can collectively deny the realities of bordering and wash our hands of the deaths it contributes to.

Denial at home

> *When they are travelling by boat on water, many, many things will happen to them. It is not an easy way you are coming and just claiming asylum. Once you are struggling and reaching, it is survival of fittest, survival of just getting life and extending life, there is nothing that you will not do. If they saw us here, why they are not allowing us life?*
>
> (Hawwi)

Back to Britain, and we can see that similar strategies are employed that allow the British asylum system to continue inflicting harms that are otherwise reframed, renamed and denied. Denial takes hold both structurally and through individuals. Spatial and temporal isolation, for example, is enabled through detention, imprisonment for immigration-related crimes, and dispersal to predominantly poorer areas and this enables collective and individual denial. As we have seen, asylum housing is often in areas away from city centres or in the most deprived councils. Theresa May, who has instigated so many policies regarding immigration welfare, has never even visited asylum housing (Devlin, 2016). *She has not seen it.* Likewise, Immigration Removal Centres are, like many prisons, far from the gaze of the public, often situated near industrial estates miles from major cities or towns. IRC The Verne, a former prison, is probably the most extreme example of this spatial isolation. Situated on the Isle of Portland, it is as close to external as one could get, short of taking on Australia's example of offshore detention processing.

As Cohen argued, denial requires cognition, which facilitates the knowing or unknowing of suffering or harm. Problems or problematic aspects can cognitively be separated out or rationalised so that they are disconnected from each other. Consider the below statement from the UKBA director I introduced some chapters ago:

> *We would not knowingly make somebody homeless, without support, however if somebody has reached a point with their claim where they have no right to remain in UK, then we would terminate single person's support to encourage them to return to their home country. If they don't voluntarily return, then we may enforce their return. That would involve detention, possible forced removal on a flight.*

Logically, if or when a person who has no right to work has welfare or financial support removed, the only options become illegalised working, destitution and possibly homelessness, dependence on family or friends, or – the preferred outcome for the Home Office – deportation. This juxtaposed statement at once denies deliberately or knowingly inflicting social harm while rationalising the actual process of it. As Cohen argued:

> Rationalisation is another matter when you know what can and should be done, you have the means to do this, and there is no risk. This is not a refusal to acknowledge reality, but a denial of its significance or implications.

> (2001: 8)

There is therefore disconnect between how the state responds to women, men and children seeking asylum and how it claims to respond to suffering. This was made clear in Chapter 2 in the context of the Global Summit to End Sexual Violence in Conflict. While Britain has championed ending rape in war through advocating the development of UN Security Council Resolutions the state can still categorically overlook the correlation between rape in conflict elsewhere and survivors of conflict rape seeking asylum in Britain (Singer, 2016). By all accounts, they have been signatories on relevant conventions and have developed Gender Issues in the Asylum Claim guidelines (2010) but still fails to fully implement them at ground level. Still, at least they exist. Those responsible for undertaking interviews and reviewing asylum claims cannot be accused of not addressing the problems I raise throughout this book: they have been reframed, responded to and thus problems developing from 'gender issues' become structurally deniable.

The bystander state?

Whether or not Britain is guilty of contributing to the ongoing crisis in responding to refugees depends on one's perspective of its role in international relations. Britain, indeed the UK, contributed significantly to war, conflict and airstrikes in some of the key regions from which refugees are currently fleeing including Libya, Syria and most notably Afghanistan and Iraq. While it is fair to say that other significant political factors have contributed, including political uprising, armed challenges to multiple dictatorships, and the role of other international aggressors and capitalist states in regions of Africa and the Middle East, Britain has played its part in dismantling stability in key countries (Green and Ward, 2009; Kelly, 2012; Whyte, 2007, 2015). As highlighted in Chapter 1, even former Prime Minister Tony Blair recently admitted that the occupation of Iraq contributed to the formation of ISIS. Britain has thus arguably played its role in perpetrating violences that have facilitated further violence in regions from which hundreds of thousands of people have fled.

However, the extent to which Britain might be held accountable for the ongoing refugee crisis – or border mismanagement – is likely to be minimal. This in part relates to the distance between Britain and refugees that I discussed in Chapter 1. Although many illegalised migrants and refugees might indicate their objectives to reach Britain and countries such as Sweden, Denmark and Germany, they are not literally dying at these borders in significant numbers, as so many have done in trying to reach Greece and Italy. States beyond the peripheries of these countries are therefore inherently able to wash their hands of border deaths (Weber and Pickering, 2011). Likewise, there are increased reports of violence against refugees by border guards, and the expansion of border camps has been marred with the documentation of violence, particularly the gendered exploitation of women (Amnesty International, 2016a; Joshi, 2016). Britain is not accountable to these: they are not British perpetrators; it is not a British problem (see also Kelly, 2012).

This brings me to consider the role of Britain as a bystander state. Certainly, it would not be the first time that such a title has been ascribed to Britain or other countries in Europe. Perhaps one of the most well-documented examples of states 'turning a blind eye' was in the years leading up to and during the Holocaust, but this was not the last time. Britain increased border restrictions in the aftermath of the Bosnian War, and as the Kosovan war continued. Rather than actively facilitate the granting of refugee status at the time, Britain increased carrier sanctions, developed further ways to outsource the responsibility of visa controls to external borders, and reduced the rights of asylum seekers once they arrived in the

UK (Aas and Bosworth, 2013; Aliverti, 2012; Bloch and Schuster, 2002, 2005a; Webber, 2012).

A question here arises from the definition of 'bystander'. Clarkson (1996: 6) argues, 'A bystander is the descriptive name given to a person who does not become actively involved in a situation where someone requires help' (Clarkson, 1996, in Cohen, 2001: 69). Considering the *active* involvement that the British state has taken to decrease refugee intakes, bystander becomes a complex term to ascribe. The UK is not in the passport-free Schengen zone, it has not taken part in a common European asylum policy, and according to (now former Prime Minister) David Cameron 'we have an absolutely rock-solid opt-out from these things' (quoted in Reuters, 2016). Unlike Western European countries such as Germany, Austria, and Sweden, the UK drew less than 40,000 asylum applications in 2016, a year with the largest number of migrants moving across Europe since the Second World War. The central British state has *actively* worked hard to be able to deny accountability and deflect responsibility in the event of such as crisis. As Cameron went on to argue, 'We will have our own way of doing things, keeping our own borders. It underlines the best of both worlds, the special status we have' (ibid., 2016).

The silent silencing of everyday suffering

Similar to Stanley Cohen's efforts to grasp and theorise the denial of suffering is Thomas Mathiesen's analysis of silent silencing (2004). Although there are profound differences between the two approaches,[3] a key similarity lies in their objective to look at states and corporations to understand how certain problems go unfixed or how suffering can be denied or ultimately ignored. Mathiesen in particular highlighted step-by-step processes through which identifiable problems become recognised, superficially responded to and 'fixed' without truly addressing structural causes or contributors. Rather than seeing systems or practices as being inherently flawed, issues are individualised and action is taken in a way that ensures that those who benefit from the given process or practice will continue to do so, while those whose concerns are raised might be gradually co-opted into assuming or accepting that adequate action is taken without wholesale change: societies and individuals within them are acquiesced.

This brings me to the 'maintenance of hidden silencing' (Mathiesen, 2004: 25) in the context of the British asylum system as a way to continue expansion and deflect responsibility from the state when identifiable problem occur. This includes aspects of individualisation, normalisation, co-option, superficial endorsement and displacement of responsibility. To do this, the remainder of this chapter will analyse a number of 'scandals' or 'tragic events' that have occurred across the British asylum system have been responded to through these processes, specifically as a way to avoid meaningful structural change.

Individualisation of 'the issue'

A number of controversies have plagued the Home Office over the past few years. In 2010, UKBA caseowner and whistleblower Louise Perrett exposed institutional racism at Cardiff UKBA office (staff had kept a toy gorilla as a 'grant monkey' to put on officers' desks when they granted refugee status to applications).[4] As discussed in Chapters 3 and 4, further allegations have included sexist, racist and sexual abuse in IRC Yarl's Wood (Canning, 2014b; Channel 4 News, 2014; Girma *et al.*, 2014); and death during deportation (Fekete, 2015). In all of these cases, the primary reaction was to call for an investigation or review. In Cardiff, recommendations were made to change processes at the centre, including introducing a disciplinary offence for individual staff or management who fail to challenge inappropriate behaviour. Those found to have perpetrated violence in Yarl's Wood were dismissed, both in the cases of racist and sexist remarks, and in cases where guards had 'sexual relations' with women in detention. In terms of the two deaths due to excessive restraint during efforts to deport, each was followed up with an investigation and criminal trial, but neither resulted in conviction. As discussed in Chapter 3, the key decision was to change the ways in which deportees were to be restrained. Although 'improvements' in this were noted by Nick Hardwick, there remained clear evidence that certain practices were still being undertaken (Hardwick, 2013).

What we can see here is a process of *individualisation*: instances of sexual violence or racist abuse are acknowledged as one-off events – they are reviewed and dealt with efficiently and effectively by removing the 'bad apples' (see Sim, 2009: 132) who had made cause for complaint. It is not that deportation is inherently violent, but rather that there were potentially violent actions committed by individuals who took the use of force too far (Bhatia and Canning, 2016). Even then, as with deaths in custody or at the hands of police (Couvée, 2013), actions were not found to be deliberate. These were 'accidents'. Racism in immigration office is not endemic; it was just that Cardiff needed to reconfigure some of the ways that it approached handling its staff and processing asylum claims.

Normalisation

As Mathiesen argued, 'normalisation' is made into something that should be expected under certain circumstances (2004: 26). No substantial change is needed, as the event or problem is a consequence of the very nature of a certain type of scenario. Perhaps this is most recognisable in the case of deaths in custody. Of the 21 deaths in IRCs from 2004–2014, 10 were counted as natural causes, and eight as self-inflicted, and of the 22 deaths of immigration detainees in prisons, 12 were natural causes and nine self-inflicted (INQUEST, 2016). The argument often comes to be that there are some people with underlying illnesses or undiagnosed health problems that contribute to their death. With over 30,000 people being detained each year in the UK, it should come as no surprise that there may be deaths in custody.

If we scratch deeper into the surface of this, there are allegations of neglect, poor treatment, and slow responses to complaints of illness or feeling unwell. The evidence of increased suicide attempts in 2016, up by 11 per cent from the year before, is a clear suggestion that life in IRCs is in itself harmful (Taylor, 2016). As argued earlier and elsewhere (Canning and Bhatia, 2016), immigration detention has become normalised but simultaneously the most controversial aspect of border controls in Britain and other areas (specifically Australia – see Grewcock, 2013). However, and as with the normalisation of prisons in so-called crime control (Scott and Codd, 2010; Sim, 2009), immigration detention has proliferated despite evidence to suggest it is deeply harmful, indeed structurally violent. This is in part, at least, because they have become normalised. Deaths and other harms that occur within them are approached as serious problems and incur serious investigations, but are ultimately an extension of normative life for people living and dying within them, despite evidence to the contrary.

Displacement of responsibility

According to Mathiesen, displacement of responsibility occurs when 'a criticisable condition has been exposed, or when a criticisable event has occurred, and when the criticism is so strong or so radical that it cannot be met just by individualisation, normalisation, co-option or superficial endorsement' (2004: 28). What Mathiesen goes on to identify is the way in which states or corporations can use events to make drastic changes which become difficult to contest – a welcome alternative, in a way. I want to argue that rather than there being one incident or identifiable problem, displacement of responsibility is the foundation of the way in which the asylum system, and indeed immigration and border control agendas and practices more broadly, function. Such displacement is fundamental to the operation of corporate expansion in border controls. As Fekete (2001) and Tyler (2013) argue, the politicisation of immigration has been prolific: if we look at immigration procedures and practices since at least the early 1970s but specifically since the 1990s, immigration has been centralised in party debates, law development and policy proliferation. Simultaneously, state handling of immigration has been systematically critiqued from commentators across a spectrum of political opinion and party politics, some for not being stringent enough, others for being inefficient or 'not fit for purpose' (Vaz, 2012) and more again for being harmful or inhumane (Athwal, 2014; Bhatia and Canning, 2016; Bloch and Schuster, 2005b).

What this has facilitated is the legitimate expansion of private and corporate control of border controls immigration procedures: if the state cannot be trusted to do its job efficiently and cost-effectively, then the appropriate alternative is to have someone else do it for them. Considering the criticisms I have waged against the Home Office in this book, even I might struggle to contest that. However, this has dualistically shifted responsibility away from the state in some areas, while allowing other (corporate, profiteering) entities to do the state's bidding for them. As I argued in relation to the allegations of sexual abuse in Yarl's Wood some time ago (Canning, 2014b), when problems surface, accountability is already deflectable to the non-state actor responsible. Often a review or investigation ensues. However, these actors are still state reliant: they work within the confines of the policies and legislation developed by the state. As Aliverti (2012, 2013), Bosworth (2014), Carr (2012), Grewcock (2013), Turnbull (2016) and Webber

(2006, 2012) all document, and as argued in Chapters 1 and 2, ever-restrictive immigration and asylum policies and legislation are what ultimately governs the everyday experiences and entitlements of people seeking asylum. From the macro to the micro-levels, from welfare, to funding decisions, to maternity entitlement, to detention, to deportation. Non-state actors may be responsible for abuses or violence but ultimately this displacement of responsibility only runs so deep: state accountability, including actions instigated or facilitated by the Home Office and their law enforcement division, Border Force.

The expansion of control through coercion and absorption

Immigration controls in Britain, as well as Australia, North America and other neoliberal economies, are fundamentally tied in with capitalist interest, encouraging tides of specific workforces during periods of need (Gilroy, 1987) and withdrawing this when economic and workplace patterns shift. In Britain this is most commonly recognised during the post-war reconfiguration and epitomised in images of Empire Windrush's arrival from the West Indies to London in 1948, facilitating economic immigration from British Colonies (Phillips and Phillips, 2009). Since these early days, the shifts in border controls are no less self-serving or capitalistic, which is perhaps why and how statistics for seeking asylum in Britain have significantly reduced since the mid-1990s, while economic migration has increased.[5]

In any case, there have been clear economic benefits to securitisation, the privatisation of border controls and the immigration detention estate (Andersson, 2014; Lowenstein, 2015). In 2015, G4S alone – the self-defined 'leading global integrated security company' – had a global revenue of £6.4 billion and was the largest employer listed on the London stock exchange (G4S, 2015). As Ruben Andersson argues, although wider evidence relating to 'funding figures remains opaque' (2014: 14), 'The European Union has allocated 60 percent of its total Home Affairs budget for 2007–13, or four billion euros to the "solidarity and management of migratory flows"' (ibid.). As he goes on to point out, the *illegality industry* of border crossing – and the number of people crossing – are not reduced the more money that is spent, but instead expand.[6] Consider that this industry has multiple beneficiaries from producing and distributing materials for border controls: technology to scan bodies and take fingerprints; bricks to build IRCs; wire to go around them, and across borderlines. From a corporate perspective, the expansion of border controls is a neoliberal dream come true.

Although IRCs have a long history of corporate involvement – even the first detention centre in the UK, IRC Harmondsworth, had been commissioned to Securior by 1971 (see Canning and Bhatia, 2016) – the scale to which border management lies with corporate interest is quite astounding. To quote Mathiesen, corporations are 'continually more encompassing' (Mathiesen, 2004: 14) in terms of the border services they offer and the contracts they are offered. At the time of research, out of 11 centres, two are operated by Her Majesty's Prison Service. Conjectures between criminalisation and border control aside, this means that the remaining nine are operated by private companies, as is evidenced in Table 7.1.

Table 7.1 Who is responsible for Immigration Detention in the United Kingdom?

IRC	Opened	Gender	Capacity	Operated By	Escort/travel provider	Health service provider
Brook House	2009	M	448	G4S	Tascor	G4S
Campsfield House	1993	M	276	Mitie	Tascor	The Practice (commissioned by Mitie)
Colnbrook	2004	Mostly M	420	Serco Ltd	Tascor	Serco Health
Dungavel House (Scotland)	2001	Mostly men (14 women)	249	GEO Group UK Ltd	Tascor	Med-Co Secure Healthcare Services Ltd (Commissioned by GEO)
Harmondsworth	2000 (original in 1970)	Mixed	615	GEO Group UK Ltd	Tascor	Primecare
Larne House (NI)	2011	Mixed	19	Tascor	Tascor	Mitie (changed from Tascor in 2016)
Morton Hall	2011	M	392	Prison Service	Tascor	G4S
Pennine House	2008	Mixed	32	Tascor	Tascor	Tascor Medical Services, then Spectrum Community Health CIC (social enterprise)
The Verne	2015	M	580	Prison Service	Tascor	Dorset Healthcare University Foundation Trust
Tinsley House	1996	Mixed	154	G4S	Tascor	G4S Policing Support and Medical Services
Yarl's Wood	2001	W, families	410	Serco Ltd	Tascor	G4S Justice Health; GP is Saxonbrook

As we can see, other services within these are also mostly privately run – including health services. Even escort travel services are generally private companies, often operating between airports and detention facilities or even prisons, or to and from asylum accommodation. One of the key companies involved in this is Tascor (formerly Reliance), who claim to, 'manage more than 70,000 'secure movements' of individuals within the UK each year and are responsible for the safe and secure escorting and removal of more than 18,000 individuals from the UK each year' (Tascor, 2013). The tallying up of outsourced responsibilities makes immigration arrival and removal particularly interesting, in that little of it is actually actioned by the state itself. Imagine being a person seeking asylum in Britain today. Arriving at the airport, you might be met by UK Border Force, and any asylum claim will be handled by Home Office immigration officers. You may, however, be initially greeted by someone from G4S, Securitas or another private company. If you are detained, you might be transferred by Tascor or G4S to a Short Term Holding Facility or IRC operated by Serco or G4S. If you are moved to asylum accommodation, in Liverpool for example, this will likely be run by Serco again. Any initial health assessments are commonly undertaken by a private provider or social enterprise, rather than public service providers. Quite basically, with the exception of asylum interviews your contact with the state is minimised, even though it is the British state – not corporate providers – that is signatory to international legislation relating to refugees. Perhaps this is the closest example of Mathiesen's definition of 'dynamic' in relation to silencing, in the sense that, 'in our society it spreads and becomes continually more encompassing' (2004: 14). Who can argue that healthcare or learning services are not positive elements in society, specifically in confinement or asylum accommodation, and particularly in lieu of what I have discussed relating to mental and physical health thus far? The 'softer' aspects of company involvement are ever absorbed into border management as something 'normal' or even positive – there to offer support to people in need of it, while simultaneously creeping into the realms of punitive control.

Of course, law, regulation and policy all stringently exists within the parameters of 'service provision' where border controls are concerned, so I am not suggesting that corporations are inherently lawless (see Tombs and Whyte, 2015, for further discussion). However, corporations are intrinsically more slippery to hold to account where regulation is concerned, primarily because they are not always answerable to the same forms of regulation as the state. In Britain, privately run IRCs do not have to respond to Freedom of Information requests, which exist to facilitate transparency. All citizens are able to request information publicly through an FOI, but private corporations are exempt from this obligation, including requests for statistical data. Likewise, as discussed earlier in relation to Yarl's Wood and Rashida Manjoo's refused entry to the centre, privately run centres are not obliged to respond positively to access requests.

Immigration removal centres as a case of silent silencing[7]

We can see then that certain processes of silent silencing are recognisable in varying aspects of the British asylum system. Perhaps the best way to draw these all together is to take immigration detention reviews as a case study. Although the intricacies of these points are developed in more depth elsewhere (Bhatia and Canning, 2016), 'independent reviews' – a process to document and review certain aspects of an identified issue or concern as a way to advise change or make recommendations for improvement – arguably offer the most elucidating access to understanding the maintenance of hidden silencing. I will focus on the first three: individualisation, co-option and normalisation as the most relevant aspects here.

The most recent set of reviews into detention to be published in 2016 were The Review into the Welfare in Detention of Vulnerable Persons (by Stephen Shaw, the former Prison and Probation Ombudsman for England and Wales) and the Independent Investigation into Concerns about Yarl's Wood Immigration Removal Centre (by Kate Lampard and Ed Marsden, both investigators with the independent investigation company Verita). The former of these was commissioned by Theresa May in response to concerns about the wellbeing of detainees and the mental health impacts of confinement on people who are deemed vulnerable and should legally not be detained in the first place (see Shaw, 2016). The latter was commissioned by Serco to investigate institutional attitudes at Yarl's Wood in the face of the allegations outlined above (see Lampard and Marsden, 2016).

Both reviews undeniably went a long way in documenting problems and recommending change. Although the remit for instigating structural change had been excluded for both, Shaw recommended some significant changes: an end to the detention of pregnant women and advocating a 'presumption against detention' of sexual violence survivors, victims of Female Genital Mutilation, people with learning difficulties, those with PTSD and transgender people. As a number of commentators acknowledged, this was more than could have been anticipated since his scope for investigation had been limited by the commissioner. In all, he made 64 recommendations, while Lampard and Marsden made 35.

At surface level, these reviews are positive steps towards addressing structural change that can improve the lives of people who are detained in IRCs. That it would take such a process to even come to the conclusion that detention is not healthy for pregnant women or survivors of trauma is perhaps telling of the state of border controls in the first place. Thus the recommendations made are timely, appropriate and important in the lives of those living day to day in IRCs. If we begin to apply Mathiesen's concept of silent silencing, however, a very different picture develops. The first is that these reviews – and Lampard and Marsden's in particular – *individualise* the problems identified during the investigations. The management of certain centres was addressed as problematic, thus the way in which some facilities run need reform. Simultaneously, the reviews normalise life in IRCs as part of the broader landscape of border controls: there are problems to be addressed which are typical of life in confinement, but since the landscape of detention is embedded in the securitisation of borders, this is expected, accepted and ultimately improved at surface level.

Co-option is recognisable in two ways – the first being the inclusion of an in-depth expert-led literature review into the impacts of confinement in Shaw's review, which acknowledged that detention is not going to go away. Perhaps inarguably, the most logical form of action would be to make systematic changes, and support detainees in coping with the effects of confinement (Bosworth, in Shaw, 2016: 324). Secondary to that concern is the lack of alternative: where else should refused asylum seekers and illegalised immigrants be 'kept'? Surely the risk of absconding would be too great to allow for release and, in any case, the populist advocating of stringent border controls condones the use of detention as control, in some pockets of society at least. What is advocated then is increased layers of management to ensure the smooth running of IRCs, and the care of those within them. This might then be interpreted as the expansion of the IRC management agenda.

There is no doubt that these reviews – Shaw's in particular – were critical of various processes and conditions in the immigration detention estate. They drew some timely and important conclusions that were broadly welcomed across activist, campaign and pressure groups. What they also do, however, is deflect from the exploration of a true alternative and provide superficial endorsement. Overall, certain criticisms were 'too strong just to be punctured through individualisation, normalisation or co-option. It is expressed through thoughtful and responsible – judiciously formulated – agreement that something particular is the matter, and should be corrected' (Mathiesen, 2004: 27). Only four months after the reviews were published, the Immigration Act 2016 – which will absolutely cause more harms similar to those highlighted in Chapters 3 and 4 – set in motion a time limit of 72 hours for detaining pregnant women. As I will argue in the concluding chapter, this is no doubt positive, but it is not wholesale change.

Overall, neither review was given the capacity to discuss the lack of a time limit on days spent in detention, even though the House of Lords had only recently rejected the case for a 28-day limit (see Bhatia and Canning, 2016). It is perhaps here that silent silencing and denial intersect: when something can be denied as structurally harmful because this process of review and recommendation is the means through which systems can be legitimated. This below observation nicely encapsulates this – an interview response from a GP who worked in initial asylum accommodation:

> *The Home Office borders agency are very good at public relations, they're always very well dressed, very well turned out and they sound very suave and they sound very accommodating. But when you've heard the same story year after year that this particular event occurred in a detention centre or somebody died during deportation or some asylum seekers are very badly treated and they say well that happened last year, we've looked into it, we've sorted it out and we're going to have better service this time round, then start disbelieving them very much ... I think they lie to themselves and I think that people are good basically, but they're caught up in a system.*

To reiterate a point I made in Chapter 3, confinement is inherently harmful. It removes autonomy from a person in all of the ways I described in Chapters 3 and 4. The threat of detention can put fear into those seeking asylum, including those who are awaiting appeal, those who have weekly or bimonthly meetings with immigration officers, and of course those who engage in illegal work or overstaying on visas. Ultimately, detention in and of itself can cause harm – no amount of reform can undo the impacts of losing ones' liberty, autonomy and access to outside society. To add to this, the focus on detention alone also has the capacity to deflect from the broader issues addressed in this book: that the asylum system itself is also harmful, and causes significant harm to many women, men and indeed children who pass through it. Reviews, however critical, cannot change this.

Chapter conclusion

There are many ways to attempt to view or understand the infliction of harms documented throughout this book. Silencing in the feminist sense of the word is certainly one of these, and draws us right back to Chapter 2 in relation to sexual violence and torture. This chapter reflects briefly on this, but also draws in processes and structures through which harms of the British asylum system, and central British responses to the ongoing refugee crisis, are denied or silenced.

The incremental impact of bordering Europe situates Britain as a bystander state rather than having been active in facilitating the outsourcing of death at Europe's borders. In the UK more broadly there is a real risk that the aspects of denial and silencing addressed in this chapter will facilitate further superficial changes rather than structural reconfiguration of a harmful system. As we saw in Chapters 3 and 4, it is not only the identifiable or most prolific problems that are structurally violent, but aspects which affect the banal or everyday existence of people awaiting asylum. Exclusionary practices and punitive processes which people regularly face in the British asylum system do, as we have seen, contribute to emotional, physical and mental health harms. They compound problems that may have otherwise developed in response to violence or fear of persecution. Although such problems are acknowledged, they are arguably peripheral to interest or consciousness because the harms they cause are not part of the lives that those enforcing them actually lead: they are *spatially isolated.* Temporal limbo, threat of detention, fear of deportation: all of these can have profound impacts, as the women whose voices are embedded in the previous chapters indicate. The asylum system is harmful and although change is welcome, superficial endorsement should not suffice.

Notes

1 This form of coverage was exacerbated after attacks in Paris on 13 November 2015 during which nine terrorists killed 130 people. Media outlets suspected the perpetrators had been terrorists pretending to be asylum seekers, a claim that was momentarily substantiated when Egyptian and Syrian passports were found near bodies of the dead. Once identified, it transpired that all of the perpetrators had been EU citizens, although some had travelled freely through borders to work with terror groups in Syria.

2 This was after the UK withdrew support from the Mediterranean migrant rescue mission *Mare Nostrum* in October 2014 (Travis, 2014).

3 Although Mathiesen's text *Silently Silenced: Essays on the Creation of Acquiescence in Modern Society* was published in 2004, the essays themselves date back to 1977 and arguably influenced Cohen's work on denial (1993, 2001).

4 According to *The Guardian*, Perrett said some of her colleagues expressed anti-immigration views and took pride in refusing asylum applications. She said that a toy gorilla nicknamed the 'grant monkey' was placed as a badge of shame on the desk of any officer who approved an asylum application. Former child soldiers were forced to lie on the office floor and demonstrate how they shot people in the bush, she said, while a test to determine the authenticity of people who claimed to be from North Korea was to ask them if they ate chop suey. When she asked advice about the legitimacy of a Congolese woman's asylum claim, a legal official apparently replied: 'Umbongo, umbongo, they kill them all in the Congo' (Taylor, 2010).

5 The most recent statistics from the Office of National Statistics show 41,563 claims for asylum from April 2015–March 2016.

6 In his book *Illegality, Inc.* Andersson reflects on hundreds of interviews with migrants, NGOs and border guards across North Africa and Southern Europe and concludes that 'The workings of the illegality industry … are absurd' (2014: 273).

7 This section develops from a short article published for the Institute of Race Relations News: Bhatia and Canning, (2016).

Conclusion
Resisting the spiral of silence

Introduction

The complexity of women's lives has been made evident throughout this book, and the forms of intersectional violence, oppressions and harms that women seeking asylum often face have been intricately documented. At the heart of the work is addressing systemic and structural oppressions which facilitate violence against women, but also which socially hinder the wellbeing of people seeking asylum once they have reached relative safety. Ultimately, I am arguing that the British asylum system is structurally harmful in that it is built to regulate, control and dehumanise those who pass through its processes and whose lives depend on its policies. There is no one aspect that is singularly harmful – not detention, not destitution – but a culmination of procedures which reduce or eradicate autonomy, produce existential banality, and cause further emotional, physical and relational harms to survivors of violence and persecution. Importantly, many of these processes mirror or are mirrored in the global arena of securitisation and border controls, and expansion rather than reduction is increasingly the main objective of states and nations across the world (Aliverti, 2012, 2013; Bosworth, 2008; Bowling and Sheptycki, 2015; Weber and Pickering, 2011; Webber, 2012).

As Stanley and McCulloch argue, critical research is important in drawing attention to state crimes and harms; it is vital for moving towards accountability, in the hope that such harms will be reduced or eradicated (2013). The same can be said for feminist objectives of challenging patriarchal violence and control, since naming, documenting and challenging silence around sexual and domestic violence have been integral to feminist movements in activist, practitioner and academic realms. Much of this has been the aim of this book, to document otherwise invisible forms of violence and harm that are prolific in women's lives, as well as the broader harms that people seeking asylum face in Britain and other countries with similar punitive approaches to asylum.

However Stanley and McCulloch also point out that the failure to include 're-sistance as a core aspect of the study of state crime may lead to feelings of despair, disinterest … states of mind that facilitate passivity, even in the face of irrefutable knowledge about state crimes' (2013: 2). I will go on to address state crime and state harm (Lasslett, 2010) in the next section, but central to this book has been *state power*, particularly the manifestation of this through structural violence and harm. As Stanley and McCulloch perhaps imply, the culmination of these are not happy existences – not to read about, not to research or write about, and certainly not to live through.

This book has not *only* been about power, violence and harm. Embedded in the background of each chapter is survival and resistance: survival through conflict, persecution, violence, sexual abuse, and through everyday harms in seeking asylum. I have aimed to avoid undermining agency, and focus instead on experience and the violences of state actors and institutions. The voices which have weaved through the previous chapters are in themselves resistance: women and men who have spoken up and spoken out about their experiences or political opinions, as well as injustices they see external to their own lives. The development of platforms from which otherwise powerless voices are heard is important – it is what critical criminology and feminist scholarship have been built upon. From an activist perspective, however, academia cannot fully address the multiple modes of resistance required to challenge societal oppressions and state-sanctioned abuses (Schostak and Schostak, 2008). Books, and the many journal articles, blogs, conference presentations and papers which are likely to have proceeded them take a lot of work and are often invaluable, but other actions and acts of resistance are integral to challenging state crime, harms and violence. Direct action, counter movements, protests, activist events, radical arts,[1] organisational involvement: all of these have their place in activism, and all have helped inform how I view and participate in resistance outside or alongside academic work.

To conclude then, I will thus focus on resistance and survival. Much of this book probably seems quite hopeless, and I often feel like that is the case – just as one challenge is fought and won or lost, another seems to begin. This is perhaps even more the case as Britain begins its exit strategy from the European Union post-EU Referendum, a point in time that has seen unparalleled negative representations of asylum and immigration. However, to echo the sentiments of Frances Webber, the contemporary response to Europe's refugee crisis has been enlightening. While there are of course disparaging misrepresentations of asylum seekers, refugees and economic migrants, and although political moves to close borders have escalated, there is also an ever-growing pro-refugee movement across parts of Europe and in the UK and Ireland. Support networks to provide assistance at border camps; street protests for the rights of asylum seekers; refugee welcome groups forming at train stations in Germany, Sweden and other countries (*The Local*, 2015). As I will document below, in Britain there are increasing tides of people across all sectors – refugees and asylum seekers, students, lawyers, teachers, religious groups – who are campaigning and demonstrating for people's right to asylum, and for the freedom of all immigrants from detention. Not always successful, and not always flawless but *the first sustained pro-immigration movement in our lifetime* (Webber, in conversation, 2016). That is surely something to embrace, and a point to reflect upon when considering the value and necessity of acts of resistance – however big or small.

State crime, harm and violence

The previous chapter framed aspects of structural violence and social harm in Britain's asylum system within Cohen's framework of denial (2001). Since 'naming the state as criminal and exposing the way states work to hide or obscure state perpetrated crimes challenges this denial' (Stanley and McCulloch, 2013: 2), this has been a necessary feat to bridge the gap between violence and resistance, which the latter part of this book does. What I have avoided so far, however, is reproducing debates around naming state crime and state harm in ways that have been done in great depth before this (Ballinger, 2009; Green and Ward, 2000, 2004, 2009; Hillyard and Tombs, 2004, 2007; Cain and Howe, 2007; Lasslett, 2010; Pantazis and Pemberton, 2009). The reason for this is the nature of the exertions of power evidenced throughout. Some are arguably state harm, such as legislation restricting asylum or controlling autonomy; cuts to welfare that disproportionally affect women and those seeking asylum; legal but nonetheless harmful deportations and removals. Some are morally dubious but still harmful, such as the detention of people seeking asylum, which is based on a narrow reading of the Refugee Convention but arguably goes against the fundamental right to liberty (Grewcock, 2013). In any case, and as the previous chapter argued in depth, the overlapping of responsibilities between the state and the corporate can facilitate displacement of responsibility and accountability when identifiable crimes or harms are committed (see Andersson, 2014; Burnett; 2009; Canning and Bhatia, 2016; Tombs and Whyte, 2015).

Defining state crime is thus complex in the context of asylum in Britain. Indeed even when the state has been found in contravention of its own laws or policies (such as in the case of asylum welfare – see Chapter 3) it is difficult – but not impossible, as we will later see – to have changes made. There are two points worth picking up on here: the first is that state crime might be viewed as the 'Infliction of pain, injury or death in contravention of legal or moral norms' (Green and Ward, 2009: 116). While Green and Ward refer specifically to states that perpetrate physical and mass scale violence such as war crimes or genocide, a broad reading allows us to look critically at the issues developed in relation to the 'bystander state' and the refugee crisis in Chapter 7. As Pickering and Cochrane argue, the:

> fatalities of irregular border crossers raise serious questions concerning state obligations, at least in relation to the foreseeability of these deaths, if not also in connection to state culpability in and the legality of border control efforts that directly or indirectly result in deaths.
>
> (Pickering and Cochrane, 2013: 28; see also Weber and Pickering, 2011)

It also lets us critically consider what I called the *deliberate* infliction of harm in Chapter 4: harms which affect the mental, emotional and physical wellbeing of people seeking asylum but that are portrayed as immigration deterrents or by-products of border control. As argued, decisions that have been made over the past three decades at least have developed outcomes that were wholly foreseeable and foreseen, and this continues to be the case even despite the increased documentation of harm, and capacity for challenging denial that we now have. These are intentional, and pain, injury and death are subsequently inflicted on varying scales.

The second point draws us closer to key arguments made by Chambliss more than 20 years ago: that 'state crime' should incorporate 'behaviour that violates international agreements and principles established in the courts and treaties of international bodies' (Chambliss, 1995 in Canning, 2011b: 29). Under this wider definition of state crime, it could be argued that in wrongly refusing protection under the Refugee Convention (among others), which is clear in some cases as we have seen, then governmental agencies fit this description. As Webber recently argued, the British state increasingly sees 'human rights *obligations* as *optional*' (Webber, 2016). Since 'crime is not a rigid legal category but a fluid and contested construct' (Green and Ward, 2013: 28) there is scope to move towards criminal accountability, something which has increasingly been advocated by critical lawyers and other parties who have brought High Court challenges against the Home Office. Drawing from perspectives such as Chambliss and Webber then we can see that although state *harms* and state *power* are the most recognisable elements of the points highlighted earlier, there is still scope to address and challenge some harms as crimes.

The contemporary challenge to the 'spiral of silence'[2]

As is documented throughout, the illegalisation of asylum has long been in train (Dauvergne, 2013). Much of this has been within the realms of policy and law and thus out of the gaze of most of the general public for most of the time. Juxtaposed with silencing has been the very loud public disparaging of people seeking asylum, and of immigrants generally. The increased politicisation of asylum in the 1980s went hand in hand with disproportionately negative coverage of asylum seekers that spiralled into the 1990s and 2000s (Tyler, 2006). As we have seen, this era simultaneously saw the constriction of asylum welfare and support and the expansion of visa controls and offshore processing, underhandedly reducing the possibility of seeking asylum in the United Kingdom and increasing the potential for illegalisation. While this was highly public, based on populist assumptions around asylum and welfare and riding on increasingly xeno-racist sentiments (Fekete, 2005), quite a bit of behind the scenes work was done ever so silently: the gradual expansion of profitable border controls, increases in immigration detention, and the erosion of rights and liberties that might otherwise gain widespread criticism or resistance.

For some time then, out of sight has been out of mind. However, this frame of mind has been rapidly changing. Throughout the course of this research and particularly in the past few years, the public sphere has been increasingly perforated by dissenting voices challenging otherwise dominant assumptions around immigration. Some of this is rightly received with scepticism, for example when political commentators or news media advocate numbered allowances for specific social groups rather than sustained acceptance of refugees (for example 20,000 Syrian refugees by 2020 – see Wintour, 2015). Of course these would be welcome advances, but we are at a crossroads between real and sustained resistance to the harms of borders, and accepting once again discourses of the deserving and undeserving refugee. The above examples, two of many, have the propensity to negatively affect refugees from other regions, including those from countries with the highest levels of asylum applications in Britain and the UK generally. It also affects refugee men who are increasingly demonised as illegal, criminal and even dangerous (Bhatia, 2014).

However, for the first time that I can recall, it is not only the most controversial elements of the asylum system which have drawn sustained public criticism recently – such as death during deportation, or the detention of pregnant women – but aspects which had previously, deliberately been silenced. This has included public protests at Immigration Removal Centres, encompassing numerous days of action across the UK and Europe which have seen thousands of people travel hundreds of miles (such is the spatial isolation of IRCs) to voice their criticism and show their solidarity with detainees (Figure C.1, below). Organisations that have been supporting illegalised immigrants and people seeking asylum, or challenging certain aspects of the asylum system for many years have become more and more prominent in wider areas of media than before, increasing their visibility in public consciousness. Right to Remain, (formerly National Coalition of Anti-Deportation Campaigns, established 1995), the Unity Centre in Glasgow (established in 2005) and other members of the No Borders network, even localised organisations such as Asylum Link in Merseyside have become increasingly well recognised and their objectives picked up upon across wider networks and campaigns, including prison abolitionist networks and even religious groups. By all accounts, the increased visibility afforded by social media no doubt has its role in this unsilencing, but so does the political tide of resistance which has grown in the face of complicacy, complacency and the recognition of harms that people face in Britain's asylum system.

Figure C.1 'Shut Down Yarl's Wood' protest, 2016.

Resistance from within[3]

As with many social movements, including anti-violence movements and Rape Crisis movements, much of this resistance has developed autonomously and from within. In the context of Australian detention for example, Grewcock argues that despite the 'government's deliberate strategy of physically isolating refugees ... the social isolation is not total and the detainees' humanity is not completely destroyed' (2013: 63). Although the spatial isolation of which he speaks is markedly different from the British context, the underlying argument is the same: isolation is not absolute. People seeking asylum who are in or out of detention face multiple layers of isolation and exclusion but autonomous acts of resistance have always played out in and out of the gaze of the public eye, and not only in the recent surge of pro-refugee campaigns. Some have ranged from physical protests, such as multiple hunger strikes, including in 2015 in IRC Harmondsworth that spread to IRC Moreton Hall (see Green, 2015), and periodic strikes in Yarl's Wood over the past 15 years. Yarl's Wood has seen many other eras of unrest and resistance and dissent, which included being set on fire shortly after opening in protest to the maltreatment of a fellow detainee. Other acts of resistance include petitions for individuals to be granted asylum or for structural reform, and the forming of protective barriers between deportees and Border Force or immigration officers. Some have been less public and more sustained, such as campaigning against conditions in IRCs, and localised campaigns regarding inadequate housing in parts of Britain (including Liverpool, Glasgow, Manchester, Sheffield and Leeds, all of which are dispersal areas).

Furthermore, and as argued elsewhere in relation to sexual violence in detention:

> Survivors of sexual violence are often faced with a wall of silence, be it through social stigma, shame, or fear of reporting. Add to this a perpetrator who has the power to detain, restrain, search or report you, who can exploit a fear of forced return to the country you have fled and you have what some women seeking sanctuary have been made to face.'
>
> (Canning, 2014b: 11)

Yet even in the face of this, *women have still spoken out.* Many women speak out against their own subjections to violence, as Hawwi and others have done, but also against violence so that their counterparts might not face sexual or domestic violence elsewhere. Organisations such as Southall Black Sisters, Women Asylum Seekers Together (WAST) and Merseyside Refugee and Asylum Seekers Pre and Post Natal Support Group (MRANG) have spoken, protested and written their criticisms of a system which facilitates vulnerability to exploitation, which curbs women's capacities to leave violent relationships, and which undermines the impacts of previous violences that women disproportionately experience prior to and during migration. In the face of expanding controls, such levels of grassroot organising probably face more threats – political and financial – than ever before but they continue, they challenge, they grow and they *resist.*

Everyday survival as resistance

In any case, responding to singular aspects of the process of seeking asylum as problematic and in need of change is important in the short term. However, the all-encompassing nature of asylum through destitution, temporal limbo, and the harms discussed in Chapters 3 and 4, all require sustained and systematic resistance to ensure the rights, long-term wellbeing and liberties of women, men and children seeking asylum. Short-term responses are limiting, an issue that is made difficult by the current funding structures in place which short-sightedly incur inadequate provisions from state sources.

This brings me then to the forms of resistance that have been the backbone to the women and organisations I have worked with over the past decade. To echo the sentiments of Stanley and McCulloch:

> we argue that it [resistance] should include assertive or creative acts … Resistance can be about *becoming* or *creating* something – it may produce alternatives for harmful products or processes … it may reinvigorate traditions or reaffirm values, such as cultural identity, integrity or sense of self; it can invoke a competing claim of universalism or attempt to set the boundaries of a 'viable' or 'liveable' life.
>
> (Stanley and McCulloch, 2013: 5)

They are speaking specifically of resistance to state crime, but I argue that the same aspects resonate with resisting harm, power and structural or patriarchal violence. For the duration of this research, I have witnessed incredible acts of solidarity that have supported the wellbeing and survival of women and men seeking asylum. A weekly Muslim women's group at a Mosque which gave food collections to other women who were awaiting asylum or the outcome of an asylum appeal; daily foodbanks at an asylum support organisation which did everything it could to ensure people were not malnourished; birthing partners among refugee and non-refugee women so that single pregnant women did not have to face childbirth alone in an unfamiliar country; a woman giving up her own bed so another could sleep in it with her two daughters when Section Four funds did not come through in time from the Home Office; petitions – some successful, others not – to stop the deportation of friends and fellow activists; group phonecalls on loudspeaker to women in detention so they did not feel isolated or forgotten; cookathons to raise legal funds for a member of a mutual aid group who could not afford to have a report produced to documents the prevalence of gendered violence in her country of origin. As with Weber's arguments around non-compliance among custody officers (2005), various forms of support that facilitate survival come from the outside. Health visitors who make sure to prescribe the same standard of vitamins or creams that they would for themselves over cheaper and less effective counterparts; lawyers who spend more and more of their spare time on cases for which they are not paid but that they take on out of a sense of moral obligation – all of these points are creative and facilitate survival. This is not simply a list of good deeds: it is the recording of acts of solidarity and resistance among autonomous groups and in the face of poverty, destitution and imminent uncertainty on their own behalf. For some, just being here and surviving is an indicator of resistance.[4] As Grewcock said, 'humanity is not completely destroyed', and nor can it be (2013: 63).

Addressing state harm: the value and limits of human rights

Similar can be said within more formal spheres, and in particular in some areas of legal practice. The multiple legal challenges discussed throughout have drawn together activist groups with legal practitioners and concerned or dissenting politicians to challenge aspects of immigration detention and welfare. Although not all challenges are successful, marked legal shifts include the introduction of a 72-hour time limit for the detention of pregnant women and the inclusion of automatic judicial oversight in cases of immigration detention in the Immigration Act 2016. The challenges in this act will be addressed later, but these remain positive and substantial gains for women affected by these issues.

Law and criminology have highly administrative histories and for some critical criminologists and postmodern feminists the propensity to resort to law or aspects of criminal justice means embedding elitist state practices in otherwise critical forums (Smart, 1990; Hillyard and Tombs, 2004). This can promote an assumption that the state and agencies affiliated with the state have democratic accountability or indeed the best interests of civilians at heart, which is certainly not always the case. These assumptions have been contested throughout this book with regard to everyday wellbeing; sexual violence support; asylum decision making; and the rights of refugees – which are regularly compromised. Human rights in particular can be critiqued as individualistic in essence, since cases are often taken singularly to challenge legal decisions.

From my own activist perspective, the concept of civil liberties is vital to resistance movements, to acknowledge that the system as it stands is consuming, confining and harmful, and that it erodes *collective* civil liberties which should be afforded to people generally, and to those seeking sanctuary from persecution specifically. However, as Pantazis and Pemberton argue:

> the human rights framework has directly challenged the encroachment of individual liberty by the state by invoking human rights norms and instruments. These have been mobilized and have formed critical sites of resistance for a diverse range of actors, including politicians, judges and non-governmental organisations.

(2013: 115)

Indeed, as earlier chapters show, the Human Rights Act, Joint Committee on Human Rights and European Court of Human Rights have allowed for appeals and the over-turning of decisions in many asylum and immigration cases. It is perhaps for this reason that multiple state representatives, particularly the Prime Minister, have argued for a 'British Bill of Rights' to replace the 'red tape bureaucracy' that has been fundamental to contesting and resisting the debasement of asylum seekers rights. It is thus also a likely contributor to reducing the rights under which asylum seekers can appeal their decision, to have influenced the 'deport now, appeal later' action facilitated by the Immigration Act 2014 and extended in the Immigration Act 2016. Although clearly a negative progression and one with serious consequences, as discussed in the previous chapters, it is also arguably an indicator that *legal resistance in relation to human rights has been working.* To counteract the successes identified by Pantazis and Pemberton (2013), the ever-shifting state (Fletcher, 2015) has tightened its legal grip. I view this, perhaps optimistically, as an indicator of state power being challenged and 'power needs no justification, as it is inherent in the very existence of political communities; what, however, it does need is legitimacy' (Arendt, 1969: 31). Perhaps these changes indicate that certain aspects of the asylum system have lost their legitimacy.

Embedding rights and wellbeing through practice and collectivity

One key focus of this book has been on gendered violence, and I have highlighted that gaps in consciousness are embedded in state and organisational responses to refugees with regard to sexual violence, domestic abuse, and ongoing gendered violences in the asylum system. These are substantive issues that often seem secondary to first responses, but are integral to ensuring the wellbeing of women and men who are faced with structural challenges throughout the whole of the asylum process. In some cases, this requires recognition and consciousness. For example, Chapters 5 and 6 in particular emphasised that the consequences of historic or ongoing abuses can be severe and prolonged – lifelong for some survivors. They are also disproportionately experienced by women, thus requiring gendered consideration for support.

As Wonders and Danner argue, 'many harms against women can be viewed as political crimes, predominantly characterised by failing to protect women's basic human rights' (2006: 54). From a rights perspective, this means adhering to gendered conventions and guidelines in asylum review, but also going beyond the reactive to be proactive, for example in offering a female caseworker and interpreter, or ensuring adequate childcare for initial and substantive interview. By gendered, I do not mean blanket segregation across networks or service providers, but simply a recognition of *disproportionality in subjection to gendered and interpersonal violence* when responding to groups seeking asylum. This therefore also means provision of space for intersectional identities where men, queer people or transgender women and men, and lesbian, gay or bisexual people can also feel enabled to engage in support free from stigmatisation or social exclusion. Much of this can be portrayed as peripheral, particularly in the aftermath of structurally violent austerity measures, as this research shows, is not only necessary for the wellbeing of individuals but also strengthens the value and dynamicy of networks and organisations working to support survivors of violence and persecution in all areas. This also means that organisations working to support survivors or end violence do not see asylum and immigration as an add-on, but as *part of what they do*.

As outlined in Chapter 6, one key barrier to support provision or collective organisation lies in funding provision. While expenditure for counter-terrorism[5] and border securitisation has proliferated throughout the duration of this research, domestic violence refuges and non-state affiliated rape support organisations have depleted. For Black and Minority Ethnic women, the impact of cuts have been even more severe, since there were disproportionately fewer support resources to begin with (James and Patiniotis, 2013). The current climate in restricting borders and reducing rights to asylum, paired with violent austerity measures (Cooper and Whyte, 2017), even further reduces the opportunity to support survivors of violence and persecution. As such, the significance of funding cannot be undermined. However, this research not only attests to the importance of financial sustainability, but for governmental and non-governmental organisations to address gaps in consciousness with regard to intersectional differences and multiple oppressions: to recognise that varying forms of support are required for different people, that women's and men's subjections to violence – and the impacts thereof – are not necessarily the same, and that homophobic and transphobic ideologies persist within and across cultures in ways that require further barriers to be broken down and autonomous spaces to be created. One shoe does not fit all with regard to responding to refugee groups or survivors of violence generally, and these differences require serious consideration and positive reformation.

Resistance and survival, come what may

> When the Immigration Act comes into force, many people's lives will be a lot worse, and we need to evidence this, challenge it, and work to overturn these measures.
>
> (Matthews, 2016)

Having emphasised some of the successes of resistance movements and collective legal and social action, it is fundamentally important that this wave of resistance is not allowed to ride away or silence other aspects of refugee lives. The barriers in place to supporting the wellbeing of women seeking asylum, and the harms highlighted throughout this book, will almost inevitably be amplified by forthcoming challenges. The most obvious of these is in entering a period of intense uncertainty in relation to Britain's decision to leave the European Union in June 2016. How or when this might be completed is unknown, which means that forthcoming policy or legislative change is unforeseeable. However, considering that much of the propaganda developed by the political right in the 'Leave' campaign was based on fears around immigration and the ongoing refugee crisis, and since most of the claims were not effectively countered by the 'Remain' campaign, it is fair to anticipate further stringent measures being placed around Britain's borders.

Additionally, as Right to Remain indicate above, recent legal shifts in immigration law, namely the Immigration Act 2016, are geared towards making life harder for people seeking asylum. The cementing of the 'deport now, appeal later' agenda has potential to affect survivors of sexual violence or torture who have not disclosed persecution or abuse and whose claims are initially rejected, and this group is predominantly women. Further recent restrictions to welfare, reductions in funding for refuges and sexual violence support, and legal aid cuts will no doubt complicate the process of seeking asylum with further negative effects.

In post-EU Referendum Britain, the campaign focus placed on immigration, is likely to place further exclusionary barriers to people seeking asylum. Drawing from Webber (2016) earlier allows for another key recognition: that this is not only an era of immigration demonisation, but of counter-collective support for the rights of refugees, people seeking asylum and economic migrants. Likewise, the increased legal and Parliamentary challenges to a number of key legislative decisions, including cases against the Home Office, are a reminder of these fundamental shifts in collective consciousness. They also serve to remind us that states are not monolithic – they are made of diverse actors, are highly complicated and in some areas even fractured and it is within these fractures that seeds of resistance have increasingly grown.

Stemming back to Mathiesen's arguments on silencing (2004), there is a very real risk of further co-option and superficial endorsement as organisations and individuals struggle to support people seeking asylum. The depletion in rights and welfare with simultaneous increases in detention mean that superficial improvements – often on the back of independent reviews – provide a lifeline to specific groups, such as pregnant women in detention or people who fall into the quota of specified refugee numbers to be accepted by the British state. Improvement and change is always welcome, but to these we are required to stay focussed on the value of individuals' rights within the context of broader collective civil liberties. Surface-level support will not reduce the plethora of social and gendered harms outlined throughout this book, but sustained collective social and legal action can, as we have seen.

This brings me full circle, to draw back to encouraging recognition of intersectional continuums of violence in many women's lives, and to address the impacts of such violence among survivors seeking sanctuary. As pointed out in Chapters 5 and 6, formal and informal support can range between participation in friendship groups or collective action, to counselling or psychotherapy. Importantly, the needs of the individual should be central, not peripheral, to support agendas and for this to be the case, there are two key requirements: sustainable funding for support provision, and organisational consciousness of the intersectional oppressions women seeking asylum face. Each facilitates implementation of the specific needs of asylum populations into policy and practice, from the provision of gendered space, to adequate interpretation, or the recognition of social silencing in relation to gendered harms. Government and state/corporate agendas to increase punitive responses to people seeking asylum reduce these, but wholesale eradication of these requirements is impossible in the face of sustained resistance from autonomous migrants groups, critical legal practitioners, academics and non-governmental service providers. The multiple oppressions some women face and survive in the domestic sphere, within relationships, in conflict, during migration and in seeking asylum are utterly profound; surely a minimum obligation is the enabling of survival through sanctuary, without the infliction of further harm.

Notes

1 To give an example of this, I have been involved in a mutual aid choir since 2013. For this, migrant women meet every week and rehearse songs in various languages. As someone who is perhaps more academically than artistically minded, this initially seemed an apolitical exercise. After being involved for some years, I now see the opposite is true – weekly meetings draw women together in ways that build lasting relationships and political networks. Singing in public has offered different opportunities to draw audiences that academic events cannot, with members of the public coming to ask more about the group and about the challenges of the asylum system. It is also a way for women to come together beyond traditional or more formal support frameworks, facilitating ways for women to discuss everything from Home Office decision appeals to finding a dentist, thus developing autonomously effecting resistance.

2 This term draws from Elisabeth Noelle-Neumann's phrase from a 1974 article. This was subsequently developed by Thomas Mathiesen in the context of his 'silent silencing' arguments (2004: 103–108).

3 The Institute of Race Relations have developed a 'Calendar of Resistance' which documents various acts across the United Kingdom which can be followed on their news services here: www.irr.org.uk/news/, last accessed 05/12/2016.

4 Thanks to Bree Carlton and Jude McCulloch for highlighting this in a seminar I gave at Monash University in 2015. At the time my exasperation at the asylum system had left me overlooking this simple but integral point.

5 For example, former Chancellor George Osbourne (2010–2016) dedicated £15.1 billion to counter-terrorism efforts in 2015, even though there were zero deaths in Britain related to terrorism in this year.

Bibliography

Aas, K. F. and Bosworth, M. (2013), *The Borders of Punishment: Migration, Citizenship and Social Exclusion*, Oxford: Oxford University Press.

Ackerman, S. (2015), *Drone Strikes by UK and Pakistan Point to Obama's Counter-Terror Legacy*, The Guardian, available at: www.theguardian.com/us-news/2015/sep/09/obama-drone-strikes-counterterror-uk-pakistan, last accessed 06/04/2016.

Ackerman, S. (2016), *US Says Airstrikes on Syrian City Manbij to Continue Despite Civilian Deaths*, The Guardian, 22 July 2016.

Agamben, G. (1998), *Homo Sacer: Sovereign Power and Bare Life*, Stanford, CA: Stanford University Press.

Ahrens, C. E. (2006), *Being Silenced: The Impact of Negative Social Reactions on the Disclosure of Rape*, American Journal of Community Psychology, Vol. 38, No. 3–4: 263–274.

Alemu, B. and Mengitsu, A. (2009), *Women's Empowerment in Ethiopia: New Solutions to Ancient Problems*, available at: www.pathfinder.org/publications-tools/pdfs/Womens-Empowerment-in-Ethiopia-New-Solutions-to-Ancient-Problems.pdf, last accessed 10/06/2016.

Ali, H. C., Querton, C. and Solard, E. (2012), *Gender Related Asylum Claims in Europe*, Brussels: Director-General for Internal Policies, European Parliament.

Aliverti, A. (2012), *Making People Criminal: the Role of the Criminal Law in Immigration Enforcement*, Theoretical Criminology, Vol. 16, No. 4: 417–434.

Aliverti, A. (2013), *Sentencing in Immigration-Related Cases: The Impact of Deportability and Immigration Status*, Prison Service Journal, Vol. 205: 39–44.

Aliverti, A. (2015), *Criminal Immigration Law and Human Rights in Europe*, in Pickering, S. And Ham, J. (eds.), The Routledge Handbook on Crime and International Migration, Oxford: Routledge.

Allen, K. (2010), *Rape in Iran's Prisons: the Cruellest Torture*, The Telegraph, 1 November 2010.

Allnock, D., Hynes, P. and Archibald, M. (2015), *Self-Reported Experiences of Therapy Following Child Sexual Abuse: Messages from a Retrospective Survey of Adult Survivors*, Journal of Social Work, Vol. 15. No. 2: 114–137.

Allsopp, J., Sigona, N. and Phillimore, J. (2014), *Poverty Among Refugees and Asylum Seekers in the UK*, IRIS Working Paper Series No. 1.

Amnesty International (1997), *Refugees: Human Rights Have No Borders*, London: Amnesty International.

Amnesty International (2010), *Dangerous Deals: Europe's Reliance on 'Diplomatic Assurances' Against Torture*, London: Amnesty International.

Amnesty International (2015), *World Leaders' Neglect of Refugees Condemns Millions to Death and Despair*, available at: www.amnesty.org/en/latest/news/2015/06/world-leaders-neglect-of-refugees-condemns-millions-to-death-and-despair/, last accessed 21/06/2016.

Amnesty International (2016a), *Female Refugees Face Physical Assault, Exploitation and Sexual Harassment on their Journeys through Europe*, available at: www.amnesty. org/en/latest/news/2016/01/female-refugees-face-physical-assault-exploitation-and-sexual-harassment-on-their-journey-through-europe/, last accessed 07/04/2016.

Amnesty International (2016b), *Turkey: Illegal Mass Returns of Syrian Refugees Expose Fatal Flaws in EU-Turkey Deal*, available at: www.amnesty.org/en/press-releases/2016/04/turkey-illegal-mass-returns-of-syrian-refugees-expose-fatal-flaws-in-eu-turkey-deal/, last accessed 21/06/2016.

Amnesty International and Southall Black Sisters (2008), *'No Recourse' No Safety*, London: Amnesty International.

Amos, V. and Parmar, P. (1984), *Challenging Imperial Feminism* in Bhavnani, K. (2001), Feminism and 'Race', Oxford: Oxford University Press.

Anderson, B. (1991), *Imagined Communities: Reflections on the Origins and Spread of Nationalism*, London: Verso.

Andersson, R. (2014), *Illegality INC.: Clandestine Migration and the Business of Bordering Europe*, California: University of California Press.

Annan, K. (2005), *A Comprehensive Strategy to Eliminate Future Sexual Exploitation and Abuse in United Nations Peacekeeping Operations*, available at: https://cdu.unlb. org/Portals/0/Documents/KeyDoc5.pdf, last accessed 20/06/2016.

Anthias, F. and Yuval-Davis, N. (1983), *Contextualising Feminism: Gender, Ethnic and Class Division*, Feminist Review, Vol. 15: 62–75.

Anthias, F. and Yuval-Davis, N. (1989), *Women-Nation-State*, New York: St. Martin's Press.

Arcel, L. T. (2003), *Introduction*, in Arcel, L.T., Popovic, S., Kucukalic, A., and Bravo-Mehmedbasic, A. (eds.), Treatment of Torture and Trauma Survivors in a Post-War Society, Sarajevo: Association for Rehabilitation of Torture Victims.

Arendt, H. (1969), *Reflections on Violence*, in Besteman, C. (2002), Violence: a Reader, Basingstoke: Palgrave MacMillan.

Arieff, A. (2009), *Sexual Violence in African Conflicts*, US: Congressional Research Service.

Askin, K. D. (1997), *War Crimes Against Women: Prosecution in International War Crimes Tribunals*, The Hague: Kluwer Law International.

Asociación EXIL and Comissió Catalana d'Ajuda al Refugiat (2016), *Good Practices with Victims of Torture*, Barcelona: European Union.

Asylum Aid (2011), *Unsustainable: The Quality of Initial Decision Making in Women's Asylum Claims*, London: Asylum Aid.

Asylum Aid (2016), *Refugee Charities Point out Double Standards for Survivors as Lords Report on Sexual Violence in Conflict*, available at: www.asylumaid.org.uk/press-release-refugee-charities-point-double-standards-survivors-lords-report-sexual-violence-conflict/, last accessed 23/06/2016.

Athwal, H. (2014), *Deaths in Immigration Detention, 1989–2014*, Institute of Race Relations News, available at: www.irr.org.uk/news/deaths-in-immigration-detention-1989-2014/, last accessed 17/05/2016.

Atkinson, R. (1998), *The Life Story Interview*, London: Sage.

Bacon, C. (2005), *The Evolution of Immigration Detention in the UK: The Involvement of Private Prison Companies*, Refugee Studies Centre Working Paper No. 27, Oxford University.

Baker, J. and Rytter, T. (2014), *Conditions for Women in Detention: Needs, Vulnerabilities and Good Practice*, Copenhagen: Danish Institute Against Torture.

Ballinger, A. (2009), *Gender, Power and the State: Same as it Ever Was?* in Coleman, R., Sim, J., Tombs, S. and Whyte, D. (eds.), State, Power, Crime, London: Sage.

Bastia, T. (2014), *Intersectionality, Migration and Development*, Progress in Development Studies, Vol. 14, No. 3: 237–248.

Bastick, M., Grimm, K. and Kunz, R. (2007), *Sexual Violence in Armed Conflict: Global Overview and Implications for the Security Sector*, Geneva: Geneva Centre for the Democratic Control of Armed Forces.

Bates, L. (2014), *Everyday Sexism …*, London: Simon and Schuster Ltd.

Bauman, Z. (1998), *Globalisation: The Human Consequences*, New York: Columbia University Press.

Bauman, Z. (2000), *Liquid Modernity*, Cambridge: Polity Press.

BBC (2011), *Theresa May Under Fire for Cat Claim*, BBC News, available at: www.bbc.co.uk/news/uk-politics-15160326, last accessed 06/01/2016.

BBC (2013), *Staff Fired After Sex with Detainee at Yarl's Wood Immigration Centre*, available at: www.bbc.co.uk/news/uk-england-beds-bucks-herts-24719300, last accessed 05/12/2016.

BBC (2015a), *Asylum Appeal Fast-Track System Unlawful, Says Court of Appeal*, available at: www.bbc.co.uk/news/uk-33704163, last accessed 06/01/2016.

BBC (2015b), *Liverpool Mayor Criticises 'Asylum Apartheid'*, BBC News available at: www.bbc.co.uk/news/uk-england-merseyside-31353963, last accessed 05/01/2016.

Becker, H. (1967), *Whose Side Are We On*, Social Problems, Vol. 14, No. 3: 239–247.

Berry, M., Garcia-Blanco, I. and Moore, K. (2015), *Press Coverage of the Refugee and Migrant Crisis in the EU: A Content Analysis of Five European Countries*, UNHCR Report, available at: www.unhcr.org/56bb369c9.html, last accessed 10/04/2016.

Bennett, C. (2008), *Relocation, Relocation: The Impact of Internal Relocation on Women Asylum Seekers*, London: Asylum Aid.

Besteman, C. (2002), *Violence: A Reader*, Basingstoke: Palgrave MacMillan.

Bhatia, M. (2014), *Creating and Managing 'Mad', 'Bad' and 'Dangerous': The Role of the Immigration System* in Canning, V. (ed.), Sites of Confinement: Prisons, Punishment and Detention Weston-Super-Mare: European Group for the Study of Deviance and Social Control.

Bhatia, M. (2015), *Turning Asylum Seekers into 'Dangerous Criminals': Experiences of the Criminal Justice System of those Seeking Sanctuary*, International Journal for Crime, Justice and Social Democracy, Vol. 4, No. 3: 97–111.

Bhatia, M. and Canning, V. (2016), *Immigration Detention: a Tale of Two Reviews*, The Institute of Race Relations, available at: www.irr.org.uk/news/immigration-detention-a-tale-of-two-reviews/, last accessed 08/06/2016.

Blinder, S. (2015), *Deportations, Removals and Voluntary Departures from the UK*, available at: www.migrationobservatory.ox.ac.uk/sites/files/migobs/Briefing-Deportations.pdf, last accessed 05/04/2016.

Blinder, S. and Betts, A. (2016), *Deportations, Removals and Voluntary Departures from the UK*, available at: www.migrationobservatory.ox.ac.uk/resources/briefings/deportations-removals-and-voluntary-departures-from-the-uk/, last accessed 05/12/2016.

Blinder, S. and McNeil, R. (2016), *Migration to the UK: Asylum*, available at: http://migrationobservatory.ox.ac.uk/briefings/migration-uk-asylum, last accessed 29/07/2016.

Bloch, A., Galvin, T. and Harrell-Bond, B. (2000), *Refugee Women in Europe: Some Aspects of the Legal and Policy Dimension*, Vol. 38, No. 2: 169–188.

Bloch, A. and Schuster, L. (2002), *Asylum and Welfare: Contemporary Debates*, Critical Social Policy, Vol. 22, No. 3: 393–414.

Bloch, A. and Schuster, L. (2005a), *Asylum Policy under New Labour*, Benefits, Vol. 13, No. 2: 115–118.

Bloch, A. and Schuster, L. (2005b), *At the Extremes of Exclusion: Deportation, Detention and Dispersal*, Ethnic and Racial Studies, Vol. 28, No.3: 491–512.

Bögner, D., Brewin, C. and Herlihy, J. (2010), *Refugees' Experiences of Home Office Interviews: A Qualitative Study on the Disclosure of Sensitive Personal Information*, Journal of Ethnic Migration Studies, Vol. 36, No. 3: 519–535.

Boffey, D. (2016), *Five Cabinet Ministers' Constituencies 'Least Hit by Council Budget Cuts'*, The Observer, 24 April 2016.

Bosworth, M. (2008), *Border Control and the Limits of the Sovereign State*, Social Legal Studies, Vol. 17, No. 2: 199–215.

Bosworth, M. (2014), *Inside Immigration Detention*, Oxford: Oxford University Press.

Bosworth, M. (2015), *Border Criminologies*, available at: http://britsoccrim.org/new/sites/default/files/Bosworth2015.pdf, last accessed 05/01/2016.

Bosworth, M. and Guild, M. (2008), *Governing Through Migration Control: Security and Citizenship in Britain*, British Journal of Criminology, Vol. 48, No. 6: 703–719.

Bosworth, M. and Turnbull, S. (2015), *Immigration Detention, Punishment and the Criminalisation of Migration*, in Pickering, S. And Ham, J. (eds.), The Routledge Handbook on Crime and International Migration, Oxford: Routledge.

Bourke, J. (2007), *Rape: A History from 1869 – Present*, London: Virago.

Bowcott, O. (2014), *Asylum Seeker Subsistence Payments Defeat for Government in High-Court*, The Guardian, available at: www.theguardian.com/politics/2014/apr/09/asylum-seeker-subsistence-payments-defeat-government-theresa-may, last accessed 24/02/2016.

Bowling, B. and Sheptycki, J. (2015), *Global Policing, Mobility and Social Control*, in Pickering, S. And Ham, J. (eds.), The Routledge Handbook on Crime and International Migration, Oxford: Routledge.

Box, S. (1983), *Power, Crime and Mystification*, London: Tavistock.

Brindle, D. (2015), *NHS Cannot Take More Cuts to Social Care, Say Healthcare Leaders*, The Guardian, 2 June 2015.

Briscoe, L. and Lavender, T. (2009), *Exploring Maternity Care for Asylum Seekers and Refugees*, British Journal of Midwifery, Vol. 17, No. 1: 17–23.

British Red Cross (2015), *Not So Straight-forward: the Need for Qualified Legal Support in Refugee Family Reunion*, available at: www.redcross.org.uk/~/media/BritishRedCross/Documents/About%20us/Not%20so%20straightforward%20refugee%20family%20reunion%20report%202015.pdf, last accessed 07/04/2016.

Brooks-Pollock, T. (2015), *Nauru: Guards at Australian-run detention camp 'filmed themselves getting sexual favours from Refugees*, The Independent, 20 June 2015.

Brownmiller, S. (1975), *Against Our Will: Men, Women and Rape*, Harmondsworth: Penguin.

Burnett, J. (2009), *Racism and the State: Authoritarianism and Coercion*, in Coleman, R., Sim, J., Tombs, S. and Whyte, D. (eds.), State, Power, Crime, London: Sage.

Burnett, J., Carter, J., Evershed, J., Bell Kohli, M., Powell, C. and de Wilde, G. (2010), *State Sponsored Cruelty: Children in Immigration Detention*, London: Medical Justice.

Burnett, A. and Peel, M. (2001), *Health Needs of Asylum Seekers and Refugees*, British Medical Journal, Vol. 322: 544–547.

Burnett, J. and Whyte, D. (2010), *The Wages of Fear: Risk, Safety and Undocumented Work*, Leeds: PAFRAS.

Butler, J. (2004), *Precarious Life: The Powers of Mourning and Violence*, London: Verso.

Butler, J. (2009), *Frames of War: When is Life Grievable?* London: Verso.

Butler, P. (2015), *Thousands have Died After Being Found Fit to Work, DWP Figures Show*, The Guardian, 27 August 2015.

Bywaters, P., Ali, Z., Fazil, Q., Wallace, M. and Singh, G. (2003*), Attitudes towards Disability amongst Pakistani and Bangladeshi Parents of Disabled Children in the UK: Considerations for Service Providers and the Disability Movement*, Health and Social Care in the Community, Vol. 11, No. 6, pp. 502–509.

Cain, M. and Howe, A. (2008), *Women, Crime and Social Harm: Towards a Criminology for the Global Era*, Oxford and Portland: Hart Publishing.

Caldwell, R. A. (2012), *Fallgirls: Gender and the Framing of Torture at Abu Ghraib*, Farnham: Ashgate.

Cameron, D. (2013), *David Cameron's immigration speech* available at: www.gov.uk/ government/speeches/david-camerons-immigration-speech, last accessed 08/01/2016.

Cancian, F. M. (1993), *Conflicts between Activist Research and Academic Success: Participatory Research and Alternative Strategies*, The American Sociologist, Vol. 24, No. 1: 92–106.

Canning, V. (2010), *Who's Human? Developing Sociological Understandings of the Rights of Women Raped in Conflict*, International Journal of Human Rights, Vol. 14, Nos. 6–7: 847–862.

Canning, V. (2011a), *Transcending Conflict: Exploring Sexual Violence Support for Women Seeking Asylum in Merseyside*, LJMU PhD, December 2011.

Canning, V. (2011b), *Women Seeking Sanctuary: Questioning State Responses to Violence against Women in the Asylum System*, Criminal Justice Matters, September 2011, Vol. 85: 29–30.

Canning, V. (2013), *Illusions of Freedom: The Paradox of Border Confinement*, Oxford University Border Criminologies, available at: http://bordercriminologies.law.ox.ac. uk/illusions-of-freedom/, last accessed 17/02/2014.

Canning, V. (2014a), *International Conflict, Sexual Violence and Asylum Policy: Merseyside as a Case Study*, Critical Social Policy, Vol. 34, No. 1: 23–45.

Canning, V. (2014b), *Women, Asylum and the Harms of Detention*, Criminal Justice Matters, December 2014, Vol. 98: 10–11.

Canning, V. (2015), *I Would Build... a Humane Asylum System*, in Allison, C. and McMahon, W. (eds.), Discussing Alternatives to Criminal Justice, London: Centre for Crime and Justice Studies.

Canning, V. (2016a), *Unsilencing Sexual Torture: Responses to Refugees and Asylum Seekers in Denmark*, British Journal of Criminology, Vol. 56, No. 3: 438–456.

Canning, V. (2016b), *The Criminalisation of Asylum*, available at: www.open.edu/ openlearn/people-politics-law/politics-policy-people/timeline-the-criminalisation-asylum, last accessed 29/07/2016.

Canning, V. and Bhatia, M. (2016), *Immigration Detention: What's the Problem with Privatisation?* Society Matters, available at: www.open.edu/openlearn/people-politics-law/immigration-detention-whats-the-problem-privatisation, last accessed 14/06/2016.

Carr, M. (2012), *Fortress Europe: Inside the War Against Immigration*, London: Hurst and Co.

Carroll, A. and Itaborahy, L. P. (2015), *State Sponsored Homophobia: A World Survey of Laws: Criminalisation, Protection and Recognition of Same-Sex Love*, available at: http://old.ilga.org/Statehomophobia/ILGA_State_Sponsored_Homophobia_2015. pdf, The International Lesbian, Gay, Bisexual, Trans and Intersex Association, last accessed 20/06/2016.

Chambliss, W. (1995), *Commentary*, Society for the Study of Social Problems, Vol. 26, No. 1: 9.

Channel 4 News (2014), *Is the UK Doing Enough for Gay Asylum Seekers?*, Channel 4, 28 March 2014.

Chase, S. E. (2008), *Narrative Inquiry: Multiple Lenses, Approaches, Voices*, in Denzin, N. K. and Lincoln, Y. S. (eds.), Collecting and Interpreting Qualitative Materials, London: Sage.

Chigwada-Bailey, R. (2004), *Black Women and the Criminal Justice System*, in McIvor, G. (ed.), Women Who Offend, London: Jessica Kingsley Publishers.

Christie, N. (2000), *Crime Control as Industry: Towards Gulags, Western Style*, London: Routledge.

Churchill, H. and Canning, V. (2011), *Maternity and Asylum: The Right to Maternal Healthcare in Merseyside*, British Sociological Association Annual Conference, April 2011, London School of Economics.

Cohen, S. (1985), *Visions of Social Control*, Cambridge: Polity Press.

Cohen, S. (2001), *States of Denial*, Cambridge: Polity.

Cohen, S. (1993), *Human Rights and Crimes of the State: The Culture of Denial, Australian and New Zealand Journal of Criminology*, Vol. 26, No, 2: 97–115.

Collier, B. (2007), *Country of Origin Information and Women: Researching Gender and Persecution in the Context of Asylum and Human Rights Claims*, London: Asylum Aid.

Convention on the Elimination of all forms of Discrimination Against Women (2014), *General Recommendation No. 32 on the Gendered Dimension of Refugee Status, Asylum, Nationality and Statelessness of Women*, available at: http://daccess-dds-ny.un. org/doc/UNDOC/GEN/N14/627/90/PDF/N1462790.pdf?OpenElement, last accessed 19/08/2015.

Connell, R.W. (1987), *Gender and Power*, Cambridge and Oxford: Polity Press.

Connelly, A. (2016), *Why is Europe Closing its Borders to Afghans?* Al Jazeera News, available at: www.aljazeera.com/indepth/features/2016/02/europe-closing-borders-afghans-160225151702251.html, last accessed 21/06/2016.

Coole, C. (2002), *A Warm Welcome? Scottish and UK Media Reporting of an Asylum Seeker Murder*, in Media, Culture and Society, Vol. 24, No. 6: 839–852.

Cooper, V. (2014), *Gendered Geographies of Punishment*, in V.Canning (ed.), Sites of Confinement: Prisons, Punishment and Detention, Weston-Super-Mare: European Group for the Study of Deviance and Social Control.

Cooper, V. (2015), *Austerity as Organised and Bureaucratised Violence*, Open Democracy, available at: www.opendemocracy.net/ourkingdom/vickie-cooper/ austerity-as-bureaucratized-and-organized-violence, last accessed 21/06/2016.

Cooper, V. and Whyte, D. (2017), *The Violence of Austerity*, London: Pluto Press.

Copelon, R. (1994), *Intimate Terror: Understanding Domestic Violence as Torture*, in Cook, R. (ed.), Human Rights of Women: National and International Perspectives, Pennsylvania: University of Pennsylvania Press.

Copelon, R. (2004), *Surfacing Gender: Reengraving Crimes Against Women in Humanitarian Law*, in Dombrowski, N. A. (ed.), Women and War in the Twentieth Century: Enlisted With or Without Consent, Oxford: Routledge.

Corporate Watch (2015), Harmonsworth Immigration Detention Centre, available at: https://corporatewatch.org/news/2015/mar/04/harmondsworth-immigration-detention-centre-secret-filming-mitie, last accessed 21/06/2016.

Couvée, K. (2013), *Deaths in British Police Custody: No Convictions Since 1969*, Open-Democracy available at: www.opendemocracy.net/opensecurity/deaths-in-british-police-custody-no-convicted-officers-since-1969, last accessed 12/04/2016.

Crack, A. M. (2013), *Language, Listening and Learning: Critically Reflective Accountability for INGOs*, International Review of Administrative Sciences, Vol. 79, No. 4: 809–828.

Crawley, H., Hemmings, J. and Price, N. (2011), *Coping with Destitution: Survival and Livelihood Strategies of Refused Asylum Seekers Living in the UK*, Oxfam Research Report, UK: Swansea University and Oxfam.

Crawley, H., Guemar, L. and Hintjens, H. (2011), *Thematic Review on the Coverage of Women in Country of Origin Information (COI), Reports*, Swansea and London: Swansea University: CMPR.

Crawley, H., Hemmings, J. and Price, N. (2011), *Coping with Destitution: Survival and Livelihood Strategies of Refused Asylum Seekers Living in the UK*, Swansea: Oxfam.

Crawley, H. and Sigona, N. (2016), *European Policy is Driving Refugees to More Dangerous Routes Across the Med*, The Conversation, available at: https://theconversation.com/european-policy-is-driving-refugees-to-more-dangerous-routes-across-the-med-56625, last accessed 16/05/2016.

Crenshaw K. (1989), *Demarginalizing the Intersection of Race and Sex: A Black Feminist Critique of Antidiscrimination Doctrine, Feminist Theory and Antiracist Politics*, 1989 University of Chicago Legal Forum, Issue 1: 139–167.

Crenshaw, K. (1991), *Mapping the Margins: Intersectionality, Identity Politics, and Violence Against Women of Color*, Stanford Law Review, Vol. 43, No. 6: 1241–1299.

Dauvergne, C. (2013), *The Troublesome Intersections of Refugee Law and Criminal Law*, in Aas, K. F. and Bosworth, M. (eds.), *The Borders of Punishment: Migration, Citizenship and Social Exclusion*, Oxford: Oxford University Press.

Demmers, J. (2012), *Theories of Violent Conflict*, Oxford: Routledge.

Denzin, N. K. (2008), *Emancipatory Discourses and the Ethics and Politics of Interpretation*, in Denzin, N. K. and Lincoln, Y. S. (eds.), Collecting and Interpreting Qualitative Materials, London: Sage.

Department for Communities and Local Government (2015), *2015 English Indices of Deprivation*, available at: www.gov.uk/government/uploads/system/uploads/attachment_data/file/465791/English_Indices_of_Deprivation_2015_-_Statistical_Release.pdf, last accessed 05/01/2015.

Detention Action (N.D.), *The Legal Challenge*, available at: http://detentionaction.org.uk/campaigns/end-the-fast-track-to-despair/legal-challenge, last accessed 25/04/2016.

Devessa, N., Kassaye, M., Demeke, B. and Taffa, N. (1998), *Magnitude, Type and Outcomes of Physical Violence Against Married Women in Butajira, Southern Ethiopia*, Ethiopia Medical Journal, Vol. 36, No. 2: 83–92.

Devlin, K. (2016), *Theresa May: I have Never Visited Asylum Seeker Accommodation*, Herald Scotland, available at: www.heraldscotland.com/news/14376625.Theresa_May__I_have_never_visited_asylum_seeker_accommodation/, last accessed 16/05/2016.

Dobash, R. and Dobash, R. E. (2004), *Women's Violence to Men in Intimate Relationships: Working on a Puzzle*, British Journal of Criminology, Vol. 44, No. 3: 324–349.

Dorling, D. (2008), *Prime Suspect: Murder in Britain*, in Dorling, D., Gordon, D., Hillyard, P., Pantazis, C., Pemberton, S. and Tombs, S. (eds), *Criminal Obsessions: Why Harm Matters More Than Crime*, London: Centre for Crime and Justice Studies.

Dorling, D. (2014), *Inequality and the 1%*, London: Verso.

Dorling, K., Girma, M. and Walter, N. (2012), *Refused: The Experiences of Women Denied Asylum in the UK*, London: Women for Refugee Women.

DIGNITY (2012), *Field Manual on Rehabilitation*, Copenhagen: Danish Institute Against Torture.

Duggan, O. (2014), *Asylum Seekers in Liverpool Forced into Dirty, Cramped and Dangerous Housing*, The Liverpool Echo, 16 March 2014.

Dumper, H. (2002), *Is it Safe Here? Refugee Women's Experiences in the UK*, available at: www.refugee-action.org.uk/assets/0000/5475/Is_It_Safe_Here_Report_2002_ Refugee_Action.pdf, last accessed 20/06/2016.

Edley, N. and Wetherall, M. (1995), *Men in Perspective: Practice, Power and Identity*, London: Harvester Wheatsheaf.

Elbe, S. (2002), *HIV/AIDS and the Changing Landscape of War in Africa*, International Security, Vol. 27, No. 2: 159–177.

European Commission (2016), *Country Responsible for Asylum Application (Dublin)*, available at: http://ec.europa.eu/dgs/home-affairs/what-we-do/policies/asylum/examination-of-applicants/index_en.htm, last accessed 29/07/2016.

Farmer, P. (1996), *On Suffering and Structural Violence: A View from Below*, Daedalus, Vol. 125, No. 1: 261–283.

Fekete, L. (2001), *The Emergence of Xeno-Racism*, Race & Class, Vol. 43, No. 23: 23–40.

Fekete, L. (2005), *The Deportation Machine: Europe, Asylum and Human Rights*, Race and Class, Vol. 47, No. 1: 64–78.

Fekete, L. (2015), *Another Deportation Death in Europe*, Institute of Race Relations, available at: www.irr.org.uk/news/another-deportation-death-in-europe/, last accessed 06/04/2016.

Finnegan, A. (2016), *Welfare Reform: Voices from the Voluntary Sector*, London: National Council for Voluntary Organisations.

Fisk, R. (2016), *When We Mourn the Passing of Prince But Not 500 Migrants, We Have to Ask: Have We Lost All Sense of Perspective?*, available at: www.independent.co.uk/voices/when-we-mourn-the-passing-of-prince-but-not-500-migrants-we-have-to-ask-have-we-lost-all-sense-of-a6997581.html, last accessed 23/06/2016.

Fitzpatrick, S., Bramley, G., Sosenko, F., Blenkinsopp, J., Johnsen, S., Littlewood, M., Netto, G. and Watts, B. (2016), *Destitution in the UK*, York: Joseph Rowntree Trust.

Fletcher, S. (2015), *The Occupy Movement Vs, Capitalist Realism: Seeking Extraordinary Transformations in Consciousness*, in Sollund, R. (ed.), Green Harms and Crimes: Critical Criminology in a Changing World, Hampshire: Palgrave MacMillan.

Flyvberg, B. (2006), *Five Misunderstandings About Case Study Research*, Qualitative Inquiry, Vol. 12, No. 2: 219–245.

Freedom from Torture (2009), *Justice Denied*, London: Freedom from Torture.

Freedom from Torture (2011), *Body of Evidence: Treatment of Medico-Legal Reports for Survivors of Torture in the UK Asylum Tribunal*, available at: www.freedomfromtorture. org/sites/default/files/documents/body-of-evidence.pdf, last accessed 23/02/2016.

Freedom from Torture (2013), *The Poverty Barrier: The Right to Rehabilitation for Torture Survivors in the UK*, available at: www.freedomfromtorture.org/sites/default/files/documents/Poverty%20report%20FINAL%20a4%20web.pdf, last accessed 31/03/2015.

Friedan, B. (1963), *The Feminine Mystique*, London: Gollancz.

G4S (2015), *Financial Statements*, available at: www.g4s.com/en/Investors/Financial%20 Statements/, last accessed 11/05/2016.

Galtung, J. (1969), *Violence, Peace, and Peace Research*, Journal of Peace Research, Vol. 6, No. 3: 167–191.

Gender Identity Issues in the Asylum Process (2011), available at: www.ukba.homeoffice. gov.uk/sitecontent/documents/policyandlaw/asylumpolicyinstructions/apis/ genderissueintheasylum.pdf?view=Binary, last accessed 20/10/2014.

Ghelani, S. (2014), *Government in the Dock: Destitution and Asylum in the UK*, Open Democracy, available at: www.opendemocracy.net/5050/sonal-ghelani/government-in-dock-destitution-and-asylum-in-uk, last accessed 24/02/2016.

Gibney, M. J. (2008), *Asylum and the Expansion of Deportation in the United Kingdom*, Government and Opposition, Vol. 42, Vol. 2: 146–167.

Gibney, M. J. (2013), *Deportation, Crime, and the Changing Character of Membership in the United Kingdom*, in Aas, K. F. and Bosworth, M. (eds.), The Borders of Punishment: Migration, Citizenship and Social Exclusion, Oxford: Oxford University Press.

Gilmore, J. (2010), *Policing Protest: An Authoritarian Consensus*, Criminal Justice Matters, Vol. 82, No. 1: 21–23.

Gilmore, J. (2012), *Criminalizing Dissent in the 'War on Terror': The British State's Reaction to the Gaza War Protests of 2008–2009*, in Poynting, S. and Morgan, G. (eds.), Global Islamophobia: Muslims and Moral Panic in the West, Farnham: Ashgate.

Gilmore, J., Jackson, W. and Monk, H. (2016), *Keep Moving: Report on the Barton Moss Community Protection Camp*, Liverpool: Centre for the Study of Crime, Criminalisation and Social Exclusion.

Gilroy, P. (1987), *There Ain't No Black in the Union Jack*, London: Routledge.

Girma, M., Radice, S., Tsangarides, N. and Walter, N. (2014), *Detained: Women Asylum Seekers Locked Up in the UK*, London: Women for Refugee Women.

Gladwell, C., Bowerman, E., Norman, B., Dickson, S. and Ghafoor, A. (2016), *After Return: Documenting the Experiences of Young People Being Forcibly Removed to Afghanistan*, London: Refugee Support Network.

Gouldner, A. (1968), *The Sociologist as Partisan*, in Gouldner, A., For Marx, London: Allen Lane.

Gov.uk (N.D.) *Global Summit to End Sexual Violence in Conflict*, available at: www.gov. uk/government/topical-events/sexual-violence-in-conflict, last accessed 05/12/2016.

Green, C. (2015), *Harmondsworth: Asylum Seekers' Hunger Strike Spreads to Second Centre*, The Independent, available at: www.independent.co.uk/news/uk/politics/ harmondsworth-asylum-seekers-hunger-strike-spreads-to-second-centre-10099111. html, last accessed 23/05/2016.

Green, P. and Ward, T. (2000), *State Crime, Human Rights and the Limits of Criminology*, Social Justice, Vol. 27, No. 1: 101–115.

Green, P. and Ward, T. (2004), *State Crime: Governments, Violence and Corruption*, London: Pluto Press.

Green, P. and Ward, T. (2009), *The Transformation of Violence in Iraq*, British Journal of Criminology, Vol. 49, No. 5: 609–627.

Green, P. and Ward, T. (2013), *Civil Society, Resistance and State Crime*, in Stanley, E. and McCulloch, J. (eds.), State Crime and Resistance, Oxford: Routledge.

Gregory, J. and Lees, S. (1999), *Policing Sexual Assault*, London: Routledge.

Grewcock, M. (2013), *The Great Escape: Refugees, Detention and Resistance*, in Stanley, E. And McCulloch, J. (eds.), State Crime and Resistance, Oxford: Routledge.

Grewcock, M. (2015), *Reinventing 'The Stain': Bad Character and Criminal Deportation in Contemporary Australia*, in Pickering, S. And Ham, J. (2015), The Routledge Handbook on Crime and International Migration, Oxford: Routledge.

Grierson, J. (2015), *Ex-BA Flight Attendant Sues G4S after Witnessing Death of Jimmy Mubenga*, The Guardian, 30 September 2015.

Grzanka, P. (2014), *Intersectionality: A Foundations and Frontiers Reader*, Colorado: Westview Press.

Harding, S. (1986), *The Science Question in Feminism*, Milton Keynes: Open University Press.

Harding, S. (1987), *Feminism and Methodology*, Milton Keynes: Open University Press.

Hardwick, N. (2013), *Detainees under Escort: Inspection of Escort and Removals to Nigeria and Ghana*, available at: www.justiceinspectorates.gov.uk/hmiprisons/wp-content/uploads/sites/4/2014/04/nigeria-ghana-escorts-2013-rps.pdf, last accessed 06/04/2016.

Harris, J. (2003), *'All Doors are Closed to Us': A Social Model Analysis of the Experiences of Disabled Refugees and Asylum Seekers in Britain*, Disability and Society, Vol. 18, No. 4: 395–410.

Herman, J. L. (1992), *Trauma and Recovery: From Domestic Abuse to Political Terror*, London: Pandora.

Hillyard, P. and Tombs, S. (2004), *Introduction*, in Hillyard, P., Tombs, S. and Gordon, D. (eds.), Beyond Criminology: Taking Harm Seriously, London: Pluto Press.

Hillyard, P. and Tombs, S. (2008), *Introduction*, in Dorling, D., Gordon, D., Hillyard, P., Pantazis, C., Pemberton, S. and Tombs, S. (eds), Criminal Obsessions: Why Harm Matters More Than Crime, London: Centre for Crime and Justice Studies.

Home Office (2010a), *Country of Origin Information Service*, available at: http://webarchive.nationalarchives.gov.uk/20101208171359/http:/rds.homeoffice.gov.uk/rds/country_reports.html, last accessed 05/12/2016.

Home Office (2010b), *Gender Issues in the Asylum Claim*, available at: www.gov.uk/government/uploads/system/uploads/attachment_data/file/257386/gender-issue-in-the-asylum.pdf, last accessed 23/06/2016.

Home Office (2011), *Immigration and Passports*, available at: www.homeoffice.gov.uk/passports-and-immigration/, last accessed 23/06/2016.

Home Office (2013), *Asylum Support Application Form*, available at: www.gov.uk/government/uploads/system/uploads/attachment_data/file/261498/asylumsupport-form.pdf, last accessed 24/02/2016.

Home Office (2015a), *National Statistics: Asylum*, available at: www.gov.uk/government/publications/immigration-statistics-april-to-june-2015/asylum#nationalities-applying-for-asylum, last accessed 17/02/2016.

Home Office (2015b), *Asylum Policy Instruction: Assessing Credibility and Refugee Status*, available at: www.gov.uk/government/uploads/system/uploads/attachment_data/file/397778/ASSESSING_CREDIBILITY_AND_REFUGEE_STATUS_V9_0.pdf, last accessed 03/05/2016.

hooks, b. (1981), *Ain't I a Woman*, Boston: South End Press.

hooks, b. (1984), *Black Women: Shaping Feminist Theory*, in Bhavnani, K. (2001) (ed.), Feminism and 'Race', Oxford: Oxford University Press.

hooks, B. (1990), *Postmodern Blackness*, Vol. 1, No. 1.

Hopkins, K. (2015), *Rescue Boats? I'd Use Gunships to Stop Migrants*, The Sun, 17 April 2015.

Human Rights Act, Article 8: Right to a Private and Family Life.

Human Rights Watch (1996), *Shattered Lives: Sexual Violence during the Rwandan Genocide and its Aftermath*, available at: www.hrw.org/report/1996/09/24/shattered-lives/sexual-violence-during-rwandan-genocide-and-its-aftermath, last accessed 16/06/2016.

Human Rights Watch (2004), *Struggling to Survive: Barriers to Justice for Rape Victims in Rwanda*, available at: www.hrw.org/report/2004/09/30/struggling-survive/barriers-justice-rape-victims-rwanda, last accessed 16/06/2016.

Human Rights Watch (2010), *Fast Tracked Unfairness: Detention and Denial of Women Asylum Seekers in the UK*, available at: www.hrw.org/node/88671, last accessed 10/01/2016.

Human Rights Watch (2015), *World Report 2015: Australia*, available at: www.hrw.org/world-report/2015/country-chapters/australia, last accessed 07/04/2016.

Hynes, P. (2010), *Understanding the 'Vulnerabilities', 'Resilience' and Processes of the Trafficking of Children and Young People into, within and out of the UK*, Youth & Policy, Vol. 104: 97–118.

Hynes, P. (2011), *The Dispersal and Social Exclusion of Asylum Seekers: Between Liminality and Belonging*, Bristol: Policy Press.

Hynes, P. (2015), *No 'Magic Bullets': Children, Young People, Trafficking and Child Protection in the UK*, International Migration, Vol. 53, No. 4: 62–76.

Immigration Act 2014, available at: www.legislation.gov.uk/ukpga/2014/22/contents/enacted, last accessed 23/06/2016.

Immigration Act 2016, available at: www.legislation.gov.uk/ukpga/2016/19/contents/enacted, last accessed 23/06/2016.

INQUEST (2016), *Deaths of Immigration Detainees*, available at: www.inquest.org.uk/statistics/deaths-of-immigration-detainees, last accessed 17/05/2016.

Inman, P. (2013), *Army of Workers Trapped in Insecure, Badly Paid 'Jobs'*, The Guardian, 30 July 2013.

International Centre for Health and Human Rights (2014), *Monitoring and Evaluation of Rehabilitation Services for Torture Survivors*, London: ICHHR.

International Commission of Jurists (2016), *Refugee Status Claims Based on Sexual Orientation and Gender Identity*, Geneva: ICJ.

International Organisation for Migration (2016), *IOM Counts 3,771 Migrant Fatalities in the Mediterranean in 2015*, IOM, available at: www.iom.int/news/iom-counts-3771-migrant-fatalities-mediterranean-2015, last accessed 08/01/2015.

James, L. and Patiniotis, J. (2013), *Women at the Cutting Edge: Why Public Sector Spending Cuts are a Gender Equality Issue*, Liverpool: Liverpool Charity and Voluntary Services and Liverpool John Moores University.

Jefferson, A. (2014), *Performances of Victimhood, Allegation, and Disavowal*, in Jensen, S. and Rønsbo, H. (eds.), Histories of Victimhood, Philadelphia: University of Pennsylvania Press.

Jensen, S. and Rønsbo, H. (2014), *Introduction*, in Jensen, S. and Rønsbo, H. (eds.), Histories of Victimhood, USA: University of Pennsylvania Press.

Jewkes, R., Sikweyiya, Y., Morrell,R. and Dunkle, K. (2009), *Understanding Men's Health and Use of Violence: Interface of Rape and HIV in South Africa*, Pretoria: Medical Research Council.

Joint Committee on Human Right (2007), *The Treatment of Asylum Seekers*, available at: www.publications.parliament.uk/pa/jt200607/jtselect/jtrights/81/81i.pdf, last accessed 20/10/2014.

Jones, H. and Cook, K. (2008), *Rape Crisis: Responding to Sexual Violence*, London: Russell House Publishing.

Jones, O. (2011), *CHAVS: The Demonisation of the Working Class*, London: Verso.

Jones, S. (2015), *UN Human Rights Chief Denounces Sun over Katie Hopkins 'Cockroach' Column*, 24 April 2015, available at: www.theguardian.com/

global-development/2015/apr/24/katie-hopkins-cockroach-migrants-denounced-united-nations-human-rights-commissioner, last accessed 28/04/2015.

Jordan, J. (2012), *Silencing Rape, Silencing Women*, in Brown, J. and Walklate, S. (eds.), Handbook on Sexual Violence, Oxford: Routledge.

Joshi, P. (2015), *Migrant Crisis: Women Sold for Sex for 10 Euros in German Refugee Camps*, International Business Times, available at: www.ibtimes.co.uk/migrant-crisis-women-sold-sex-10-german-refugee-camps-1524515, last accessed 07/04/2016.

Jurado, E., Brochmann, G. and Dølvik, J. E. (2013), *Immigration, Work and Welfare: Towards an Integrated Approach*, London: Policy Network.

Karumba, C. (2010), *Rape Capital of the World*, The New Statesman, available at: www.newstatesman.com/blogs/the-staggers/2010/07/congo-drc-women-war-violence last accessed 20/06/2016.

Kastrup, M. C. and Arcel, L. T. (2004), *Gender-Specific Treatment*, in Wilson, J. P and Drozdek, B. (eds.), Broken Spirits: The Treatment of Traumatised Asylum Seekers Refugees and War and Torture Victims, London: Brunner-Routledge.

Kedir, A. and Admasachew, L. (2010), *Violence Against Women in Ethiopia*, Gender, Place and Culture, Vol. 17, No. 4: 437–452.

Keefe, A. (2014), *Abysmal Asylum Support Rates Are Hampering Torture Survivors' Recovery from Trauma*, Freedom from Torture, available at: www.freedomfromtorture.org/news-blogs/8012, last accessed 13/05/2015.

Kelly, L. (1988), *Surviving Sexual Violence*, Minneapolis: University of Minnesota Press.

Kelly, L. (1990), *Journeying In Reverse: Possibilities and Problems in Feminist Research on Sexual Violence*, in Gelsthorpe, L. and Morris, A. (eds.), Feminist Perspectives in Criminology, Buckingham: Open University Press.

Kelly, L. (2000), *Wars against Women: Sexual Violence, Sexual Politics and the Militarised State*, in Jacobs, S., Jacobson, R. and Marchbank J. (eds.), States of Conflict: Gender, Violence and Resistance, New York: St. Martin's Press.

Kelly, L. (2011), *Reasonable Responses to Unreasonable Behaviour?: Medical and Sociological Perspectives on the Aftermath of Sexual Violence*, BSA Sociology of Mental Health Study Group, Edge Hill University, 7 June 2011.

Kelly, T. (2012), *This Side of Silence: Human Rights, Torture, and the Recognition of Cruelty*, Philadelphia: Pennsylvania University Press.

Kelly, L., Burton, S. and Regan, L. (1994), *Researching Women's Lives or Studying Women's Oppression? Reflections on What Constitutes Feminist Research*, in Maynard, M. and Purvis, J. (2004) (eds.), Researching Women's Lives from a Feminist Perspective, London: Taylor and Francis.

Kelly, L. and Radford, J. (1987), *The problems of men: Feminist perspectives on sexual violence*, in Scraton, P. (ed.), Law, Order and the Authoritarian State: Readings in Critical Criminology, Milton Keynes: Open University Press, pp. 237–253.

Kelly, L. and Westmarland, N. (2016), *Naming and Defining 'Domestic Violence' Lessons from Research with Violent Men*, Feminist Review, Vol. 112, No. 1: 113–127.

Kirkup, J. and Winnett, R. (2012), *Theresa May Interview: We're Going to Give Illegal Immigrants a Really Hostile Reception*, The Telegraph, 25 May 2012.

Kisson, P. (2010), *From Persecution to Destitution: A Snapshot of Asylum Seekers' Housing in Canada and the United Kingdom*, Journal of Immigrant and Refugee Studies, Vol. 8, No. 1: 4–31.

Lampard, K. and Marsden, E. (2016), Independent Investigation into Concerns about Yarl's Wood Immigration Removal Centre, Veritas.

Lansley, S. and Mack, J. (2015), *Breadline Britain: The Rise of Mass Poverty*, London: OneWorld Publications.

Lasslett, K. (2010), *Crime or Social Harm? A Dialectical Perspective*, State Crime, Vol. 1: 1–19.

Leatherman, J. (2011), *Sexual Violence in Conflict*, Cambridge: Polity Press.

Lees, S. (1996) *Carnal Knowledge: Rape on Trial*, London: Hamish Hamilton.

Lewis, R., Sharp, E., Remnant, J. and Redpath, R. (2015), *'Safe Spaces': Experiences of Feminist Women-Only Spaces*, Sociological Research Online, Vol. 20, No. 4: 9.

London Rape Crisis Centre (1984), *Sexual Violence: The Reality for Women*, London: Women's Press.

Lowenstein, A. (2015), *Disaster Capitalism: Making a Killing Out of Catastrophe*, London: Verso.

Mail Online (2016), *The OTHER Victims of Red Door Apartheid: Asylum Seekers are Angry at Their Homes Having Distinctive Red Doors. But Locals Who've Seen Their Town Lose Its Soul (AND Been Branded Racist) Are Just as Bitter*, available at: www.dailymail.co.uk/news/article-3411117/The-victims-red-door-apartheid-Asylum-seekers-angry-homes-having-distinctive-red-doors-locals-ve-seen-town-lose-soul-branded-racist-just-bitter.html#ixzz4CCkJnUYF, last accessed 21/06/2016.

MacKinnon, C. (1994), *Rape, Genocide, and Women's Human Rights*, in Stiglmayer. A. (ed.), Mass Rape: The War Against Women in Bosnia-Herzegovina, Lincoln: University of Nebraska Press.

MacKinnon, C. A. (2006), *Are Women Human? And Other International Dialogues*, Harvard: Harvard University Press.

MacPherson, P. (2014), *People Seeking Asylum and Refugees in Liverpool: Needs Assessment*, Liverpool City Council.

Marmot, M. (2010), *Fair Societies, Healthy Lives*, London: UCL Institute of Health Equity.

Masmas, T. N., Møller, E., Buhmann, C., Bunch, V., Jensen, J. H., Nørregård Hansen, T., Møller Jørgensen, L.; Kjær, C., Mannstaedt, M., Oxholm, A., Skau, J., Theilade, L., Worm, L. and Ekstrøm, M. (2008), *Asylum Seekers in Denmark: A Study of Health Status and Grade of Traumatization of Newly Arrived Asylum Seekers*, Torture, Vol. 18, No. 2: 77–86.

Mason, J. (2002), *Qualitative Researching*, London: Sage.

Mathiesen, T. (2004), *Silently Silenced: Essays on the Creation of Acquiescence in Modern Society*, Winchester: Waterside Press.

Maternity Action and the Refugee Council (2013), *When Maternity Doesn't Matter: Dispersing Pregnant Women Seeking Asylum*, available at: www.refugeecouncil.org.uk/assets/0002/6402/When_Maternity_Doesn_t_Matter_-_Ref_Council__Maternity_Action_report_Feb2013.pdf, last accessed 07/01/2016.

Matthews, L. (2016), *The Bill Becomes and Act... What's Been Won, and What's Been Lost'*, Right to Remain, available at: www.righttoremain.org.uk/blog/the-bill-becomes-an-act-whats-been-won-and-whats-been-lost/, last accessed 05/12/2016.

Mauthner, N. and Doucet, A. (1998), *Reflections on a Voice-centred Relational Method: Analysing Maternal and Domestic Voices*, in Ribbens, J. and Edwards, R. (eds.), Feminist Dilemmas in Qualitative Research: Public Knowledge and Private Lives, London: Sage.

Mays, M. (2006), *Feminist Disability Theory: Domestic Violence Against Women with a Disability*, Disability and Society, Vol. 21, No. 2: 147–158.

May, T. (2011), *Foreword* in HM Government (2011), *Human Trafficking: The Government's Strategy*, available at: https://ec.europa.eu/anti-trafficking/sites/antitrafficking/files/human-trafficking-strategy_1.pdf, last accessed 23/06/2016.

Maynard, M. and Purvis, J. (2004), *Researching Women's Lives from a Feminist Perspective*, London: Taylor and Francis.

McClenaghan, M. (2016), *Theresa May Wins Right to Deport Failed Asylum Seekers to Afghanistan after Judges Remove Court Injunction*, available at: www.thebureau-investigates.com/2016/03/03/theresa-may-wins-right-deport-failed-asylum-seekers-afghanistan-judges-remove-court-injunction-returns, last accessed 06/04/2016.

McCulloch, C. (2015), *500 Seeking Asylum in Northern Ireland*, The Belfast Telegraph, 3 October 2015.

McVeigh, T. (2015), *Austerity a Factor in Rising Suicide Rate Among Men*, The Guardian, 12 November 2015.

McVeigh, T. and Smith, H. (2016), *Double Crisis Deepens Despair in Greece's 'Warehouse of Souls'*, The Guardian, 27 February 2016.

Meintjes, S., Pillay, A. and Turshen, M. (2001), *The Aftermath: Women in Post-Conflict Transformation*, London: Zed Books.

Melossi, D. (2003), *"In a Peaceful Life": Migration and the Crime of Modernity in Europe/Italy*, Punishment and Society, Vol. 5, No. 4: 371–397.

Michalowski, R. (2013), *The Master's Tools: Can Supranational Law Confront Crimes of Powerful States?* in Stanley, E. and McCulloch, J. (eds.), State Crime and Resistance, Oxford: Routledge.

Michalowski, R. and Kramer, R. (2006), *A Critique of Power*, in Michalowski, R. and Kramer, R. (eds.), State-Corporate Crime: Wrongdoing at the Intersection of Business and Government, New Brunswick: Rutgers University Press.

Migrant Rights Network (2015), *New ESOL Funding Reductions Will See 16,000 Places cut*, available at: www.migrantsrights.org.uk/news/2015/new-esol-funding-reductions-will-see-16000-places-cut, last accessed 05/01/2016.

Mills, E. and Nachega, J. (2006), *HIV as a Weapon of War*, The Lancet, Vol. 6: 752.

Mirza, M. (2011), *Disability and Humanitarianism in Refugee Camps: The Case for a Traveling Supranational Disability Praxis*, Third World Quarterly, Vol 2, No. 8: 1527–1536.

Mitie, (2016), *Detainee Custody Officer* job advertisement, available at: www.totaljobs.com/JobSearch/JobDetails.aspx?JobId=64942579, last accessed 09/03/2016.

Montgomery, E. and Foldsprang, A. (2005), *Predictors of Authorities' Decision to Grant Asylum in Denmark*, Journal of Refugee Studies, Vol. 18, No. 4: 454–467.

Mookherjee, N. (2006), *'Remembering to Forget': Public Secrecy and Memory of Sexual Violence in the Bangladesh War of 1971*, Journal of the Royal Anthropological Institute, Vol. 12: 433–450.

Mookherjee, N. (2010), *The Spectral Wound: Sexual Violence and Public Memories and the Bangladesh War of 1971*, New York: Duke University Press.

Moore, K. (2013), *'Asylum Shopping' in the Neoliberal Social Imaginary*, Media, Culture & Society, Vol. 35, No. 3: 348–365.

Moore, K. and Clifford, S. (2007), *The Gendered Use of the Media by Asylum Seekers in Britain*, Gender and Development, Vol. 15, No. 3: 451–466.

Morris, L. (2010), *Asylum, Welfare and the Cosmopolitan Ideal: A Sociology of Rights*, Abingdon: Routledge.

Murray, G. and Abu-Hayyeh, R. (2014), *Asylum in Switzerland: Out of Sight, Out of Mind*, IRR News, available at: www.irr.org.uk/news/asylum-in-switzerland-out-of-sight-out-of-mind/, last accessed 21/06/2016.

Mythen, G. (2007), *Cultural Victimology: Are We All Victims Now?*, in Walklate, S. (ed.), Handbook on Victims and Victimology, Devon: Willan.

Naples, N. (2003), *Feminism and Method: Ethnography, Discourse Analysis and Activist Research*, Oxford: Routledge.

Nesabai, C. (2005), *Marital Violence*, in Jeyaraj, N. (ed.), Women and Society: A Reader in Women's Studies, Delhi: Cambridge Press.

National Crime Agency (2016), *National Referral Mechanism Statistics – End of Year Summary 2015*, available at: www.nationalcrimeagency.gov.uk/publications/676-national-referral-mechanism-statistics-end-of-year-summary-2015/file, last accessed 05/12/2016.

NHS (2014), *Your Choices in the NHS*, available at: www.nhs.uk/choiceintheNHS/Yourchoices/GPchoice/Pages/GPappointments.aspx, last accessed 07/01/2016.

NHS (2016) *Talking Therapies Explained*, available at: www.nhs.uk/conditions/stress-anxiety-depression/pages/types-of-therapy.aspx, last accessed 05/12/2016.

O'Carroll, S. and Jones, L. (2016), *'It was a Fake Meeting': Byron Hamburger Staff on Immigration Raid*, The Guardian, 28 July 2016.

Oakley, A. (2010), *The Social Science of Biographical Life-Writing: Some Methodological and Ethical Issues*, International Journal of Social Research Methodology, Vol. 13, No. 5: 425–439.

Office for National Statistics (2013), *An Overview of Sexual Offending in England and Wales*, available at: http://webarchive.nationalarchives.gov.uk/20160105160709/https://www.gov.uk/government/uploads/system/uploads/attachment_data/file/214970/sexual-offending-overview-jan-2013.pdf, last accessed 23/06/2016.

Osley, R. (2015), *Tony Blair Apologises For 'Mistakes' over Iraq War and Admits 'Elements of Truth' to View That Invasion Helped Rise of Isis*, The Independent, 24 October 2015.

Owen, J. (2010), *Immigrant Children Still Being Detained, Figures Show*, The Independent, available at: www.independent.co.uk/news/uk/politics/immigrant-children-still-being-detained-figures-show-9966155.html, last accessed 05/12/2016.

Paget, A. (2015), *Merseyside Police Recorded Some of the Highest Numbers of Hate Crimes Last Year, Figures Reveal*, The Liverpool Echo, available at: www.liverpoolecho.co.uk/news/liverpool-news/merseyside-police-recorded-highest-numbers-10326459, last accessed 25/04/2016.

Palmary, I. (2005), *Engendering Wartime Conflict: Women and War Trauma*, Braamfontein: Centre for the Study of Violence and Reconciliation.

Palmary, I. (2007), *Positioning Feminist Research Politically: A Reflection on Tensions and Standpoints in African Feminist Research*, POWS Review, Vol. 9, No.1: 23–33.

Pantazis, C. and Pemberton, S. (2009), *Policy Transfer and the UK's "War on Terror": A Political Economy Approach*, Policy & Politics, Vol. 37, No. 3: 363–387.

Pantazis, C. and Pemberton, S. (2013), *'Frameworks of Resistance': Challenging the UK's Securitization Agenda*, in Stanley, E. And McCulloch, J. (eds.), State Crime and Resistance, Oxford: Routledge.

Pasquali, V. (2016), *The Poorest Countries in the World*, Global Finance, available at: www.gfmag.com/global-data/economic-data/the-poorest-countries-in-the-world?page=3, last accessed 26/04/2016.

Patel, N. and Mahtani, A. (2004), *Psychological Approaches to Rape as Torture*, in Peel, M. (ed.), Rape as a Method of Torture, London: Freedom from Torture.

Patel, T. and Tyrer, D. (2011), *Race, Crime and Resistance*, London: Sage.

Peel, M. (2004), *Rape as a Method of Torture*, London: Freedom from Torture.

Peel, M., Mahtani, A., Hinshelwood, G. and Forrest, D. (2000), *The Sexual Abuse of Men in Detention in Sri Lanka*, The Lancet, Vol. 355, No. 10: 2069–2070.s.

Pemberton, B. (2015), *The Most Powerful Passports in the World Revealed*, Mail Online, available at: www.dailymail.co.uk/travel/travel_news/article-3021237/ The-powerful-passports-world-revealed-ones-barely-let-travel-anywhere.html, last accessed 25/07/2016.

Pemberton, S. (2015), *Harmful Societies*, Bristol: Policy Press.

Phillips, M. and Phillips, T. (2009), *Windrush: The Irresistible Rise of Multi-Racial Britain*, London: HarperCollins Publishers.

Pickering, S. (2005), *Refugees and State Crime*, Sydney: The Federation Press.

Pickering, S. (2010), *Women, Borders and Violence: Current Issues in Asylum, Forced Migration, and Trafficking*, New York: Springer.

Pickering, S. and Cochrane, L. (2013), *Irregular Border-Crossing Deaths and Gender: Where, How and Why Women Die Crossing Borders*, Theoretical Criminology, Vol. 17. No. 1: 27–48.

Pickering, S. and Ham, J. (2015), *The Routledge Handbook on Crime and International Migration*, Oxford: Routledge.

Pickering, S. and Weber, L. (2013), *Hardening the Rule of Law and Asylum Seekers: Exporting Risk and the Judicial Censure of State Illegality*, in Stanley, E. and McCulloch, J. (eds.), State Crime and Resistance, Oxford: Routledge.

Price, R. (2015), *Theresa May: Economic Migrants Fleeing across Mediterranean Should Be Returned to Africa*, The Telegraph, 13 May 2015, online interview available at: www.telegraph.co.uk/news/politics/conservative/11601628/Theresa-May-economic-migrants-fleeing-across-Mediterranean-should-be-returned-to-Africa.html, last accessed 05/12/2016.

Prime Minister's Office (2016), *PM Announces UK Depoloyment for NATO Mission in Aegean Sea to Tackle Migrant Crisis*, available at: www.gov.uk/government/news/pm-announces-uk-deployment-for-nato-mission-in-aegean-sea-to-tackle-migrant-crisis, last accessed 16/05/2016.

Prison Reform Trust (2009), *Too Little, Too Late: An Independent Review of Unmet Mental Health Need in Prison*, London: Prison Reform Trust.

Ramazanoglu, C. and Holland, J. (2002), *Feminist Methodology: Challenges and Choices*, London: Sage.

Rape Crisis Network Ireland, (2014), *Asylum Seekers and Refugees Surviving on Hold*, available at: www.rcni.ie/wp-content/uploads/RCNI-Asylum-Seekers-and-Refugees-Surviving-on-Hold.pdf, last accessed 20/06/2016.

Ray, L. (2010), *Refused Sanctuary then Deprived of their Health*, Leeds: Positive Action for Refugees and Asylum Seekers.

Red Cross (2016), *Refugee Facts and Figures*, available at: www.redcross.org.uk/What-we-do/Refugee-support/Refugee-facts-and-figures, last accessed 20/06/2016.

Refugee Council (2007), *The New Asylum Model*, London: British Refugee Council.

Refugee Council, The Vulnerable Women's Project (2009), *Refugee and Asylum Seeking Women Affected by Rape or Sexual Violence*, London: British Refugee Council.

Refugee Council (2009), *Change To The Way UKBA Registers In-Country Asylum Applications And Further Submissions On Asylum Claims*, available at: www.refugeecouncil. org.uk/policy/briefings/2009/25112009, last accessed 16/06/2016.

Refugee Council (2010), *Rape and Sexual Violence: The Experiences of Refugee Women in the UK*, UK: British Refugee Council.

Refugee Council (2013), *Asylum Statistics*, available at: www.refugeecouncil.org.uk/assets/0002/7887/Asylum_Statistics_May_2013.pdf, last accessed 16/02/2016.

Refugee Council (2015), *Asylum Statistics*, available at: www.refugeecouncil.org.uk/assets/0003/4620/Asylum_Statistics_May_2015.pdf, last accessed 20/06/2016.

Refugee Women's Strategy Group (2014), *Speak for Yourself: Report From Our Engagement with 100 Refugee and Asylum Seeking Women between June and November 2013*, Scottish Refugee Council, available at: www.scottishrefugeecouncil.org.uk/assets/0000/8001/Speak_for_Yourself_report29414.pdf, last accessed 29/04/2016.

Refugees, Survivors and Ex-Detainees (N.D.), *Who We Are*, available at: http://riserefugee.org/, last accessed 20/07/2016.

Rejali, D. (2007), *Torture and Democracy*, Princeton: Princeton University Press.

Reuters (2016), *Britain Will Not Join a Common EU Asylum System: Cameron*, Reuters, available at: www.reuters.com/article/us-europe-migrants-cameron-idUSKCN0W9184, last accessed 24/06/2016.

Rice, M. (1990), *Challenging Orthodoxis in Feminist Theory: a Black Feminist Critique'*, in Gelsthorpe, L. And Morris, A. (eds.), Feminist Perspectives in Criminology, Milton Keynes: Open University Press.

Right to Remain (2015), *'We Still Have Problems Talking About It'*, Right to Remain News, available at: www.righttoremain.org.uk/blog/we-all-still-have-problems-talking-about-it/, last accessed 26/04/2016.

Rights of Women (2010), *Measuring Up? UK Compliance with International Commitments on Violence Against Women*, London: Rights of Women.

Roberts, K. and Harris, J. (2002), *Disabled People in Refugee and Asylum Seeking Communities*, Bristol: Policy Press.

Rogers, S. (2012), *What do People Die of? Mortality Rates and Data for Every Cause of Death in 2011 Visualised*, The Guardian, available at: www.theguardian.com/news/datablog/2012/nov/06/deaths-mortality-rates-cause-death-2011, last accessed 24/04/2016.

RT (2014a), *ISIS Leader Says US prisons in Iraq Led to the Creation of Terrorist Organisation*, available at: www.rt.com/news/213843-isis-creation-prison-iraq/, last accessed 20/06/2016.

RT (2014b), *'New Level of Ignorance': UK Charity Blasts Farage's Call to Ban HIV-Positive Migrants*, available at: www.rt.com/uk/194876-farage-ban-hiv-migrants/, last accessed 16/02/2016.

RT (2015), *High Court: 100s of Asylum Seeker Torture Survivors Can Sue UK Government for Illegal Detention*, available at: www.rt.com/uk/271558-torture-victims-asylum-detained/, last accessed 05/04/2016.

Salazar, C. (1991), *A Third World Woman's Text: Between the Politics of Criticism and Cultural Politics*, in Berger Gluck, S. and Patai, D. (eds), Women's Words: The Feminist Practice of Oral History, London: Routledge.

Sales, R. (2002), *The Deserving and the Undeserving? Refugees, Asylum Seekers and Welfare in Britain*, Critical Social Policy, Vol. 22, No. 3: 456–478.

Sales, R. (2007), *Understanding Immigration and Refugee Policy: Contradictions and Continuities*, Bristol: Policy Press.

Sambamoorthi, U., Walkup, J., Olfson, M. and Chrystal, S. (2001), *Antidepressant Treatment and Health Service Utilization Among HIV Medicaid Patients Diagnosed with Depression*, Journal of General Internal Medicine, Vol. 15, No. 5: 311–319.

Schostak, J. and Schostak, J. (2008), *Radical Research: Designing, Developing and Writing Research to make a Difference*, Oxford: Routledge.

Schuster, L. and Solomos, J. (2004), *Race, Immigration and Asylum: New Labour's Agenda and its Consequences*, Ethnicities, Vol. 4, No. 2: 267–300.

Scott, D. and Codd, H. (2010), *Controversial Issues in Prisons*, Buckingham: Open University Press.

Segrave, M. and Carlton, B. (2011), *Counting the Costs of Imprisonment: Researching Women's Post-Release Deaths in Victoria*, Australian and New Zealand Journal of Criminology, Vol. 44, No. 1: 41–55.

Sexual Violence Research Initiative (2015), *Sexual Violence and Women's Vulnerability to HIV*, available at: www.svri.org/hiv.htm, last accessed 16/02/2016.

Sharma, S. (2016), *Activism Panel Presentation*, Holding the State to Account on Violence Against Women, Sylvia Pankhurst Gender Research Centre, 22 July 2016.

Shaw, S. (2016), *Review into the Welfare in Detention of Vulnerable Persons*, available at: www.gov.uk/government/uploads/system/uploads/attachment_data/file/490782/ 52532_Shaw_Review_Accessible.pdf, last accessed 24/06/2016.

Showalter, E. (1985), *The Female Malady: Women, Madness, and English Culture, 1830–1980*, New York: Pantheon Books.

Silverman, S. and Hajela, R. (2015), *Immigration Detention in the UK*, available at: http:// migrationobservatory.ox.ac.uk/briefings/immigration-detention-uk, last accessed 05/01/2016.

Sim, J. (1990), *Medical Power in Prisons: Prison Medical Services in England, 1774–1988*, Buckingham: Open University Press.

Sim, J. (2009), *Punishment and Prisons*, London: Sage.

Singer, D. (2016), *Protection Gap Campaign Reaches Europe*, Asylum Aid: Women's Asylum News, available at: www.asylumaid.org.uk/wp-content/uploads/2016/03/ WAN_134.pdf?utm_source=WAN+134&utm_campaign=Wan+134&utm_medium= email, last accessed 23/06/2016.

Sivakumaran, S. (2007), *Sexual Violence against Men in Armed Conflict*, The European Journal of International Law, Vol. 18, No. 2: 253–276.

Smart. C. (1989), *Feminism and the Power of Law*, London: Routledge.

Smart, C. (1990), *Law, Crime and Sexuality*, London: Sage.

Smith, A. (2005), *Conquest: Sexual Violence and American Indian Genocide*, Cambridge, MA: South End Press.

Smith, D. (1987), *The Everyday World as Problematic: A Feminist Sociology*, Boston: Northeastern University Press.

Smith, E. (2004a), *Right First Time? Home Office Asylum Interviewing and Reasons for Refusal Letters*, London: Medical Foundation for the Care of Victims of Torture (Now Freedom from Torture).

Smith, E. (2004b), *A Legal Analysis of Rape as Torture*, in Peel, M. (ed.), Rape as a Method of Torture, London: Freedom from Torture.

Smith, A. (2005), *Looking to the Future: Domestic Violence, Women of Colour, The State, and Social Change*, in Sokoloff, N. and Pratt, C. (eds), Domestic Violence at the Margins, New Brunswick: Rutgers University Press.

Sokoloff, N. (2008), *Expanding the Intersectional Paradigm to Better Understand Domestic Violence in Immigrant Communities*, Critical Criminology, Vol. 16, No. 4: 229–255.

Somerville, W. (2007), *Immigration Under New Labour*, Bristol: Policy Press.

Spanjers, S. (2013), *Legal Implications of Zero-Hour Contracts*, HR Magazine, available at: www.hrmagazine.co.uk/article-details/legal-implications-of-zero-hours-contracts, 23 July 2013, last accessed 09/03/2016.

Spiegel Online (2015), *Asylum Shelters in Germany Struggle with Violence*, available at: www.spiegel.de/international/germany/asylum-shelters-in-germany-struggle-with-refugee-violence-a-1056393.html, last accessed 07/04/2016.

Stanko, E. (1985), *Intimate Intrusions*, London: Routledge and Kegan Paul.

Stanko, E. (1990), *Everyday Violence: How Women and Men Experience Sexual and Physical Danger*, London: Pandora Press.

Stanley, E. (2008), *Torture and Terror*, in Anthony, T. and Cuneen, C. (eds,), The Critical Criminology Companion, California: Hawkins Press.

Stanley, E. and McCulloch, J. (2013), *Resistance to State Crimes*, in Stanley, E. and McCulloch, J. (Eds.), State Crime and Resistance, Oxford: Routledge.

Stanley, L. and Wise, S. (1993), *Breaking Out Again: Feminist Ontology and Epistemology*, London: Routledge.

Stiglmayer, A. (1994), *Mass Rapes: The War Against Women in Bosnia Herzegovina*, Lincoln and London: University of Nebraska Press.

Stonewall (2010), *No Going Back: Lesbian and Gay People in the Asylum System*, available at: www.stonewall.org.uk/documents/no_going_back_1.pdf, last accessed 20/10/2014.

Somerville, W. (2007), *Immigration under New Labour*, Bristol: Policy Press.

Stumpf, J. (2006), *The Crimmigration Crisis: Immigrants, Crime and Sovereign Power*, American University Law Review, Vol. 52, No. 2: 367–419.

Tascor Ltd. (2013), *What We Do*, available at: www.tascor.co.uk/what-we-do/immigration-and-border/, last accessed 11/05/2016.

Taylor, D. (2009), *Britain Sending Refused Congo Asylum Seekers Back to the Threat of Torture,* The Guardian, 27 May 2009.

Taylor, D. (2010), *Border Staff Humiliate and Trick Asylum Seekers - Whistleblower*, The Guardian, available at: www.theguardian.com/uk/2010/feb/02/border-staff-asylum-seekers-whistleblower, last accessed 12/05/2016.

Taylor, D. (2009), *Britain Sending Refused Congo Asylum Seekers Back to Threat of Torture*, The Guardian, available at: www.theguardian.com/world/2009/may/27/drc-congo-deport-torture, last accessed 06/04/2016.

Taylor, D. (2016), *Suicide Attempts at Immigration Removal Centres at an All Time High*, The Guardian, 4 April 2016.

Taylor, D. and Townsend, M. (2014), *Gay Asylum Seekers Face 'Humiliation'*, The Guardian, 8 February 2014.

Temkin, J. (1997), *Plus Ça Change: Reporting Rape in the 1990s*, British Journal of Criminology, Vol. 37, No.4: 507–528.

The Guardian Australia, (2013), *Nauru Riot: 125 Asylum Seekers Arrested*, The Guardian, available at: www.theguardian.com/world/2013/jul/21/nauru-riot-asylum-seekers-arrested, last accessed 07/04/2016.

The Independent (2015), *Theresa May's speech to the Conservative Party Conference – in full*, available at: www.independent.co.uk/news/uk/politics/theresa-may-s-speech-to-the-conservative-party-conference-in-full-a6681901.html, last accessed 21/06/2016.

The Iraq Inquiry (2016), *The Chilcot Report*, available at: www.iraqinquiry.org.uk/the-report/, last accessed 29/07/2016.

The Local Sweden (2015), *Stockholmers Gather to Welcome Refugees*, The Local, available at: www.thelocal.se/20150908/stockholmers-on-hand-to-welcome-refugees, last accessed 23/05/2016.

The Migration Observatory (2015), *Migration to the UK: Asylum*, available at: http://migrationobservatory.ox.ac.uk/briefings/migration-uk-asylum, last accessed 16/02/2016.

Thompson, P. (2000), *The Voice of the Past: Oral History*, Oxford: Oxford University Press.

Tilly, C. (1985), *War Making and State Making as Organised Crime*, in Evans, P., Rueschemeyer, D. and Skocpol, T. (eds.), Bringing the State Back In, Cambridge: Cambridge University Press.

Tombs, S. (2016), *Social Protection After the Crisis: Regulation without Enforcement*, Bristol: Policy Press.

Tombs, S. and Whyte, D. (2015), *The Corporate Criminal: Why Corporations Must be Abolished*, Oxford: Routledge.

Townsend, M. (2015a), *William Hague's Summit Against Warzone Rape Seen as 'Costly Failure'*, The Guardian, 13 June 2015.

Townsend, M. (2015b), *Yarl's Wood: UN Special Rapporteur to Censure UK Government*, The Guardian, 3 January 2015.

Travis, A. (2011), *Murder Rate Lowest for 12 Years*, The Guardian, available at: www.theguardian.com/uk/2011/jan/20/murder-rate-lowest-12-years, last accessed 05/12/2016.

Travis, A. (2013), *UK Border Agency to be Abolished, Theresa May Announces*, The Guardian, 26 March 2013.

Travis, A. (2014), *UK Axes Support for Mediterranean Migrant Rescue Operation*, The Guardian, 27 October 2014.

Turnbull, S. (2016), *'Stuck in the Middle': Waiting and Uncertaintly in Immigration Detention*, Time & Society, Vol. 25, No. 1: 65–79.

Turner, S. (2010), *Politics of Innocence*, Oxford: Berghahn Books.

Tyler, I. (2006), *'Welcome to Britain': The Cultural Politics of Asylum*, European Journal of Cultural Studies, Vol. 9, No. 2: 185–202.

Tyler, I. (2013), *Revolting Subjects: Social Abjection and Resistance in Neoliberal Britain*, London: Zed Books.

United Kingdom Border Agency (2007, 2010), *Gender Issues in the Asylum Process*, available at: www.gov.uk/government/uploads/system/uploads/attachment_data/file/257386/gender-issue-in-the-asylum.pdf, last accessed 27/07/2016.

Ugelvik, T. (2013), *Seeing Like a Welfare State: Immigration Control, Statecraft, and a Prison with a Double Vision*, in Aas, K. F. and Bosworth, M. (eds.), The Borders of Punishment: Migration, Citizenship and Social Exclusion, Oxford: Oxford University Press.

UK Visas and Immigration (2014a), *Working Whilst an Asylum Claim is Considered*, available at: www.gov.uk/government/publications/working-whilst-an-asylum-claim-is-considered/working-in-the-uk-whilst-an-asylum-case-is-considered, last accessed 13/10/2015.

UK Visas and Immigration (2014b), *Information about Your Asylum Application*, available at: www.gov.uk/government/publications/information-leaflet-for-asylum-applications, last accessed 16/10/2015.

Ullman, S. E. (2007), *Comparing Gang and Individual Rapes in a Community Sample of Urban Women*, Violence and Victims, Vol. 22, No. 1: 43–51.

United Nations (N.D.), *Refugees*, available at: www.un.org/en/globalissues/briefingpapers/refugees/, last accessed 20/06/2016.

United Nations (1948), *Universal Declaration of Human Rights* (1948), available at: www.un.org/en/documents/udhr/#atop, last accessed 20/10/2014.

United Nations (1984), *United Nations Convention Against Torture and other Cruel, Inhuman or Degrading Treatment or Punishment*, available at: www.un.org/documents/ga/res/39/a39r046.htm, last accessed 3/03/2015.

United Nations High Commissioner for Refugees (1951, 1967), *Convention and Protocol Relating to the Status of Refugees (Geneva Convention)*, available at: www.unhcr.org/3b66c2aa10.html, last accessed 20/10/2014.

United Nations High Commissioner for Refugees (2012), *Asylum Levels and Trends in Industrialized Countries*, available at: www.unhcr.org/507c000e9.html, last accessed 19/02/2015.

United Nations High Commissioner for Refugees (2013), *Country Statistics: Ethiopia*, available at: www.unicef.org/infobycountry/ethiopia_statistics.html, last accessed 26/04/2016.

United Nations High Commissioner for Refugees (2014), *UNHCR Alarmed at Death Toll from Boat Sinkings in the Mediterranean*, available at: www.unhcr.org/54184ae76.html, last accessed 20/10/2014.

United Nations High Commissioner for Refugees (2015), *Over 1 Million Sea Arrivals Reach Europe in 2015*, available at: www.unhcr.org/uk/news/latest/2015/12/5683d0b56/million-sea-arrivals-reach-europe-2015.html, last accessed 29/07/2016.

United Nations High Commissioner for Refugees (2016), *Where We Work*, available at: www.unhcr.org/pages/49c3646c206.html, last accessed 17/02/2016.

UN Women (2016), *Facts and Figures: Ending Violence Against Women*, available at: www.unwomen.org/en/what-we-do/ending-violence-against-women/facts-and-figures, last accessed 20/06/2016.

Ussher, J. (1989), *The Psychology of the Female Body*, London: Routledge.

Ussher, J. M. (2011), *The Madness of Women: Myth and Experience*, London: Routledge.

Vaz, K. (2012), *UK Border Agency 'Not Fit for Purpose'*, BBC News, available at: www.bbc.co.uk/news/uk-politics-17674101, last accessed 24/06/2016.

Vine, J. (2011), *The Use of Country of Origin Information in Deciding Asylum Applications: A Thematic Review*, available at: http://icinspector.independent.gov.uk/wp-content/uploads/2011/02/Use-of-country-of-origin-information-in-deciding-asylum-applications.pdf, last accessed 25/07/2016.

Vine, J. (2014), *An Investigation into the Home Office's Handling of Asylum Claims Made on the Grounds of Sexual Orientation*, available at http://icinspector.independent.gov.uk/wp-content/uploads/2014/10/Investigation-into-the-Handling-of-Asylum-Claims-Final-Web.pdf, last accessed 05/12/2016.

Visas and Immigration (2016), *Claim Asylum in the UK*, available at www.gov.uk/claim-asylum, last accessed 05/12/2016.

Wagner, A. (2011), *Catgate: Another Myth Used to Trash Human Rights*, The Guardian Online, available at: www.theguardian.com/law/2011/oct/04/theresa-may-wrong-cat-deportation, last accessed 10/05/2016.

Walby, S., Armstrong, J. and Strid, S. (2012), *Intersectionality: Multiple Inequalities in Social Theory*, Sociology, Vol. 46, No. 2: 224–240.

Walklate, S. (2014), *Sexual Violence Against Women: Still a Controversial Issue for Victimology?*, International Review of Victimology, Vol. 20, No. 1: 71–84.

Ward, K., Amas, N. and Lagnado, J. (2008), *Supporting Disabled Refugees and Asylum Seekers: Opportunities for New Approaches*, Refugee Support, available at: www.metropolitan.org.uk/images/Disability-Report.pdf, last accessed 28/04/2016.

Waugh, P. (2016), *Anger as Tory MPs Vote Down Plan to Take 3000 Child Refugees from Europe*, Huffington Post, available at: www.huffingtonpost.co.uk/entry/child-refugees-plan-defeated-by-tory-mps_uk_571e7e1ce4b0d6f7bed4c815, last accessed 16/05/2-16.

Webber, F. (2004), *The War on Migration*, in Hillyard, P., Tombs, S. and Gordon, D. (eds), Beyond Criminology: Taking Harm Seriously, London: Pluto Press.

Webber, F. (2006), *Border Wars and Asylum Crimes*, Statewatch, available at: www.statewatch.org/analyses/border-wars-and-asylum-crimes.pdf, last accessed 05/12/2016.

Webber, F. (2012), *Borderline Justice: The Fight for Refugee and Migrant Rights*, London: Pluto Press.

Webber, F. (2014), *Justice Blindfolded? The Case of Jimmy Mubenga*, Institute for Race Relations, available at: www.irr.org.uk/news/justice-blindfolded-the-case-of-jimmy-mubenga/, last accessed 06/04/2016.

Webber, F. (2016), *Keynote Speech*, Sites of Confinement: Confines, Controls and Resistance at the Border, University of Turin, 17 March 2016.

Weber, L. (2005), *The Detention of Asylum Seekers as a Crime of Obedience*, Critical Criminology, Vol. 13, No. 1: 89–109.

Weber, L. (2015), *Deciphering Deportation Practices across the Global North*, in Pickering, S. and Ham, J. (2015), The Routledge Handbook on Crime and International Migration, Oxford: Routledge.

Weber, L. and Pickering, S. (2011), *Globalisation and Borders: Death at the Global Frontier*, Basingstoke: Palgrave Macmillan.

Weber, M. (1946; 2002), *Politics as a Vocation*, in Besteman, C. (2002), Violence: A Reader, Basingstoke: Palgrave MacMillan.

Westmarland, N. and Alderson, S. (2013), *The Health, Mental Health and Well-being Benefits of Rape Crisis Counselling*, Journal of Interpersonal Violence, Vol. 28, No. 17: 3265–3282.

Whyte, D. (2007), *The Crimes of Neoliberal Rule in Occupied Iraq*, British Journal of Criminology, Vol. 47, No. 2: 177–195.

Whyte, D. (2015), *How Corrupt is Britain?*, London: Pluto Press.

Wickes, R. and Sydes, M. (2015), *Immigration and Crime*, in Pickering, S. and Ham, J. (eds.), The Routledge Handbook on Crime and International Migration, Oxford: Routledge.

Williams, P. (2015), *Criminalising the Other: Challenging the Race and Gang Nexus*, Race and Class, Vol. 56, No. 3: 18–35.

Williams, Z. (2015), *Katie Hopkins Calling Migrants Vermin Recalls the Darkest Events of History*, The Guardian, 19 April 2015.

Wilson, D. (2015), *Border Militarisation, Technology and Crime Control*, in Pickering, S. and Ham, J. (eds.), The Routledge Handbook of Crime and Migration Studies, Oxford: Routledge.

Wilson, J. P and Drozdek, B. (2004), *Broken Spirits: The Treatment of Traumatised Asylum Seekers, Refugees and War and Torture Victims*, London: Brunner-Routledge.

Wilson, D. and Weber, L. (2008), *Surveillance, Risk and Preemption on the Australian Border*, Surveillance and Society, Vol. 5, No. 2: 124–141.

Wintour, P. (2011), *Theresa May Accused of Lifting Cat Anecdote from UKIP Leader*, The Guardian, 7 October 2011.

Wintour, P. (2015), *UK to Take up to 20,000 Syrian Refugees Over Five Years*, The Guardian, 7 September 2015.

Women Against Rape (2014), *Rape Survivors Protest at the Global Summit to End Sexual Violence in Conflict*, available at: www.womenagainstrape.net/content/rape-survivors-protest-global-summit-end-sexual-vi, last accessed 18/02/2016.

Women's Resource Centre (2010), *Power & Prejudice - Combating Gender Inequality Through Women's Organisations*, London: Women's Resource Centre.

Wonders, N. and Danner, M. (2006), *Globalisation, State-Corporate Crime and Women*, in Michalowski, R. and Kramer, R. (eds.), State-Corporate Crime: Wrongdoing at the Intersection of Business and Government, New Brunswick: Rutgers University Press.

Wood, E. J. (2006), *Variations in Sexual Violence During World War Two*, Politics and Society, Vol. 34, No. 3: 307–342.

Wood, E. J. (2009), *A Theoretical Framework for Explaining the Variation in Wartime Sexual Violence*, Paper presentation delivered at Rape in Wartime: A History to be Written, University of Paris 1, 11 May 2009.

Woodiwiss, A. (2005), *Human Rights*, Oxford: Routledge.

World Bank, (2014), *Gross Domestic Product 2014*, available at: http://databank.worldbank.org/data/download/GDP.pdf, last accessed 20/06/2016.

World Without Torture (2014), *World's Largest Collection of Documents on Torture Still a Well-Kept Secret*, available at: http://worldwithouttorture.org/2014/11/20/worlds-largest-collection-of-documents-on-torture-still-a-well-kept-secret/, last accessed 3/03/2015.

Wright, O. (2014), *Ban on HIV Positive Immigrants Entering the UK Proposed for Immigration Bill by Tory MPs*, The Independent, 30 January 2014.

Wright, O. (2015), *Women Targeted as Hate Crime Against British Muslims Soars Following Terrorist Atrocity*, The Independent, 22 November 2015.

Yuval-Davis, N. (1994), *Women, Ethnicity and Empowerment*, Feminism and Psychology, Vol. 4, No. 1: 179–197.

Yuval-Davis, N. (2006a), *Belonging and the Politics of Belonging*, Patterns of Prejudice, Vol. 40, No. 3: 197–214.

Yuval-Davis, N. (2006b), *Intersectionality and Feminist Politics*, European Journal of Women's Studies, Vol. 13, No. 3: 193–209.

Zawati, H. M. (2007), *Impunity or Immunity: Wartime Male Rape and Sexual Torture as a Crime Against Humanity*, Torture, Vol. 17, No. 1: 27–47.

Zedner, L. (2013), *Is the Criminal Law Only for Citizens? A Problem at the Borders of Punishment*, in Aas, K. F. and Bosworth, M. (2013), The Borders of Punishment: Migration, Citizenship and Social Exclusion, Oxford: Oxford University Press.

Index